Education Is Politics

CRITICAL
TEACHING
ACROSS
DIFFERENCES,
K–12

EDITED BY

Ira Shor & Caroline Pari

FOREWORD BY BOB PETERSON

Boynton/Cook
HEINEMANN
Portsmouth, NH

Boynton/Cook Publishers, Inc.
A subsidiary of Reed Elsevier Inc.
361 Hanover Street
Portsmouth, NH 03801–3912
www.boyntoncook.com

Offices and agents throughout the world

The editors and publisher wish to thank those who have generously given permission to reprint borrowed material:

Portions of "Multiculturalism, Social Justice, and Critical Teaching" by Sonia Nieto originally appeared in *Affirming Diversity: The Sociopolitical Context of Multicultural Education, 2nd Edition.* Copyright © 1992, 1996 by Longman Publishers USA. Reprinted by permission of Addison-Wesley Educational Publishers Inc.

"Life After Death: Critical Pedagogy in an Urban Community" by J. Alleyne Johnson originally appeared as "Life After Death: Critical Pedagogy in an Urban Classroom" in *Harvard Educational Review,* 65:2 (Summer 1995): 213–230. Copyright © 1995 by the President and Fellows of Harvard College. All rights reserved.

"Empowerment Education: Freire's Ideas Adapted to Health Education" by Nina Wallerstein and Edward Bernstein originally appeared in *Health Education Quarterly* 1988 15(4): 379–394. Reprinted by permission of Nina Wallerstein.

"A Gay-Themed Lesson in an Ethnic Literature Curriculum: Tenth Graders' Responses to 'Lear Anita'" by Steven Z. Athanases originally appeared in *Harvard Educational Review,* 66:2 (Summer 1996): 231–256. Copyright © 1996 by the President and Fellows of Harvard College. All rights reserved.

Acknowledgments for borrowed material continue on p. 260.

Library of Congress Cataloging-in-Publication Data
Education is politics : critical teaching across differences, K–12 / edited by Ira Shor
  and Caroline Pari ; foreword by Bob Peterson.
    p.   cm.
  Includes bibliographical references.
  ISBN 0-86709-465-6
   1. Critical pedagogy—United States.   2. Multicultural education—United States.
  3. Educational equalization—United States.   I. Shor, Ira, 1945– .   II. Pari, Caroline.
  LC196.5.U6E36   1999
  370.11′5—dc21   99-26638
                                                                       CIP

Editor: Lisa Luedeke
Production: Vicki Kasabian
Cover design: Catherine Hawkes/Cat and Mouse
Manufacturing: Louise Richardson

Printed in the United States of America on acid-free paper
Docutech T & C 2006

In memory of Paulo Freire, 1921–1997
Teacher, mentor, friend

Paulo Freire at home, Sâo Paulo, Brazil, 1987.

"This is a great discovery, education is politics! . . . [T]he teacher has to ask, What kind of politics am I doing in the classroom? That is, in favor of whom am I being a teacher? By asking in favor of whom am I educating, the teacher must also ask against whom am I educating."
—*A Pedagogy for Liberation* (1987, p. 46)

"Any educational practice based on standardization, on what is laid down in advance, on routine in which everything is predetermined, is bureaucratizing and thus anti-democratic."
—*Learning to Question* (1989, p. 41)

"Maybe so many people emerge from your school systems illiterate because they are resisting, refusing to read the world the way they're being taught it."
—*OMNI* magazine interview (1990, p. 79)

Contents

Preface

Two Rivers of Reform

Ira Shor

" . . . the medium of exchange in which education is conducted—
language—can never be neutral . . . it imposes a point of view not
only about the world to which it refers but toward the use of mind in
respect of this world."

—Jerome Bruner,
Actual Minds, Possible Worlds

"We must always take sides. Neutrality helps the oppressor, never
the victim."

—Elie Wiesel

Two great rivers of reform are flowing in opposite directions across the im-
mense landscapes of American education. One river flows from the top down
and the other from the bottom up. The top-down river has been the voice of authority proposing conservative agendas that support inequality and traditional
teaching; the bottom-up flow contains multicultural voices speaking for social
justice and alternative methods. These two rivers represent different politics,
different models for teaching and learning, and finally different visions of the
people and the society we should build through education. Will conservative
agendas succeed in imposing more control, more rote learning, and more unequal funding on public education? Or will emerging groups and networks de-
mocratically remake school systems especially divided by race and class, from
impoverished inner cities to affluent suburbs to depressed rural areas?

Democratic educators who speak from the bottom-up river of reform see
the classroom work of teachers and students shaped by the larger social context. "Whether schools are public or private," wrote Deborah Meier in 1995,
"the social class of the students has been and continues to be the single most
significant factor in determining how a school works and the intellectual values it promotes. The higher the student body's economic status, the meatier the
curriculum, the more open-ended the discussion, the less rote and rigid the pedagogy, the more respectful the tone, the more rigorous the expectations, the
greater the staff autonomy" (78). Meier found that the SAT scores of her Central

Park East High School students in New York were an "overwhelming" measure of their family's class status. Her observations echo those of her reform colleague Ted Sizer from a decade earlier. After a national tour of American high schools, Sizer wrote that "Among schools there was one important difference, which followed from a single variable only: the social class of the student body. If the school principally served poor adolescents, its character, if not its structure, varied from sister schools for the more affluent. It got so I could say with some justification to school principals, Tell me about the incomes of your students' families and I'll describe to you your school" (1984, 6). Sizer also found that the *theme* of social class was absent from the secondary curriculum, despite the massive impact of economic status on learning. The broad exclusion of the subject of class—as well as gender and race bias—reveals the politics of the status quo dominating curriculum.

There is a special intersection of class and race in this curricular exclusion because black and Hispanic families have a poverty rate nearly three times that of white households. About half of all American families live on less than $42,000 a year while 41 percent of *all* American families live on less than $35,000; but if these figures are broken down racially we find that more than 60 percent of black and Hispanic families live on less than $35,000 while only 37 percent of white families are at this low economic level (Statistical Abstract of the U.S. 1998). Racism means that students of color are far more likely to be from lower income homes (surely not news to anyone reading this book) making them stakeholders in schools that need funding equal to that in affluent suburbs. Many years ago, John Dewey focused on the unresolved issue of class inequality in *Democracy and Education* (1916). More recently, Jonathan Kozol described in poignant detail the racial impact of unequal funding in *Savage Inequalities* (1991). Further, the problem of gender equity has also received important attention in the bottom-up river of democratic reform, especially around the daily sexual harassment of girls in schools (Stein, Marshall, and Tropp 1993) and the lesser access for girls to technology.

The fate of democracy in school and society will be decided by the funding and curriculum wars now under way. Teachers, students, and parents are stakeholders in this debate over educational and economic policies. Official agendas are maintaining tracking, imposing more standardized testing, legislating more restrictive courses, and continuing unequal funding of urban public schools while promoting vouchers, privatization, and tax monies for private and religious units. These top-down policies put most American kids at risk in schools that get less than they need, where teachers are underpaid and overworked thanks to large classes, heavy course loads, and limited resources. This unequal school landscape will look very different should bottom-up reforms succeed with student-based curricula, critical teaching and learning, multicultural and gender-conscious programs, smaller classes, and equal funding.

This book is one product of the bottom-up river of reform where many teachers, parents, groups, and networks are contending for schools that are democractic, equitable, critical, inspiring, and humane. We are at a moment when society appears to be moving left and right at the same time, becoming more authoritarian and unequal, more unstable and damaging for children, thus provoking action from below by teachers, parents, community coalitions, organized advocates, and national networks. The power of the media, schools, government, and industry to project the status quo has perhaps never been greater. At the same time, popular outrage at and mass alienation from the system is perhaps also at its peak. A long-term showdown is in the making here, and the schools are a major scene in the great contentions roiling American society.

Speaking from the bottom-up river of reform, the teachers in this volume report ways of working inside classrooms at a difficult time for them and students. The following chapters are written by teachers for teachers about critical and democratic learning that hopes to change a society not yet just or compassionate to all its children.

Works Cited

Bruner, Jerome. 1984. *Actual Minds, Possible Worlds.* Cambridge, MA: Harvard University Press.

Dewey, John. [1916] 1966. *Democracy and Education.* Reprint, New York: Free Press.

Kozol, Jonathan. 1991. *Savage Inequalities: Children in America's Schools.* New York: Crown.

Meier, Deborah. 1995. *The Power of Their Ideas: Lessons for America from a Small School in Harlem.* Boston: Beacon Press.

Sizer, Theodore. 1984. *Horace's Compromise: The Dilemma of the American High School.* Boston: Houghton Mifflin.

Stein, Nan, Nancy L. Marshall, and Linda R. Tropp. 1993. *Secrets in Public: Sexual Harassment in Our Schools.* A report written in collaboration with Wellesley College and the National Organization of Women. Washington, DC: NOW Legal Defense Fund.

U.S. Bureau of the Census. 1998. Statistical Abstract of the United States: 1998. 118th ed. Tables 745, 746, and 747. Washington, DC.

Wiesel, Elie. 1986. Nobel Prize acceptance speech, published in *Public Speaking,* 2d ed., edited by Michael Osborn and Suzanne Osborn, 456–58. Boston: Houghton Mifflin, 1991.

Foreword

My Journey as a Critical Teacher: Creating Schools as Laboratories for Social Justice

Bob Peterson

At La Escuela Fratney, a bilingual multicultural public school in Milwaukee, I often see my former fifth-grade students when they accompany younger siblings to school events or when they come to after-school programs. At times they even try to hang out in my classroom because they've been suspended from middle or high school.

When I ask these Fratney graduates how school is now, they usually answer "OK." But occasionally our conversation opens up and they tell me their real feelings. They talk of the uneven quality of their teachers, and they usually register disappointment. Sometimes I'm pleased to hear them reminisce about their time in my classroom—that they had fun with challenging topics such as child labor or putting Christopher Columbus on trial. "Come talk to our teachers," they say. "Show them how to teach. We're so bored."

These conversations are uplifting but they are also depressing. They reaffirm my conviction that good teaching can engage kids intellectually, physically, and socially, by drawing on their interests, posing controversial problems, offering meaningful activities, and encouraging an active role in the community. Some call this *critical teaching*. I also call it teaching for social justice.

Whatever we call it, the fact is that most students in public and private schools in America don't experience it. Studies by scholars like John Goodlad and Ted Sizer, among others, confirm that even some of the "best" schools in America do not challenge students to think deeply, to question fundamental social premises, or to discuss real issues with one another.[1] This miseducation of the vast majority of kids is in addition to the even more appalling undereducation of children from the most disenfranchised sections of our population.[2]

Progressive Dilemma

So what are progressive teachers to do? Should we close our doors, teach well, and ignore the wrangling in the institutions and the society we inhabit? I would answer no. Even the best teacher won't last forever by trying to stay oblivious to the surrounding storms. My teaching career has taught me that what goes on in the classroom is the core of all school change efforts, but that strategies for transforming classrooms need to be interwoven with broader efforts to change the whole school, the surrounding district, and the larger society. The conditions we face in our classrooms are a result of the political decisions made outside our classrooms. Government invests in sports stadiums and prisons while many schools are crowded and ill-equipped. Corporations relocate companies outside our communities, and even our national borders, so students and families have fewer resources and more employment problems. A school district decides to introduce a new curricular initiative or adopt a new textbook series and our teaching must adapt to the new straitjacket. We need to find ways to link such decisions, and the resistance they engender, to critical classroom teaching.

But practicing critical pedagogy for social justice in education is not easy. Given current realities, progressive teachers find themselves on the one hand defending public schools from right-wing critics, who would privatize everything,[3] and on the other, criticizing the inequalities and inadequacies of the very schools they are defending. This dilemma is not new. Public education has been contested terrain in this country ever since the first schools opened their doors. Businesspeople and some "social reformers" have viewed schools as a way to socialize unruly populations and mold a more efficient, docile workforce. Whether the students were children of immigrants, of freed slaves, of Native Americans, of speakers of languages other than English, or of rural people moving into the city, schooling was to be the great homogenizer and sorter.[4] At the same time, working-class organizations, women, and people of color have viewed schools as potential vehicles for achieving equality, enlightenment, and in some cases, social mobility. In fact, today's schools are a result of these and other unfolding struggles of the last century.

The struggles continue. Although the civil rights movement forced public schools to open their classrooms to all and to provide better services to those who had been excluded in the past, such achievements are not everlasting. Just as the 1880s witnessed a rollback of the momentous gains of the Reconstruction era, the 1990s have witnessed a similar attack on the advances of the modern civil rights and the women's movements. In education this has assumed the blatant form of resegregation in many of our schools and of attacks on bilingual education, the multicultural curriculum, and affirmative action. It has also taken a more insidious form when teachers have been pressured to align their curriculum with state tests and official standards having little sensitivity to racial and cultural issues or to how children learn. Conservative policies make it harder to do child-centered education because testing imposes direct instruction and "teacher-proof" methods.

Teachers, caught in the middle, respond in a variety of ways ranging from resignation to outrage. Under current conditions, just keeping a class intact and functioning can exhaust a teacher's energy. Mounting scheduling and curricular demands eat up class time. Given this situation, it may seem counterintuitive to suggest that success in our classrooms could be linked to further activities outside the classroom, yet that has been my experience. I've maintained a positive attitude, despite some daunting conditions, because I've brought issues of social justice into my teaching. Teaching third, fourth, and fifth graders in inner-city schools informs my efforts to create an innovative public school and my broader involvement in developing a newspaper called *Rethinking Schools* and an organization called the National Coalition for Education Activists. Our students are connected to their families just as our classrooms are connected to the broader political world beyond our classroom doors. Community activism gives my teaching purpose, motivates my students, and keeps me sane.

Classrooms as Laboratories for Social Justice

In *Rethinking Our Classrooms: Teaching for Equity and Justice* my colleagues and I describe our classrooms as "laboratories for social justice" (Bigelow et al. 1994). What do such classrooms look like? First, they are grounded in the lives of our students, whose voices deserve to be heard. The New Zealand educator Sylvia Ashton-Warner (1963) calls this "teaching organically," while Brazilian educator Paulo Freire (1990) talks of "generative themes." Whatever the label, the point is that our teaching should connect our students' lives with a particular subject matter, should link their culture and conditions to the curriculum. Most good language arts teachers do this in writing workshops, journals, or personal notebooks. In *Living Between the Lines,* Lucy Calkins (1990) explains the importance of giving voice to students when she writes, "We can't give children rich lives, but we can give them the lens to appreciate the richness that is already there in their lives." To do this, however, we ourselves must see richness and not simply deficit.

While I agree with Lucy Calkins and use her ideas in my teaching, I find her thinking insufficient because I also believe that we must help our students understand how their lives connect to the broader society, which so often limits them. We need to get students asking the big "why" questions about what they don't like and about what needs to change so that they can live fuller lives. When we do more than offer student-centered classrooms, when we connect students' experience to social issues, our teaching becomes critical. We locate ourselves and our students in history. In a society as violent and as class- and race-stratified as ours is, this is the only kind of teaching that makes sense to me. If the mass media are showing kids how to resolve their conflicts through violence or unfettered consumerism, we have to encourage them to reflect. We have a responsibility to help them question their ideas and values, to figure out where these ideas come from and whose interests they serve. In my classroom we search out bias in children's books, fairy tales, news reports, CD-ROMs, songs, and cartoons. I tell my fifth graders that it's important to examine "the messages that are trying to take over your brain" and that it's up to them to sort out which ones promote fairness and justice.

In *Rethinking Columbus* Bill Bigelow and I report how we used the 1492 "discovery" myth to demonstrate that children's literature and textbooks tend to value the lives of Great White Men over all others (1998). The traditional materials we read in class invite children into Columbus' thoughts and dreams; he gets to speak, claim territories, and rename the ancient homelands of Native Americans. In such hero-centered texts, children are implicitly encouraged to disregard the lives of women, working people, and especially people of color. They view history and current events from the standpoint of society's winners, the dominant groups. A social justice curriculum, by contrast, strives to include everyone, especially the heretofore dominated. To encourage such critical thinking we list a series of questions children can use to look at portrayals of Columbus in children's books: Whose thoughts does the author share with the reader? How many times does Columbus talk compared to Native Americans? When Bill Bigelow and Linda Christensen encourage their Oregon high school students to rewrite history from the point of view of those who have been silenced, students enact a trial in which Columbus, Spanish royalty, the crew, the Taínos, and the "system of empire" all stand accused of contributing to the genocide of the Taíno people.[5] The students then take what they have learned into elementary schools and teach the younger children.

In addition to asking critical questions of the subject matter, a social justice classroom should be participatory and it should be based on dialogue. Dialogue in this context is a structured discussion with an extended focus and a critical purpose. It makes the objects of study the mutual property of teacher and students; learning is not a one-way process that transfers knowledge from teacher to student. As Ira Shor writes, "A dialogic class begins with problem-posing discussion and sends powerful signals to students that their participation is expected and needed. . . . Dialogue calls for a teacher's art of intervention and art of restraint, so that the verbal density of a trained intellectual does not silence the verbal styles of unscholastic students" (Shor 1987, 23).

In my dialogic teaching I emphasize *conflict* in history, current events, and other subjects. In traditional school curricula, however, struggle is often omitted and conflict forgotten. Official textbook history is not about social movements. But when a common history of struggle is denied, the past is rewritten in ways that make it easier for those in power to manipulate truth. When Richard Nixon said, "History will absolve our role in Vietnam," he knew what he was talking about; corporate textbook companies continue to write Vietnam out of our national literature and history (Bibby 1993). In contrast, educators like Paulo Freire point out the positive role of struggle in history. Freire calls conflict the "midwife of real consciousness" and says it should be the focus of learning.

In approaching conflict, social justice classrooms are multicultural and antiracist. I want to help kids learn to critique the curriculum and the texts to uncover where and why these books are inadequate to deal with the realities of our multicultural society. I believe children should be taught that racism is unscientific, immoral, and damaging to our society.[6] Kids absorb racism at a young age, so it makes sense for elementary schools to zero in on this problem.

A final characteristic of a social justice classroom is that it promotes activism. The central theme in my classroom is that the quest for social justice is an ongoing struggle from which we have already benefited. By understanding this struggle kids can decide whether or not to be involved, and I weave this theme into the various disciplines.

I believe it is important to encourage students to see themselves as actors in the world, not just as acted upon. If students critique the ills of society, they also need ways to help change wrongs; otherwise, all they learn is cynicism. By providing examples of how young people and adults have fought for social change in the past and by helping students keep abreast of current social struggles, we give them a way to take such initiatives themselves, one of the most important outcomes of education for democracy. The types of transforming action possible depend, of course, on the culture, age, and interests of students, as well as on the conditions in the community and in the local school system.

The degree of action outside the classroom also depends on the confidence and the job security of the teacher. It is a big and sometimes risky step for a teacher to get involved in student action, but the results far outweigh the potential problems. Because I have chosen an activist role and have received support from other teachers and from parents who share my social justice goals, I have been able to take my students to marches demanding that Dr. King's birthday be made a national holiday, an end to nuclear arms race, and an end to child labor. My students have also testified before the City Council asking that a Jobs with Peace referendum be placed on the ballot. They've gone to the County Board demanding that a local swimming pool be kept open in spite of budget cuts. While such activities have been exciting learning experiences for us all, I also have scheduled follow-ups in the classroom to draw out more nuanced lessons and share the experience with larger numbers of students, since such overt activism is optional, not required.

Schools as Centers of Renaissance and Resistance

What I am suggesting is that critical teachers won't last long if they confine their efforts to their own classrooms. For long-term survival, we need to transform the entire school through a constructive relationship with the community. What inspires or sustains communitywide support for teachers varies from situation to situation. It might be a district or state-funded initiative. It might be a study circle working for schoolwide implementation of an antiracist curriculum. The key is seeing students and parents as local allies with whom we can share mutually supportive projects. A teacher-community alliance is the foundation for effective teaching in an effective school.

In many ravaged urban neighborhoods the only remaining stable institutions are public schools and churches. If the schools were renovated and transformed into full-service community centers, the benefits could be startling. Communities would have a center, an anchor, from which to address pressing needs. Young people would benefit from organized athletics, arts, and academic programs as constructive alternatives to gangs. Social service agencies and schools could better coordinate their work. Jobs would be provided for local parents and graduates, and job training made available to many. Most important, these community centers would kindle a sense of constructive community between school and home. The school would be a safe place for community meetings, with adequate child care and programs for putting democratic notions of community action into practice. Parents, sometimes hesitant to get involved in their children's school, might feel more comfortable if they were already coming into the facility for other activities. Such intergenerational centers would have the added benefit of putting underfunded urban and rural schools on a par with suburban schools because they would include modern libraries, art, music, and multipurpose rooms.

Just over a decade ago some teachers and parents embarked on just such an ambitious project. A school in a multiracial neighborhood of Milwaukee, where I live, was about to be closed. The kids and staff were being transferred to a newly constructed school six blocks away. The district school administration had first planned to tear down the old building, but then decided to make it into a teacher training school for "bad" teachers. Teachers, parents, and community activists in the neighborhood had other ideas. We proposed creating an integrated, bilingual (Spanish-English), antiracist, multicultural, whole language school run by a council of parents and staff. This bilingual school would be "two-way," which meant English-dominant students would learn Spanish and Spanish-dominant students would learn English while studying their native idioms as well. The ensuing two-month political struggle was short but intense, and despite the opposition of the district school superintendent we were successful. We won the right to establish a community-based school grounded in a set of progressive principles. We succeeded for several reasons: some of us were experienced organizers, we had a common vision, we were willing to play hardball with district officials, and our effort occurred at a time of relative dysfunctionality within the district. We looked like good people with a good plan for a floundering corner of public education (Peterson 1993).

The past decade has been filled with more successes and some failures, but we've learned a lot (Peterson 1995). The main lesson is that as critical teachers we work best when we work with the community to build a school based on a common pedagogical vision and allowing time to reflect on our teaching. If teachers have a unified vision and time for professional development, even large urban schools can flourish and provide a strong model of what can be, as well as a reservoir of resistance to fight for what should be. At Fratney we have made enormous efforts to build a solid academic program. Now we can work with community organizations and adjacent schools to transform our school into a "community learning center" serving the youngest and the oldest from the early morning hours into the evening.[7] We offer extensive before and after-school programs, along with academic help, drama classes, computer clubs, adult English-as-a-Second-Language and Spanish-as-a-Second-Language classes, and more. We try to be in the community and have the community in us.

Organizations as Means of Struggle

Building social justice classrooms and schools of resistance is as important as it is time consuming, but both will prove inadequate unless we connect them to even broader issues in our school districts and in society. Larger factors— such as inadequate funding for many schools and poverty for many students— directly limit learning and restrict teaching. With these broader issues in mind, several years ago a number of other teachers and I started a reading circle on the connections between social conditions and schooling. We examined the impact of class and racial stratification, the role of mass media in influencing students, and how forces outside teachers' and students' control shape the curriculum. We soon realized that we wanted to share the progressive analyses we were discussing with more people and decided to start an educational news-paper dedicated to issues of justice and equity: *Rethinking Schools* was born. We also wanted to find a way to take the offensive. We were tired of trooping to school board meetings to stave off yet another attack on teachers and educa-tion programs. School people working for change needed a forum. When we began the mass distribution of *Rethinking Schools* in 1986, our goals were to give teachers and parents a voice in reforming our public schools and to change classroom practice and educational policies. We wanted good public education for all children.

Despite the financial hardship, we decided to distribute our paper free of charge because we wanted a broad base of regular classroom teachers and administrators to read it, not just those already committed to progressive change. The paper started, literally, without any real budget; it was kept alive by volunteers and laid out on my kitchen table with the help of an Apple IIe computer. We published 6,000 copies of the first issue, which focused on read-ing, in November 1986. The attention of many classroom teachers was imme-diately caught by the bold front-page headline: "Surviving Scott, Foresman: Confessions of a Kindergarten Teacher." The author, Rita Tenorio, a bilingual kindergarten teacher, wrote that "administrators in MPS [Milwaukee Public Schools] . . . and across the country are responding to pressure to improve our schools by pushing these flawed mechanistic [basal] methods even more! Thus they are extending the questionable basal reading program downward to kindergarten" (Tenorio 1986). As an alternative she laid out what is now well known as the emergent reading—or whole language—approach.

In an editorial in the same issue, we outlined an argument that we contin-ued to develop and deepen over the next two years. We criticized the "ritualis-tic and mechanical activities" of the basal, charging that "students experience reading as a drab prelude to equally drab paper and pencil activities. They come to view books as a source of boredom, rather than as a source of discovery and stimulation." Moreover, we charged that this "systems management" approach was "de-skilling teachers," depriving them of their proper role and the chance to "grapple with the difficult tasks of figuring out what and how to teach." Finally we quoted the famous labor organizer, Joe Hill, telling teachers, "Don't Mourn, Organize." We explained that "the only realistic way for Milwaukee's elementary teachers to regain the independence they need to teach well is to organize around classroom issues. A serious effort would be to question the current basal program. . . . It is high time for the basal system to be arraigned before the court of sound educational practices, with parents, students, and teachers occupying prominent places in the jurors' box" ("Rethinking Basal Readers" 1986, 2).

The concrete struggle over the basals ultimately led to significant change within the system. Twelve pilot "whole language projects" were established and a whole language teachers council was set up across the district to help develop curriculum, design assessments, and provide inservice training. Even within those schools that continued to use the basal there was a significant shift toward reading actual literary works, toward writing workshops, and toward reading for meaning.[8]

Some of the *Rethinking Schools* editors also helped to initiate what ultimately became the National Coalition for Education Activists (NCEA), a multiracial network of teachers, parents, and community activists united around antiracist principles for transforming public education.[9] We considered it important to build this national organization based on principles of social justice and equity for the same reasons that we had launched *Rethinking Schools.* Social justice activists need to link up and learn from one another; isolation is demoralizing and destructive. The issues of equity and race also need to be placed squarely on the table of educational reform, and we thought this might be possible only by creating a multiracial organization that included teachers and parents. Over the years the NCEA has matured into one of the few national organizations strengthening local initiatives by connecting teachers, parents, and community folks around issues of schools and justice for the important goal of social change. Like our experience with *Rethinking Schools,* the success of the NCEA demonstrates that a small group of people, working together and willing to confront difficult issues such as race and power, can make a difference.

The Centrality of Race

When I look back over the dozen plus years of *Rethinking Schools,* I see that one of our strengths has been our clear political focus. Since its founding, our newspaper has emphasized issues of equity, particularly as they affect urban public schools. In our curricular articles and books (*Rethinking Columbus* and *Rethinking Our Classrooms: Teaching for Equity and Justice*) as in our policy books (Miner and Lowe 1996; Karp and Miner 1997; Miner 1998), the issue of equity, particularly racial equity, has been key. Indeed, schools must take an aggressive approach to race and inequality—from initiating antiracist classroom practices that help children see the multicultural strengths of our society to programs ensuring that all children succeed and learn at school. Henry Louis Gates Jr., chair of Afro-American studies at Harvard University, summed it up in these words: "We're worried when Johnny can't read. We're worried when Johnny can't add. But shouldn't we be worried, too, when Johnny tramples grave-stones in a Jewish cemetery or scrawls racial epithets on a dormitory wall?" (Gates 1995).

Yes, we must teach children about racism. And we must fight policies that treat children in racist ways. Sometimes I pause during the school day, look out over my students, and shake my head at the unfairness of unequal resources. Here are a group of ten-, eleven-, and twelve-year-olds, only three or four of whom have computers at home, many of whom have responsibility for siblings because parents work two jobs or odd shifts, are unable to afford the niceties of after-school lessons, and have no transportation even if they could. Yet these young people receive less public funding than suburban kids with access to so much more in their private lives. Something is wrong with this picture.[10]

As teachers concerned with our children's futures we need to look at that picture carefully at the level of classroom practice, of the school community, and of the broader society. We play a unique role in the development of our so-ciety's children. We need to make certain that our collective voices are heard, not only in our own classrooms, which might become laboratories for social justice, but in the streets of our communities and in the halls of power, to en-sure justice and equality for all of our children.

Notes

1. John Goodlad wrote in his seminal work, *A Place Called School: Prospects for the Future,* that not even one percent of the instructional time in high school is de-voted to discussion that requires some kind of response involving reasoning or perhaps an opinion from students (1984, 229). See also Ted Sizer's *Horace's Compromise: The Dilemma of the American High School.*

2. See Ann Bastian et al. (1985), *Choosing Equality: The Case for Democratic Schooling.*

3. See Barbara Miner (1998), *Classroom Crusades: Responding to the Religious Right's Agenda for Public Schools.*

4. See Michael Katz (1968), *The Irony of Early School Reform;* and Joel Spring (1972), *Education and the Rise of the Corporate State.*

5. For a complete description of the Columbus trial role play, see Bigelow and Peterson (1998), pp. 85–94.

6. See *Rethinking Our Classrooms* (Bigelow et al. 1994) and *Beyond Heroes and Holidays,* edited by Enid Lee, Deborah Menkart, and Margo Okazawa-Rey (1997).

7. In 1998 staff and parents developed and put forth a proposal, "Growing To-gether: Fratney's Building Proposal to Bridge School and Community," which calls for

the renovation of the ninety-five-year-old building and construction of a community center/school addition.

    8. For a detailed description of the antibasal struggle, see "Don't Mourn—Organize: Teachers Take the Offensive Against Basals" (Peterson 1989). For a history of the teacher council reforms within Milwaukee public schools, see "Transforming Teaching" (Peterson 1998).

    9. For more information, write to NCEA, P. O. Box 679, Rhinebeck, NY 12572–0679, or call (914) 876-4580.

    10. See Jonathan Kozol (1991), *Savage Inequalities.*

Works Cited

Ashton-Warner, Sylvia. 1963. *Teacher.* New York: Simon & Schuster.

Bastian, Ann, Norm Fruchter, Marilyn Gittell, Colin Greer, and Kenneth Haskins. 1985. *Choosing Equality: The Case for Democratic Schooling.* Philadelphia: Temple University Press.

Bibby, Michael. 1993. "'Where Is Vietnam?' Antiwar Poetry and the Canon." *College English* 55 (February): 158–78.

Bigelow, Bill, Linda Christensen, Stan Karp, and Bob Peterson, eds. 1994. *Rethinking Our Classrooms: Teaching for Equity and Justice.* Milwaukee: Rethinking Schools.

Bigelow, Bill, and Bob Peterson, eds. 1998. *Rethinking Columbus: The Next 500 Years.* Milwaukee: Rethinking Schools.

Calkins, Lucy. 1990. *Living Between the Lines.* Portsmouth, NH: Heinemann.

Freire, Paulo. 1990. *Pedagogy of the Oppressed.* New York: Continuum.

Gates, Henry Louis Jr. 1995. "Multiculturalism: A Conversation Among Different Voices." In *Rethinking Schools: An Agenda for Change,* edited by David Levine, Robert Lowe, Bob Peterson, and Rita Tenorio. New York: New Press.

Goodlad, John. 1984. *A Place Called School: Prospects for the Future.* New York: Mc-Graw Hill.

Karp, Stan, and Barbara Miner, eds. 1997. *Funding for Justice: Money, Equity, and the Future of Public Education.* Milwaukee: Rethinking Our Schools.

Katz, Michael. 1968. *The Irony of Early School Reform.* Boston: Beacon Press.

———. 1971. *Class, Bureaucracy, and Schools.* New York: Praeger.

Kozol, Jonathan. 1991. *Savage Inequalities.* New York: Crown.

Lee, Enid, Deborah Menkart, and Margo Okazawa-Rey, eds. 1997. *Beyond Heroes and Holidays.* Washington, DC: NECA.

Miner, Barbara, ed. 1998. *Classroom Crusades: Responding to the Religious Right's Agenda for Public Schools.* Milwaukee: Rethinking Schools.

Miner, Barbara, and Bob Lowe, eds. 1996. *Selling Out Our Schools: Vouchers, Markets, and the Future of Public Education.* Milwaukee: Rethinking Our Schools.

Peterson, Bob. 1989. "Don't Mourn—Organize: Teachers Take the Offensive Against Basals." *Theory into Practice* 28 (4): 295–99.

————. 1993. "Creating a School That Honors the Traditions of a Culturally Diverse Student Body: La Escuela Fratney." In *Public Schools That Work*, edited by Gregory Smith, 45–67. New York: Routledge.

————. 1995. "La Escuela Fratney: A Journey Toward Democracy." In *Democratic Schools*, edited by Michael Apple and James Bean, 58–82. Alexandria, VA: ASCD.

————. 1998. "Transforming Teaching." *Rethinking Schools* (Fall).

"Rethinking Basal Readers." 1986. Editorial. *Rethinking Schools* (Fall): 2.

Shor, Ira. 1987. *Freire for the Classroom: A Sourcebook for Liberatory Teaching*. Portsmouth, NH: Heinemann.

Sizer, Ted. 1984. *Horace's Compromise: The Dilemma of the American High School*. New York: Houghton Mifflin.

Spring, Joel. 1972. *Education and the Rise of the Corporate State*. Boston: Beacon Press.

Tenorio, Rita. 1986. "Surviving Scott, Foresman: Confessions of a Kindergarten Teacher." *Rethinking Schools* (Fall).

Rethinking Schools is a nonprofit, independent newspaper advocating for reform of public schools, with a focus on equity and social justice. It began in Milwaukee in 1986 as a quarterly journal edited by teachers and educators who .wanted to help organize a movement to reform public schools in Milwaukee. Over the years, *Rethinking Schools* has broadened its focus to include national concerns. Its fundamental mission has not changed, however. It still believes that public schools, in particular urban schools, must be reformed to meet the needs of all children. It still believes public schools are fundamental to the creation of a human, caring, multiracial democracy. *Rethinking Schools* emphasizes actual classroom practice—day-to-day realties faced by teachers, parents, and students—and the importance of equitable education opportunities. In its curriculum articles, it weaves issues of academic excellence, equity, and social justice into the life of the classroom. A special emphasis is to encourage critical teaching approaches in all subject areas. In policy analyses, *Rethinking Schools* focuses on key topics ranging from vouchers to standardized testing, in language accessible to all.

Each issue of the journal has articles on classroom practice and educational policy, along with resources, student work, analysis, and commentary. It is one of the few national educational journals put out by practicing classroom teachers.

In addition to the quarterly journal, *Rethinking Schools* has published anthologies of articles from the newspaper. Such special publications include: *Rethinking Columbus: The Next 500 Years; Rethinking Our Classrooms: Teaching for Equity; Selling Out Our Schools: Vouchers, Markets, and the Future of Public Education; The Real Ebonics Debate: Power, Language, and the*

Education of African American Children; Funding for Justice: Money, Equity and the Future of Public Education; and *Classroom Crusades: Responding to the Religious Right's Agenda for Public Schools.* The editors of *Rethinking Schools* invite inquiries and article submissions.

Subscriptions are $12.50/year. For a free catalog contact *Rethinking Schools,* 1001 E. Keefe Ave., Milwaukee, WI 53212. Call toll free 1-800-669-4192. E-mail: RSBusiness@aol.com. Visit the web site: www.rethinking schools.org.

1

Multiculturalism, Social Justice, and Critical Teaching

Sonia Nieto

Editors' Notes: We begin this volume with excerpts from Sonia Nieto's widely read *Affirming Diversity,* which connects a framework of multicultural education to critical pedagogy. Nieto believes that multicultural education in a sociopolitical context can offer hope for change, explore alternatives to traditional teaching systems, and open up awareness of the role culture and language can play in education. The first excerpt defines seven characteristics of multicultural education. The second provides a model for educators who want to incorporate multicultural education into their curriculum and instruction. A particularly useful chart showing the characteristics and levels of multicultural education concludes these excerpts. Nieto's emphasis on "social justice" in critical multiculturalism places her in the Freirean context of activist education.

I: Multicultural Education and School Reform

When multicultural education is mentioned, many people first think of lessons in human relations and sensitivity training, units about ethnic holidays, education in inner-city schools, or food festivals. If limited to these issues, the potential for substantive change in schools is severely diminished. However, when broadly conceptualized, multicultural education can have a great impact on redefining how the four areas of potential school conflict already discussed can be addressed. These are: racism and discrimination, structural factors within schools that may limit learning, the impact of culture on learning, and language diversity. This chapter focuses on how multicultural education addresses each of these areas.

Multicultural education is not being proposed as a panacea for all educational ills. It will not cure underachievement, remove boring and irrelevant curriculum, or stop vandalism. It will not automatically motivate parents to participate in schools, reinvigorate tired and dissatisfied teachers, or guarantee a lower dropout rate. Schools are part of our communities and as such reflect the stratification and social inequities of the larger society. As long as this is the case, no school program, no matter how broadly conceptualized, can change things completely and on its own. Furthermore, in our complex and highly bureaucratic school systems, no approach can yield instant and positive results for all students.

Given these caveats, we can nevertheless say that multicultural education, conceptualized as broad-based school reform, can offer hope for change. By focusing on major factors contributing to underachievement, a broadly conceptualized multicultural education permits educators to explore alternatives to a system that leads to failure for too many of its students. Such an explanation can lead to the creation of richer and more productive learning environments, diverse instructional strategies, and a more profound awareness of the role culture and language can play in education. In this way, educational success for all students can be a realistic goal rather than an impossible ideal. Multicultural education in a sociopolitical context becomes both richer and more complex than simple lessons on getting along or units on ethnic festivals.

The purpose of this chapter is to propose a definition of multicultural education, then to analyze the seven primary characteristics included in the definition. These characteristics underscore the role that multicultural education can play in reforming schools and providing an equal and excellent education for all students.

What follows is but one definition of multicultural education and thus reflects a particular understanding of the concept. My approach has been to consider multicultural education in light of the persistent problems in our schools and the lack of achievement of so many students, rather than as an add-on or luxury disconnected from the everyday lives of students and schools. In this sense, it is a comprehensive definition that emphasizes the context and process of education, not simply its outcomes. In spite of some minor differences over the past 20 years among the major theorists in the field, there has been remarkable consistency about the goals, purposes, and reasons for multicultural education.[1]

Because no definition can truly capture the complexities of multicultural education, I hope that the following will serve as a basis for dialogue and reflection. This definition reflects my own way of conceptualizing the issues. Although I have developed 7 qualities that I believe are important in multicultural education, you might come up with just 3, or with 15. The point is not to present a definitive way to understand multicultural education, but instead to start you thinking about the interplay of societal and school structures and contexts and how they influence learning. What I believe *is* essential is an emphasis on the sociopolitical context of education and a rejection of multicultural education as either a superficial adding of content to the curriculum, or alternatively, as the magic pill that will do away with all educational problems. I hope that in the process of considering my definition, you will think about multicultural education in a substantive way and develop your own priorities.

A Definition of Multicultural Education

I define *multicultural education* in a sociopolitical context as follows:

> Multicultural education is a process of comprehensive school reform and basic education for all students. It challenges and rejects racism and other forms of discrimination in schools and society and accepts and affirms the pluralism (ethnic, racial, linguistic, religious, economic, and gender, among others) that students, their communities, and teachers represent. Multicultural education permeates the curriculum and instructional strategies used in schools, as well as the interactions among teachers, students, and parents, and the very way that schools conceptualize the nature of teaching and learning. Because it uses critical pedagogy as its underlying philosophy and focuses on knowledge, reflection, and action (praxis) as the basis for social change, multicultural education promotes the democratic principles of social justice.

The seven basic characteristics of multicultural education in this definition are:

Multicultural education is *antiracist education.*

Multicultural education is *basic education.*

Multicultural education is *important for* all *students.*

Multicultural education is *pervasive.*

Multicultural education is *education for social justice.*

Multicultural education is a *process.*

Multicultural education is *critical pedagogy.*

Multicultural Education Is Antiracist Education

Antiracism, indeed antidiscrimination in general, is at the very core of a multicultural perspective. This is especially important to keep in mind when we consider that only the most superficial aspects of multicultural education are apparent in many schools, even those that espouse a multicultural philosophy. Celebrations of ethnic festivals are as far as it goes in some places. In others, sincere attempts to decorate bulletin boards or purchase materials with what is thought to be a multicultural perspective end up perpetuating the worst kind of stereotypes. And even where there are serious attempts to develop a truly pluralistic environment, it is not unusual to find incongruencies, such as the children of color as overwhelmingly visible in the lowest academic tracks and invisible in the highest. All of these are examples of multicultural education *without* an explicitly antiracist perspective.

It is important to stress multicultural education as antiracist because many people may believe that a multicultural program *automatically* takes care of racism. Unfortunately this is not always true. According to Weinberg,

> Most multicultural materials deal wholly with the cultural distinctiveness of various groups and little more. Almost never is there any sustained attention to the ugly realities of systematic discrimination against the same group that also happens to utilize quaint clothing, fascinating toys, delightful fairy tales, and delicious food. Responding to racist attacks and defamation is *also* part of the culture of the group under study.[2]

Being antiracist and antidiscriminatory thus means paying attention to all areas in which some students may be favored over others: the curriculum, choice of materials, sorting policies, and teachers' interactions and relationships with students and their communities.

To be more inclusive and balanced, multicultural curriculum must by definition be antiracist. Teaching does not become more honest and critical simply by becoming more inclusive, but this nevertheless is an important first step in ensuring that students have access to a wide variety of viewpoints. Although the beautiful and heroic aspects of our history should be taught, so must the ugly and exclusionary. Rather than viewing the world through rose-colored glasses, antiracist multicultural education forces both teachers and students to take a long, hard look at everything as it was and is, which also means considering the effects and interconnections among events, people, and things.

Confronting in an honest and direct way both the positive and negative aspects of history, the arts, and science is avoided in too many schools. Michelle Fine calls this the "fear of naming," and it is part of the system of silencing in public schools.[3] To name might become too messy, or so the thinking goes. Teachers often refuse to engage their students in discussions about racism because it might "demoralize" them. Too dangerous a topic, it is best left untouched.

Related to the fear of naming is the insistence of schools on sanitizing the curriculum, or what Kozol calls "tailoring" important men and women for school use. Schools manage to take our most exciting and memorable heroes and bleed the life and spirit completely out of them. Because it is dangerous to teach a history that he describes as "studded with so many bold, and revolutionary, and subversive, and exhilarating men and women," Kozol maintains that schools instead drain these heroes of their passions, glaze them over with an implausible veneer, place them on lofty pedestals, and then tell "incredibly dull stories" about them.[4] For example, in trying to make Martin Luther King, Jr., palatable to the mainstream, schools have made him a Milquetoast. The only thing most children know about him is that he kept having a dream. Bulletin boards are full of ethereal pictures of Dr. King surrounded by clouds. If children get to read or hear any of his speeches at all, it is his "I Have a Dream" speech. Rare indeed are the allusions to his early and consistent opposition to the Vietnam War; his strong criticism of unbridled capitalism; and the connections he made, near the end of his life, among racism, capitalism, and war. Martin Luther King, a man full of passion and life, becomes lifeless. He becomes a "safe hero."

Most of the heroes we present to our children are either those in the mainstream or those who have become safe by the process of "tailoring." Others who have fought for social justice are often downplayed, maligned, or simply ignored. For example, although John Brown's actions in defense of the liberation of enslaved people are considered noble by many, in our history books he is presented, if at all, as somewhat of a crazed idealist. Nat Turner is another example. The slave revolt that he led deserves an important place in our history, if only to acknowledge that people fought against their own oppression and were not simply passive or victimized by it. Yet his name is usually overlooked, and Abraham Lincoln is presented as the "great emancipator." Nat Turner is not safe; Abraham Lincoln is.

To be antiracist also means to work affirmatively to combat racism. It means making antiracism and antidiscrimination an explicit part of the curriculum and teaching young people skills in confronting racism. It also means that students must not be isolated, alienated, or punished for naming it when they see it. If developing productive and critical citizens for a democratic society is one of the important goals of public education, antiracist behaviors can help to meet that objective.

Racism is seldom mentioned in school (it is bad, a dirty word) and therefore is not dealt with. Unfortunately, many teachers think that simply having lessons in getting along or celebrating Human Relations Week will make students nonracist or nondiscriminatory in general. Yet it is impossible to be unaffected by racism, sexism, linguicism, ageism, anti-Semitism, classism, and ethnocentrism in a society characterized by all of them. To expect schools to be an oasis of sensitivity and understanding in the midst of this stratification is unrealistic. Therefore, part of the mission of the school becomes creating the space and encouragement that legitimates talk about racism and discrimination and makes it a source of dialogue in the schools. Part of this task includes learning the missing or fragmented parts of our history.

Multicultural education is also antiracist because it exposes the racist and discriminatory practices in schools discussed in preceding chapters. A school truly committed to a multicultural philosophy will closely examine its policies and the attitudes and behaviors of its staff to determine how these might be discriminating against some students. How teachers react to their students, whether native language use is permitted in the school, how sorting takes place, and the way in which classroom organization might hurt some students and help others are questions to be considered. In addition, individual teachers will reflect on their own attitudes and practices in the classroom and how they are influenced by their background as well as by their ignorance of students' backgrounds. Although such soul-searching is often difficult, it is a necessary step in becoming a teacher committed to an antiracist multicultural philosophy.

Nevertheless, being antiracist does not mean flailing about in guilt or remorse. One of the reasons why schools are reluctant to deal with racism and discrimination is that they are uncomfortable topics for those who have traditionally benefited by their race, gender, and social class, among other differences. These topics often place people in the role of either the victimizer or the victimized. An initial and quite understandable reaction of European American teachers and students is to feel guilty. Such a reaction, however, although probably serving a useful purpose initially, needs to be understood as only one step in the process of becoming multiculturally literate and empowered. If one remains at this level, then guilt only immobilizes. Teachers and students need to move beyond guilt to a stage of energy and confidence, where they take action rather than hide behind feelings of remorse.

Although the primary victims of racism and discrimination are those who suffer its immediate consequences, racism and discrimination are destructive and demeaning to everyone. Keeping this in mind, it is easier for all teachers and students to confront these issues. Although not everyone is directly guilty of racism and discrimination, we nevertheless are all responsible for it. Given this perspective, students and teachers can focus on discrimination as something everyone has a responsibility to confront. For example, in discussing slavery in the United States, it is important to present it not simply as slave owners against enslaved Africans. There were many and diverse roles among a great variety of people during this period: enslaved Africans and free Africans, slave owners and poor White farmers, Black abolitionists and White abolitionists, White and Black feminists who fought for both abolition and women's liberation, and so on. Each of these perspectives should be taught so that children, regardless of ethnic background or gender, see themselves in history in ways that are not simply degrading or guilt-provoking. The incident of the only Black child in a classroom who was asked by his teacher to draw himself as a character during the Civil War is a poignant example. This child drew a horse, preferring to see himself as an animal rather than as an enslaved man. The deep sense of pain and emptiness that this child felt can only be surmised. Providing alternative roles for our students is therefore another aspect of an antiracist multicultural perspective.

Multicultural Education Is Basic Education

Given the recurring concern for the "basics" in education, it is absolutely essential that multicultural education be understood as *basic* education. Multicultural literacy is as indispensable for living in today's world as are reading, writing, arithmetic, and computer literacy. When multicultural education is unrelated to the core curriculum, it is perceived as unimportant to basic education.

One of the major stumbling blocks to implementing a broadly conceptualized multicultural education is the ossification of the "canon" in our schools. The canon, as used in contemporary U.S. education, assumes that the knowledge that is most worthy is already in place. According to this rather narrow view, the basics have in effect already been defined. Knowledge, in this context, is inevitably European, male, and upper class in origin and conception, especially in the arts and social sciences. In art history, courses rarely leave France, Italy, and sometimes England in considering the "great masters." What is called "classical" music is classical only in Europe, not in Africa, Asia, or Latin America. This same enthnocentrism is found in our history books, which places Europeans and European Americans as the actors and all others as the recipients, bystanders, or bit players of history.

It is unrealistic, for a number of reasons, to expect a perfectly "equal treatment" in the curriculum. A force-fit, which tries to equalize the number of African Americans, women, Jewish Americans, and so on in the curriculum, is not what multicultural education is all about. A great many groups have in effect been denied access in the actual making of history. Their participation therefore has not been equal, at least if we consider history in the traditional sense of great movers and shakers, monarchs and despots, and makers of war and peace. The participation of diverse groups, even within this somewhat narrow view of history, has been appreciable. It therefore deserves to be included. The point is that those who *have* been present in our history, arts, literature, and science should be made visible. More recent literature anthologies are a good example of the inclusion of more voices and perspectives than ever before. Did these become "great writers" overnight, or was it simply that they had been buried for too long?

However, we are not talking here simply of the "contributions" approach to history, literature, and the arts. Such an approach may consider some small contributions from usually excluded groups and can easily become patronizing by looking for contributions to a preconceived canon. Rather, the way in which generally excluded groups have made history and affected the arts, literature, geography, science, and philosophy *on their own terms* is what is missing.

The "canon" is unrealistic and incomplete because history is never as one-sided as it appears in most of our schools' curricula. What is needed is the expansion of what we define as basic by opening up the curriculum to a variety of perspectives and experiences. The problem that a canon tries to address is a real one: Modern-day knowledge is so dispersed and compartmentalized that our young people learn very little that is common. There is no *core* to the knowledge to which they are exposed.[5] However, proposing a static list of terms, almost exclusively with European and European American referents, does little to expand our common culture.

The alternative to multicultural education is *monocultural education.* Education reflective of only one reality and biased toward the dominant group, monocultural education is the order of the day in most of our schools. What students learn represents only a fraction of what is available knowledge, and those who decide what is most important make choices that are of necessity influenced by their own limited background, education, and experiences. Because the viewpoints of so many are left out, monocultural education is at best a partial education. It deprives all students of the diversity that is part of our world.

No school can consider that it is doing a proper or complete job unless its students develop multicultural literacy. What such a conception might mean in practice would no doubt differ from school to school. At the very least, we would expect all students to be fluent in a language other than their own; aware of the literature and arts of many different peoples; and conversant with the history and geography not only of the United States but also of African, Asian, Latin American, and European countries. Through such an education, we would expect our students to develop the social skills to understand and empathize with a wide diversity of people. Nothing can be more basic than this.

Multicultural Education Is Important for All Students

There is a widespread perception that multicultural education is only for students of color, or for urban students, or for so-called disadvantaged students. This belief is probably based on the roots of multicultural education, which grew out of the civil rights and equal education movements of the 1960s. The primary objective of multicultural education was defined as addressing the needs of students who historically had been most neglected or miseducated by the schools, primarily students of color. In trying to strike more of a balance, it was felt that attention should be paid to developing curriculum and materials that reflect the reality of these students' history, culture, and experience and that this curriculum should be destined particularly for inner-city schools populated primarily by children of color. This thinking was historically necessary and is understandable even today, given the great curricular imbalance that continues to exist in most schools.

More recently a broader conceptualization of multicultural education has gained acceptance. It is that all students are *miseducated* to the extent that they receive only a partial and biased education. The primary victims of biased education are those who are invisible in the curriculum. Females, for example, are absent in most curricula, except in special courses on women's history which are few and far between. Although these courses are important and helpful in remediating the almost total lack of a female presence in curriculum and materials, they, too, are a double-edged sword. The message of these courses to both females and males is, as Shakeshaft has noted, that there are two kinds of history: women's history, which is peripheral, and American history, which is "real" history.[6] Working-class history is also absent in virtually all U.S. curricula. Anyon found, for example, that the content of the social studies curriculum was the *least* honest about U.S. history in the working-class schools than in all the others she observed.[7] The children of the working class are deprived not only of a more forthright education but, more important, of a place in history, and students of all social class backgrounds are likewise deprived of a more honest and complete view of our history.

Although the primary victims of biased education continue to be those who are invisible in the curriculum, those who figure prominently are victims as well. They receive only a partial education, which legitimates cultural blinders. European American children, seeing only themselves, learn that they are the norm; everyone else is secondary. The same is true of males. And the children of the wealthy, although generally exposed to a more comprehensive view of history, learn nevertheless that the wealthy and the powerful are the real makers of history, the ones who have left their mark on civilization.

Multicultural education is by definition expansive. Because it is *about* all people, it is also *for* all people, regardless of their ethnicity, language, religion, gender, race, or class. It can even be convincingly argued that students from the dominant culture need multicultural education more than others, for they are often the most miseducated about diversity in our society. In fact, European American youths often feel that they do not even *have* a culture, at least not in the same sense that clearly culturally identifiable youths do. At the same time, they feel that their way of living, of doing things, of believing, and of acting are simply the only possibilities. Anything else is ethnic and exotic.

Feeling as they do, these children are prone to develop an unrealistic view of the world and of their place in it. They learn to think of themselves and their group as the norm and of all others as a deviation. These are the children who learn not to question, for example, the name of "flesh-colored" adhesive strips even though they are not the flesh color of three-quarters of humanity. They do not even have to think about the fact that everyone, Christian or not, gets holidays at Christmas and Easter and that other religious holidays are given little attention in our calendars and school schedules. Whereas children from dominated groups may develop feelings of inferiority based on their school experiences, dominant group children may develop feelings of superiority. Both responses are based on incomplete and inaccurate information about the complexity and diversity of the world, and both are harmful.

Nevertheless, multicultural education continues to be thought of by many teachers and schools as education for the "culturally different" or the "disadvantaged." Teachers in predominantly European American schools, for example, may feel it is not important or necessary to teach their students anything about the civil rights movement; likewise only in scattered bilingual programs in Mexican American communities are students exposed to literature by Mexican and Mexican American authors; and only at high schools with a high percentage of students of color are ethnic studies generally taught. These are ethnocentric interpretations of multicultural education.

This thinking is paternalistic as well as misinformed. Anything remotely digressing from the "regular" (European American) curriculum is automatically considered soft. Therefore, the usual response to make a curriculum multicultural is to water it down. Poor pedagogical decisions are then based on the premise that so-called disadvantaged students need a watered-down version of the "real" curriculum, whereas more privileged children can handle the "regular" or more academically challenging curriculum. Gay suggests that the curriculum selected for learners of backgrounds different from the dominant group should be of a parallel *order*. For example, "if Robert Frost's and Emily Dickinson's works are used to teach the canons of good poetry for Anglo students, then the rapping routines of Run DMC and the Fat Boys are inappropriate to use as an Afro-American illustration of those same principles."[8] Although *all* students need to learn about the literature of many different cultures, her point is that usually *only* African American students are exposed to curriculum adaptations of this kind. Gay thus suggests that a parallel, and thus more appropriate, example would be the works of Maya Angelou and Langston Hughes. Making a curriculum multicultural should in no way dilute it; on the contrary, making it more inclusive inevitably enriches it. All students would be enriched by reading the poetry of Hughes and Angelou. One study based on extensive interviews, for instance, found that students of all backgrounds preferred a school community where differences were valued rather than feared or avoided.[9]

Multicultural education, being an alternative approach, is often considered to be most appropriate for children "at risk" of educational failure. This term has become a code word for students of color from inner-city schools or poor students of all cultural backgrounds from rural and urban schools. Yet students at risk of educational failure can and do come from all social and cultural backgrounds and find themselves on the periphery of the educational environment for a variety of reasons. Perhaps a more appropriate term for such students is *marginal,* as used by Sinclair and Ghory.[10] This term implies that the conditions for the failure of students are inherent not in the students themselves, as "at risk" implies, but rather in the learning environments created for them. By changing the environments, the so-called risk factors are reduced and marginal students again enter the educational center. A broadly conceptualized multicultural education focusing on school reform represents a substantive way of changing the curriculum, the environment, the structure of schools, and instructional strategies so that all students can benefit.

Multicultural Education Is Pervasive

Multicultural education is sometimes thought of as something that happens at a set period of the day, yet another subject area to be covered. Some school systems even have a "multicultural teacher" who goes from class to class in the same way as the music or art teacher. Although the intent of this approach may be to formalize a multicultural perspective in the standard curriculum, it is in the long run self-defeating because it tends to isolate the multicultural philosophy from everything else that happens in the classroom. By letting classroom teachers avoid responsibility for creating a multicultural approach, this strategy often alienates them by presenting multicultural knowledge as somehow contradictory to all other knowledge. The schism between what is "regular" and what is "multicultural" widens. In this kind of arrangement, classroom teachers are not encouraged, through either formal in-service programs or alternative opportunities, to develop expertise in multicultural education. It becomes exotic knowledge that is external to the real work that goes on in most classrooms. Given this conception of multicultural education, it is no wonder that teachers sometimes feel that it is a frill they cannot afford.

A true multicultural approach to education is pervasive. It permeates everything: the school climate, physical environment, curriculum, and relationships among teachers and students and community. It can be seen in every lesson, curriculum guide, unit, bulletin board, and letter that is sent home; it can be seen in the process by which books and audiovisual aids are acquired for the library, in the games played during recess, and in the lunch that is served. Thus, multicultural education is a philosophy, a way of looking at the world, not simply a program or a class or a teacher. In this comprehensive way, multicultural education helps us rethink school reform.

What might this multicultural philosophy mean in the way that schools are organized? For one, it would probably mean the end of tracking, which inevitably favors some students over others. It would also mean that the complexion of the school, both literally and figuratively, would change. That is, there would be an effort to have the entire school staff be more representative of our nation's diversity. Pervasiveness probably would also be apparent in the great variety and creativity of instructional strategies, so that students from all cultural groups, and females as well as males, would benefit from methods other than the traditional. The curriculum would be completely overhauled and would include the histories, viewpoints, and insights of many different peoples and both males and females. Topics considered dangerous could be talked about in classes, and students would be encouraged to become critical thinkers. Textbooks and other instructional materials would also reflect a pluralistic perspective. Parents and community people would be more visible in the schools because they would offer a unique and helpful perspective that the school would welcome. Teachers, parents, and students would have the opportunity to work together to design motivating and multiculturally appropriate curricula.

In other less global but no less important ways, the multicultural school would probably look vastly different as well. For example, the lunchroom might offer a variety of international meals, not because they are exotic delights but because they are the foods people in the community eat daily. Sports and games from all over the world might be played, and not all would be competitive. Letters would be sent home in the languages that parents understand. Children would not be punished for speaking their native language; on the contrary, they would be encouraged to do so and it would be used in their instruction as well. In summary, the school would be a learning environment in which curriculum, pedagogy, and outreach are all consistent with a broadly conceptualized multicultural philosophy.

Multicultural Education Is Education for Social Justice

All good education connects theory with reflection and action, which is what Paulo Freire defines as *praxis*.[11] In particular, developing a multicultural perspective means learning how to think in more inclusive and expansive ways, reflecting on what we learn, and putting our learning into action. Multicultural education invites students and teachers to put their learning into action for social justice. Whether debating an issue, developing a community newspaper, starting a collaborative program at a local senior center, or beginning a petition for the removal of a potentially dangerous waste treatment plant in the neighborhood, students learn that they have power, collectively and individually, to make change.

This aspect of multicultural education fits in particularly well with the developmental level of young people who, starting in the middle elementary grades, are very conscious of what is fair and what is unfair. Their pronounced sense of justice seldom has an opportunity to be channeled appropriately. The result can be anger, resentment, alienation from schooling, or simply dropping out physically or psychologically. Schools represent an ideal environment for tackling some of these important issues.

Students are often denied the opportunity to engage in learning that is related to the lives they lead in their communities. Although preparing students for active membership in a democracy is the basis of Deweyan philosophy and has often been cited as a major educational goal, the possibility for having schools serve as a site of apprenticeship for democracy is rarely provided.[12] For one, policies and practices such as rigid ability grouping, inequitable testing, monocultural curricula, and unimaginative pedagogy mitigate against this lofty aim. The result is that the claim of democracy is perceived as a hollow and irrelevant issue in many schools. Giroux, for example, suggests that what he calls "the discourse of democracy" has been trivialized to mean such things as uncritical patriotism and mandatory pledges to the flag.[13] In many schools, democratic practices are found only in textbooks and confined to discussions of the American Revolution, but most schools provide little chance for students to practice day-to-day democracy. Social justice becomes an empty concept in this situation.

There are numerous examples of the mismatch between students' lives and how they are disconnected from their school experiences. Commins found that the school lives of Mexican American children were not only different but almost diametrically opposed to their home lives.[14] Although the children and their families were intimately acquainted with the issues of undocumented workers, poverty, and discrimination, the school reflected an almost total lack of awareness of these problems or at least an unwillingness to reflect them in the curriculum. The children found that what they learned at school could not be applied to their lives outside of school. In contrast, Moll's research in effective classrooms for Latino students found that teachers in these classrooms encouraged their students to use personal experiences to make sense of their school experiences.[15] Topics that might be considered controversial because they concerned community issues were commonplace in these classrooms and were used to expand students' literacy. This might be the case, for example, in exploring issues of language discrimination, police brutality, or homelessness in the community.

The fact that social structures and power are rarely discussed in school should come as no surprise. Schools are organizations fundamentally concerned with maintaining the status quo and not exposing contradictions that make people uncomfortable in a society that has democratic ideals but wherein democratic realities are not always apparent. Such contradictions include the many manifestations of inequality. Yet schools are also supposed to wipe out these inequalities. To admit that inequality exists and that it is even perpetuated by the very institutions charged with doing away with it are topics far too dangerous to discuss. Nevertheless, such issues are at the heart of a broadly conceptualized multicultural perspective because the subject matter of schooling is society, with all its wrinkles and warts and contradictions. And because society is concerned with ethics and with the distribution of power, status, and rewards, education must focus on these concerns as well.

Although the connection of multicultural education with students' rights and responsibilities in a democracy is unmistakable, many young people do not learn about these responsibilities, the challenges of democracy, or the important role of citizens in ensuring and maintaining the privileges of democracy. A major study on adolescents found, for example, that most youths know little about the political process and do not make connections between the actions of government and the actions of citizens.[16] This is precisely where multicultural education can have a great impact. Not only should classrooms *allow* discussions that focus on social justice, but they should in fact *welcome* them. These discussions might center on concerns that heavily affect culturally diverse communities—poverty, discrimination, war, the national budget—and what students can do to change them. Schools cannot be separated from social justice. Because all of these concerns are pluralistic, education must of necessity be multicultural.

Multicultural Education Is a Process

Curriculum and materials represent the *content* of multicultural education, but multicultural education is above all a *process*. First, it is ongoing and dynamic. No one ever stops becoming a multicultural person, and knowledge is never complete. Thus, there is no established canon, frozen in cement. Second, it is a process because it involves relationships among people. The sensitivity and understanding teachers show their students are often more important than the facts and figures they may know about different ethnic and cultural groups. Third, and most important, multicultural education is a process because it focuses on such intangibles as teachers' expectations, learning environments, students' learning styles, and other cultural variables that are absolutely essential for schools to understand how to be successful with all of their students.

However, this process is too often relegated to a secondary position, because content is easier to handle and has speedier results. For instance, developing an assembly program on Black History Month is easier than eliminating tracking. Both are important, but the processes of multicultural education are generally more complex, more politically volatile, or more threatening to vested interests. Changing a basal reader is therefore easier than developing higher expectations for all students. The first involves changing one book for another; the other involves changing perceptions, behaviors, and knowledge, not an easy task.

Multicultural education must be accompanied by unlearning conventional wisdom as well as dismantling policies and practices that are disadvantageous for some students at the expense of others. Teacher education programs, for example, need to be reconceptualized to include awareness of the influence of culture and language on learning, the persistence of racism and discrimination in schools and society, and instructional and curricular strategies that encourage learning among a wide variety of students. Teachers' roles in the school also need to be redefined, because empowered teachers help to empower students. The role of parents needs to be expanded so that the insights and values of the community could be more faithfully reflected in the school. A complete restructuring of curriculum and of the organization of schools is called for. The process is complex, problematic, controversial, and time-consuming, but it is one in which teachers and schools must engage to make their schools truly multicultural.

Multicultural Education Is Critical Pedagogy

Knowledge is neither neutral nor apolitical, yet it is generally treated by teachers and schools as if it were. Consequently, what is presented to students tends to be knowledge of the lowest common denominator: that which is sure to offend the fewest (and the most powerful) and is least controversial. Nevertheless, history, including educational history, is full of great debates, controversies, and ideological struggles. The debate concerning the canon and cultural literacy versus the need for multicultural literacy in the curriculum is one example.[17] These controversies and conflicts are often left at the schoolhouse door. Yet every educational decision made at any level, whether by a teacher or by an entire school system, reflects the political ideology and worldview of the decision maker. Decisions to dismantle tracking, discontinue standardized tests, lengthen the school day, use one textbook rather than another, study the Harlem Renaissance, or use learning centers rather than rows of chairs—all of these decisions reflect a particular view of learners and of education.

It is important to understand that as teachers, all the decisions we make, no matter how neutral they seem, may impact in unconscious but fundamental ways the lives and experiences of our students. This is true of the curriculum, books, and other materials we provide for our students. State and local guidelines and mandates may limit what particular schools and teachers choose to teach, and this too is a political decision. What is excluded is often as telling as what is included. Because most literature taught at the high school level, for instance, is heavily male and Eurocentric, the roles of women, people of color, and those who write in other languages are thus diminished, unintentionally or not.

A major problem with a monocultural curriculum is that it gives students only one way of seeing the world. Reality is often presented in schools as static, finished, and flat. The underlying tensions, controversies, passions, and problems faced by people throughout history and today are sadly missing. To be truly informed and active participants in a democratic society, students need to understand the complexity of the world and of the many perspectives involved. They have to understand that there is not only one way of seeing things, nor even two or three. A handy number to keep in mind, simply because it reflects how complex a process it really is, is 17: There are at least 17 ways of understanding reality, and until we have learned to do that, we have only part of the truth.

What do I mean by "17 ways of understanding reality"? I mean that there are multiple perspectives on every issue. Unfortunately, most of us have been given only the "safe" or standard way of interpreting events and issues. Textbooks in all subject areas exclude information about unpopular perspectives, or the perspectives of disempowered groups in our society. For instance, there are few U.S. history texts that assume the perspective of working-class people, although it is certainly true that they were and are the backbone of our country. Likewise, the immigrant experience is generally treated as a romantic and successful odyssey rather than the traumatic, wrenching, and often less-than-idyllic situation it was and continues to be for so many. Furthermore, the experiences of non-European immigrants or those forcibly incorporated into the United States are usually presented as if they were identical to the experiences of Europeans, which they have not at all been. And finally, we can be sure that if the perspectives of women were taken seriously, the school curriculum would be altered dramatically. Unless all students develop the skill to see reality from multiple perspectives, not only the perspective of dominant groups, they will continue to think of it as linear and fixed and to think of themselves as passive in making any changes.

According to Banks, the main goal of a multicultural curriculum is to help students develop decision-making and social action skills.[18] By doing so, students learn to view events and situations from a variety of perspectives. A multicultural approach values diversity and encourages critical thinking, reflection, and action. Through this process, students can be empowered as well. This is the basis of critical pedagogy. Its opposite is what Freire calls "domesticating education," education that emphasizes passivity, acceptance, and submissiveness.[19] According to Freire, education for domestication is a process of "transferring knowledge," whereas education for liberation is one of "transforming action."[20] Liberating education encourages students to take risks, to be curious, and to question. Rather than expecting students to repeat teachers' words, it expects them to seek their own answers. Empowerment also means that students and teachers recognize their right and responsibility to take action.

What does critical pedagogy mean in terms of multicultural education? Critical pedagogy acknowledges rather than suppresses cultural and linguistic diversity. According to Cummins, because transmission models exclude and deny students' experiences, they cannot be multicultural: "A genuine multicultural orientation that promotes minority student empowerment is impossible within a transmission model of pedagogy."[21]

A few examples of how the typical curriculum discourages students from thinking critically, and what this has to do with a multicultural perspective, are in order. In most schools, students learn that Columbus discovered America; that the United States was involved in a heroic westward expansion until the twentieth century; that Puerto Ricans were granted U.S. citizenship in 1917; that enslaved Africans were freed by the Emancipation Proclamation in 1863; that the people who made our country great were the financial barons of the previous century; and if they learn anything about it at all, that Japanese Americans were housed in detention camps during World War II for security reasons.

History, as we know, is generally written by the conquerors, not by the vanquished or by those who benefit least in society. The result is history books skewed in the direction of those who are dominant in a society. When American Indian people write history books, they generally say that Columbus invaded rather than discovered this land, and that there was no heroic westward expansion but rather an eastern encroachment. Mexican Americans often include references to Aztlán, the legendary land that was overrun by Europeans during this encroachment. Puerto Ricans usually remove the gratuitous word *granted* that appears in so many textbooks and explain that citizenship was instead *imposed*, and it was opposed by even the two houses of the legislature that existed in Puerto Rico in 1917. African Americans tend to describe the active participation of enslaved Africans in their own liberation and include such accounts as slave narratives to describe the rebellion and resistance of their people. Working-class people usually credit laborers rather than Andrew Carnegie with building the country and the economy. And Japanese Americans generally cite racist hysteria, economic exploitation, and propaganda as major reasons for their evacuation to concentration camps during World War II.

Critical pedagogy is not simply the transfer of knowledge from teacher to students, even though that knowledge may contradict what students had learned before. Thus, learning about the internment of Japanese Americans during World War II is not in itself critical pedagogy. It only becomes so when students critically analyze different perspectives and use them to understand

and act on the inconsistencies they uncover. A multicultural perspective does not simply operate on the principle of substituting one "truth" or perspective for another. Rather, it reflects on multiple and contradictory perspectives to understand reality more fully. In addition, it uses the understanding gained from reflection to make changes. Thus teachers and students sometimes need to learn to respect even those viewpoints with which they may disagree, not to teach that which is "politically correct" but rather to teach students to develop a critical perspective about what they hear, read, or see.

Consider the hypothetical English literature book previously mentioned. Let us say that students and their teacher have decided to review the textbook to determine whether it fairly represents the voices and perspectives of a number of groups. Finding that it does not is in itself a valuable learning experience. However, if nothing is done with this analysis, it remains academic; it becomes more meaningful by being used as the basis for further action. Students might propose, for example, that the English department order a more culturally inclusive anthology for the coming year. They might decide to put together their own book, based on literature with a variety of perspectives. Critical pedagogy, however, does not always mean that there is a linear process from *knowledge* to *reflection* to *action*. If this were the case, it would become yet another mechanistic strategy. Furthermore, reflection and action do not take place only within high school classes. On the contrary, critical pedagogy can take place from the preschool level on.[22]

Critical pedagogy is also an exploder of myths. It helps to expose and demystify as well as dymythologize some of the truths that we have been taught to take for granted and to analyze them critically and carefully. Justice for all, equal treatment under the law, and equal educational opportunity, although certainly ideals worth believing in and striving for, are not always a reality. The problem is that we teach them as if they were always real, always true, with no exceptions. Critical pedagogy allows us to have faith in these ideals without uncritically accepting their reality.

Critical pedagogy is based on the experiences and viewpoints of students rather than on an imposed culture. It is therefore multicultural as well because the most successful education is that which begins with the learner. Students themselves are the foundation for the curriculum. Nevertheless, a liberating education takes students beyond their own particular and therefore limited experiences, no matter what their background.

Critical pedagogy is not new, although it has gone by other terms in other times. In our country, precursors to critical pedagogy can be found in the work of African American educators such as Carter Woodson and W. E. B. DuBois.[23] In Brazil, the historic work of Paulo Freire has influenced literacy and liberation movements throughout the world. Even before Freire, however, what could be called critical pedagogy was being practiced in other parts of the world. Many years ago, Sylvia Ashton-Warner, teaching Maori children in New Zealand, found that their education was completely imposed from above.[24]

The curriculum, materials, viewpoints, and pedagogy were all borrowed from a culture alien to that of the students. Because Maori children had been failed dismally by New Zealand schools, Ashton-Warner decided to develop a strategy for literacy based on the children's experiences and interests. Calling it an "organic" approach, she taught children how to read by using the words *they* wanted to learn. Each child would bring in a number of new words each day, learn to read them, and then use them in writing. Because her approach was based on what children knew and wanted to know, it was extraordinarily successful. In contrast, basal readers, because they had nothing to do with their experiences, were mechanistic instruments that imposed severe limitations on the students' creativity and expressiveness.

Other approaches that have successfully used the experiences of students are worth mentioning: Heath's work is particularly noteworthy, as are the ethnographic case studies in multiethnic classrooms documented by Saravia-Shore and Arvizu. Curriculum projects and instructional strategies based on students' languages, cultures, families, and communities are included in a valuable monograph by Menkart. May's study of the Richmond Road School in New Zealand offers another inspiring example of multicultural education in practice. Walsh's culturally affirming work with Puerto Rican youngsters is another good example. Shor's descriptions of elementary and high school classrooms, as well as the work he does in his own college classroom, are further proof of the power of critical pedagogy at all levels. Also, Darder and her colleagues have developed an entire college-level program based on critical pedagogy.[25] All of these projects use the learners' backgrounds, languages, and cultures as the basis for their education. Rather than avoid their experiences, these programs consciously seek them out and incorporate them into the curriculum.

Notes

1. See James A. Banks, "Multicultural Education: Historical Development, Dimensions, and Practice." In *Handbook of Research on Multicultural Education,* edited by James A. Banks and Cherry A. McGee Banks (New York: Macmillan, 1995).

2. Meyer Weinberg, "Notes from the Editor," *A Chronicle of Equal Education,* 4, 3 (November 1982), 7.

3. Michelle Fine, *Framing Dropouts: Notes on the Politics of an Urban Public High School* (Albany: State University of New York Press, 1991).

4. Jonathan Kozol, "Great Men and Women (Tailored for School Use)," *Learning Magazine* (December 1975), 16–20.

5. E. D. Hirsch, *Cultural Literacy* (Boston: Houghton Mifflin, 1987).

6. Charol Shakeshaft, "A Gender at Risk," *Phi Delta Kappan,* 67, 7 (March 1986), 499–503.

7. Jean Anyon, "Social Class and School Knowledge," *Curriculum Inquiry,* 11, 1 (1981), 3–41.

8. Geneva Gay, "Designing Relevant Curriculum for Diverse Learners," *Education and Urban Society,* 20, 4 (August 1988), 327–340.

9. Patricia Phelan, Ann Locke Davidson, and Hanh Thanh Cao, "Speaking up: Students' Perspectives on School," *Phi Delta Kappan,* 73, 9 (May 1992), 695–704.

10. Robert L. Sinclair and Ward Ghory, *Marginal Students: A Primary Concern for School Renewal* (Chicago: McCutchan, 1987).

11. Paulo Freire, *Pedagogy of the Oppressed* (New York: Seabury Press, 1970).

12. John Dewey, *Democracy and Education* (New York: Free Press, 1966; first published 1916).

13. Henry A. Giroux, "Educational Leadership and the Crisis of Democratic Government," *Educational Researcher,* 21, 4 (May 1992), 4–11.

14. Nancy Commins, "Language and Affect: Bilingual Students at Home and at School," *Language Arts,* 66, 1 (January 1989), 29–43.

15. Luis C. Moll, "Some Key Issues in Teaching Latino Students," *Language Arts,* 65, 5 (September 1988), 465–472.

16. S. Shirley Feldman and Glen R. Elliott, *At the Threshold: The Developing Adolescent* (Cambridge, MA: Harvard University Press, 1990).

17. See, for example, E. D. Hirsch, *Cultural Literacy;* Alan Bloom, *The Closing of the American Mind: How Higher Education Has Failed Democracy and Impoverished the Souls of Today's Students* (New York: Simon & Schuster, 1987); Rick Simonson and Scott Walker, eds., *Multicultural Literacy: The Opening of the American Mind* (St. Paul, MN: Greywold Press, 1988); James A. Banks, "The Canon Debate, Knowledge Construction, and Multicultural Education," *Educational Researcher,* 22, 5 (June/July 1993), 4–14.

18. James A. Banks, *Teaching Strategies for Ethnic Studies,* 4th ed. (Boston: Allyn & Bacon, 1987).

19. Paulo Freire, *The Politics of Education: Culture, Power, and Liberation* (South Hadley, MA: Bergin & Garvey, 1985).

20. Paulo Freire, *Pedagogy of the Oppressed.*

21. Jim Cummins, "The Sanitized Curriculum: Educational Disempowerment in a Nation at Risk." In *Richness in Writing: Empowering ESL Students,* edited by Donna M. Johnson and Duane H. Roen (White Plains, NY: Longman, 1989).

22. See, for example, Patricia G. Ramsey, *Teaching and Learning in a Diverse World: Multicultural Education for Young Children* (New York: Teachers College Press, Columbia University, 1987); Louise Derman-Sparks and the A.B.C. Task Force, *Anti-Bias Curriculum: Tools for Empowering Young Children* (Washington, DC: National Association for the Education of Young Children, 1989); Iris Santos Rivera, "Liberating Education for Little Children," *Alternativas,* 9–12 (October 1984); Suzanne Soo Hoo, "Students as Partners in Research and Restructuring Schools," *The Educational Forum,* 57, 4 (1993), 386–393; Sonia Nieto, "Lessons from Students on Creating a Chance to Dream," *Harvard Educational Review,* 64, 4 (Winter 1994), 392–426.

23. See, for instance, Carter G. Woodson, *The Miseducation of the Negro* (Washington, DC: Associated Publishers, 1933); W. E. B. DuBois, "Does the Negro Need

Separate Schools?" *Journal of Negro Education,* 4, 3 (July 1935), 328–335. For a historical analysis of multicultural education and critical pedagogy, see James A. Banks, "Multicultural Education."

24. Sylvia Ashton-Warner, *Teacher* (New York: Simon & Schuster, 1963).

25. See, for example, Shirley Brice Heath, *Ways with Words* (New York: Cambridge University Press, 1983); Marietta Saravia-Shore and Steven F. Arvizu, *Cross-Cultural Literacy: Ethnographies of Communication in Multiethnic Classrooms* (New York: Garland, 1992); Deborah Menkart, *Multicultural Education: Strategies for Linguistically Diverse Schools and Classrooms* (Washington, DC: George Washington University, National Clearinghouse for Bilingual Education Program Information Guide Series, 1993); Catherine E. Walsh, *Pedagogy and the Struggle for Voice: Issues of Language, Power, and Schooling for Puerto Ricans* (New York: Bergin & Garvey, 1991); Stephen May, *Making Multicultural Education Work* (Clevedon, England: Multilingual Matters, 1994); Ira Shor, *Empowering Education: Critical Teaching for Social Change* (Chicago: University of Chicago Press, 1992); Antonia Darder, *Culture and Power in the Classroom: A Critical Foundation for Bicultural Education* (New York: Bergin & Garvey, 1991).

II: Affirming Diversity: Implications for Schools and Teachers

Starting Out

How does a school or a teacher start a multicultural program? To say that multicultural education must be comprehensively defined, pervasive, and inclusive is not to imply that only a full-blown program qualifies. Because multicultural education is a process, we need to understand that it is always changing and never quite finished. Given that multicultural education is critical pedagogy, it must also be dynamic. A static "program-in-place" or a slick-packaged program is contrary to the very definition of multicultural education.

Let me illustrate with an example from a junior high school English teacher in a community of European American (primarily Irish, French, and Polish) and Puerto Rican students.[1] When asked how she included a multicultural perspective in her teaching, she replied that she has not yet reached that level. Rather, she said, her classroom had what she called "bicultural moments." She was very supportive of multicultural education and used curriculum and instructional strategies that emerged from this perspective, but she felt that the children in her classes did not even know about their own or one another's backgrounds, let alone about the world outside their communities. In her curriculum she focused on exploring, through reading and writing, the "little world" of her students' community before venturing beyond it. Her reasoning was logical: If students do not even understand themselves, their families, and their communities, how can they appreciate others of different backgrounds?

An example of a "bicultural moment" in writing concerned the journals her students kept. One of the central themes about which they wrote was the family, and their writings were later used as the basis for class discussions. A particularly vivid example involved two adolescent boys, one Irish American and the other Puerto Rican, and their perspectives and feelings toward their baby sisters. The Irish American boy complained about what a brat his little sister was. But the way in which he described her, hidden under the crusty surface of a young man trying to conceal his feelings, was full of tenderness. The Puerto Rican boy's journal, in contrast, was consciously sentimental. He described in great detail just how beautiful and wonderful his baby sister was and concluded that everyone in his family thanked God for sending her to them. Both of these boys loved their sisters and both were poetic and loving in their descriptions of them, but they expressed their love in widely different ways. Although not claiming that one was an Irish American and another was a Puerto Rican "way" of feeling or expression, this teacher was nonetheless using these differences as a basis for students' understanding that the same feelings are often expressed in distinct ways and that different families operate in unique but valid ways. This bicultural moment was illuminating for all students; it expanded their literacy and their way of thinking. For the teacher, to "begin small" meant to use the experiences and understandings students bring to class rather than an exotic or irrelevant curriculum that is meaningless to them.

This is a message worth remembering. In our enthusiasm to incorporate a multicultural philosophy in our teaching, we can sometimes forget that our classrooms are made up of young people who usually know very little about their own culture or that of their classmates. Starting out small, then, means being sensitive to these bicultural moments and using them as a beginning for more wide-ranging multicultural education.

Afrocentrism and Multicultural Education

Related to the issue of biculturalism is the development of what recently has been called *Afrocentrism*,[2] which refers to a philosophical worldview and values based on African cultures. In some ways, it is a direct response to *Eurocentrism*. This philosophy has become particularly visible in some schools with large African American student populations. Afrocentric curricula and educational environments have gained importance because traditional classrooms in the United States tend to put African American children at a disadvantage. This is true in the content of the curriculum, where African Americans are missing, as well as in the process of education itself, where a lack of understanding of students' communication styles by most teachers is evident.

A number of Afrocentric schools have been developed. The reasoning behind these schools is that because African American children (particularly males) suffer the consequences of miseducation in traditional schools, it is important that their culture, values, language, and communication patterns serve as the basis for their education. According to Ascher, these schools are mostly grass-roots reactions to the acute problems among those living in inner-city and poor neighborhoods, and their purpose is to protect African American young men from the many hostile forces in their environment. In addition, she cites that 86 percent of all African American children are likely to spend some time in a female-headed household and thus lack the influence of a male role model in their lives.[3] A number of the schools designed specifically for Black males are staffed almost entirely by Black male teachers, and emphasize positive identity, the value of education, parent and community involvement, and the provision of a safe haven.

It should be underscored that Afrocentrism in education represents a *range* of beliefs rather than a fixed ideology, and that it can be manifested in a variety of ways, from a sentimentalized and romantic view of culture, to an inclusive and humanistic curriculum, to a liberatory pedagogy. For example, Ladson-Billings and Henry, while supporting the use of an Afrocentric perspective in education and emphasizing its liberatory character, also caution that it can become "romantic, mythic, and monolithic."[4] Although Afrocentrism in general has come under great scrutiny for a tendency to become dogmatic and limiting, and some Afrocentric schools have been criticized for being rigidly nationalistic and exclusionary, these criticisms have probably been based on the more ideological and nationalistic models of Afrocentrism rather than on the more inclusive models. West points out its contradictory characteristics:

> Afrocentrism, a contemporary species of black nationalism, is a gallant yet misguided attempt to define an African identity in a white society perceived to be hostile. It is gallant because it puts black doings and sufferings, not white anxieties and fears, at the center of discussion. It is misguided be-cause—out of fear of cultural hybridization and through silence on the issue of class, retrograde views on black women, gay men, and lesbians, and a re-luctance to link race to the common good—it reinforces the narrow discus-sions about race.[5]

This caution is important because it points out how philosophies based on valid critiques of oppressive structures can themselves contain oppressive and limit-ing features. A similar analysis of all aspects of multicultural education, from culturally responsive strategies to bilingual programs, needs to take place if we are to move beyond sentimentality and toward a critical pedagogy.

Given the devaluation and destruction of large numbers of African Ameri-can students in traditional school settings, the reasoning behind Afrocentric schools is an understandable and even healthy response. In a similar vein, *Latinocentric, Indiancentric,* and other pedagogical approaches based on the values and perspectives of marginalized cultures provide an alternative to busi-ness as usual. Furthermore, culture-centric responses represent an important challenge to the hegemony and Eurocentrism of the curriculum and pedagogy in most schools (or, in the case of schools for females that have a feminist per-spective, to the hegemony of patriarchy). They question the promise of equal educational opportunity for all youngsters by demonstrating how this noble ideal has often been betrayed. In addition, because such schools are usually de-signed by people from the very community that they serve, they provide an im-portant example of self-determination and self-definition.[6]

Although segregation is sometimes necessary for fostering a positive iden-tity, historically it has provided few if any benefits to the most disempowered children in our society. Nevertheless, there is a crucial difference between seg-regated schools imposed by the dominant group and those developed from within subordinated communities. The goals of self-segregated schools are generally to provide excellent and affirming educational experiences for stu-dents who have too often been dismissed by traditional schools, whereas state-segregated schools were usually created to maintain one group on top and oth-ers on the bottom. In spite of such differences, however, and because we have few positive models for creating separate schools, Afrocentrism and similar approaches raise some disturbing issues. These include a tendency to create new myths in place of old ones, and segregation of students by race and gen-der. Hence, the issue becomes not whether segregation is good or bad in itself, but rather the extent to which such schools are engaged in a process of critical analysis of issues, taking into account a variety of multicultural perspectives. Without this critical analysis, self-segregated schools may simply substitute one set of myths for another, and young people will again be the losers.

Afrocentric schools are specifically aimed at alleviating the educational disadvantages of a group that has traditionally been disenfranchised and mis-educated by schools, and are thus just one option within a multicultural continuum. The need to establish special schools for any population, whether Black males, or gay and lesbian students, or females, is an indication of the nation's failure to achieve our stated multicultural goals. Such schools are examples of how particular social groups cope with society's failure to provide educational equity. The challenge for us as a society is to work toward a truly comprehensive and multicultural perspective that works for *all* of our students, while along the way responding to the very real educational needs of *some* of our students.

Becoming a Multicultural Person

Developing truly comprehensive multicultural education takes many years, in part because of our own monocultural education. Most of us, in spite of our distinct cultural and/or linguistic backgrounds, were educated in monocultural environments. We seldom have the necessary models for developing a multicultural perspective. We have only our own experiences; and no matter what our background, these have been overwhelmingly Eurocentric and English-speaking. Sleeter, for example, in a major ethnographic study of teachers involved in a two-year staff development program in multicultural education, found that because teachers share a pervasive culture and set of practices, there are limits to the extent to which they can change *without concurrent changes in their context.*[7]

Becoming a multicultural teacher, therefore, means first becoming a multicultural person. Without this transformation of ourselves, any attempts at developing a multicultural perspective will be shallow and superficial. But becoming a multicultural person in a society that values monoculturalism is not easy. It means reeducating ourselves in several ways.

First, *we simply need to learn more,* for example, by reading and being involved in activities that emphasize pluralism. This means looking for books and other materials that inform us about people and events we may know little about. Given the multicultural nature of our society, those materials are available, although sometimes they need to be sought out because we have learned not to see them.

Second, *we need to confront our own racism and biases.* It is impossible to be a teacher with a multicultural perspective without going through this process. Because we are all products of a society that is racist and stratified by gender, class, and language, we have all internalized some of these messages in one way or another. Sometimes, our racism is unconscious, as in the case of a former student of mine who referred to Africans as "slaves" and Europeans as "people" but was mortified as soon as she realized what she had said. Sometimes, the words we use convey a deep-seated bias, as when a student who does not speak English is characterized as "not having language," although she may speak her native language fluently. Our actions also carry the messages we have learned, for example, when we automatically expect that our female students will not do as well in math as our male students. Our own reeducation means not only learning new things but also unlearning some of the old. The process is difficult and sometimes painful; nevertheless, it is a necessary part of becoming multicultural.

Third, *becoming a multicultural person means learning to see reality from a variety of perspectives.* Because we have often learned that there is only one "right answer," we have also developed only one way of seeing things. A multicultural perspective demands just the opposite. We need to learn to approach reality from a variety of perspectives. Reorienting ourselves in this way can be exhausting and difficult because it means a dramatic shift in our worldview.

Although the transformation of individuals from being monocultural to being multicultural will not by itself guarantee that education will become multicultural, it would certainly lay the groundwork for it.[8] As one teacher who is thoroughly multicultural in outlook and practice told me, "Since I've developed a multicultural perspective, I just can't teach in any other way." That is, her philosophical outlook is evident in the content she teaches, the instructional strategies she uses, the environment in her classroom, the interactions she has with students and their parents, and the values she expresses in her school and community.

A Model of Multicultural Education

A monocultural perspective represents a fundamentally different framework for understanding differences than does a multicultural one. Even multicultural education, however, has a variety of levels of support for pluralism. I would classify them into at least four levels: *tolerance; acceptance; respect;* and *affirmation, solidarity, and critique.* In the process of becoming multicultural, we need to consider these levels of multicultural education and how they might be operationalized in the school.

Whenever we classify and categorize reality, as I do in this model, we run the risk that it will be viewed as static and arbitrary, rather than as messy, complex, and contradictory, which we know it to be. These categories should be viewed as dynamic and as having penetrable borders, and my purpose in using them is to demonstrate how multicultural education might be manifested in schools in various ways. I propose a model ranging from monocultural education to comprehensive multicultural education, considered vis-à-vis the seven characteristics of multicultural education described previously. This allows exploration of how multicultural education, to be truly comprehensive, demands attention to many components of the school environment and takes a variety of forms in different settings.[9]

Tolerance is the first level. To be tolerant means to have the capacity to bear something, although at times it may be unpleasant. To tolerate differences means to endure them, although not necessarily to embrace them. We may learn to tolerate differences, but this level of acceptance can be shaky. What is tolerated today may be rejected tomorrow. Tolerance therefore represents the lowest level of multicultural education in a school setting. Yet many schools have what they consider very comprehensive mission statements that stress only their tolerance for diversity. They may believe that this is an adequate expression of support, although it does not go very far in multicultural understanding. In terms of school policies and practices, it may mean that linguistic and cultural differences are borne as the inevitable burden of a culturally pluralistic society. Programs that do not build on but rather replace differences might be in place, for example, English as a second language (ESL) programs. Black History Month might be commemorated with an assembly program and a bulletin board. The life-styles and values of students' families, if different from the majority, may be considered as requiring understanding but modification.

Acceptance is the next level of support for diversity. If we accept differences, we at the very least acknowledge them without denying their importance. In concrete terms, programs that acknowledge students' languages and cultures would be visible in the school. These might include a transitional bilingual program that uses the students' primary language at least until they are "mainstreamed" to an English-language environment. It might also mean celebrating some differences through activities such as multicultural fairs and cookbooks. In a school with this level of support for diversity, time might be set aside weekly for "multicultural programs," and parents' native languages might be used for communication with them through newsletters.

Respect is the third level of multicultural education. Respect means to admire and hold in high esteem. When diversity is respected, it is used as the basis for much of the education offered. It might mean offering programs of bilingual education that use students' native language not only as a bridge to English but also throughout their schooling. Frequent and positive interactions with parents would take place. In the curriculum, students' values and experiences would be used as the basis for their literacy development. Students would be exposed to different ways of approaching the same reality and would therefore expand their way of looking at the world. *Additive multiculturalism* would be the ultimate goal for everybody.

Affirmation, solidarity, and critique are based on the premise that the most powerful learning results when students work and struggle with one another, even if it is sometimes difficult and challenging. This means accepting the culture and language of students and their families as legitimate and embracing them as valid vehicles for learning. It also means understanding that culture is not fixed or unchangeable, and thus one is able to critique its manifestations and outcomes. Because multicultural education is concerned with equity and social justice for all people, and because basic values of different groups are often diametrically opposed, conflict is inevitable. What makes this level different from the others is that conflict is not avoided, but rather accepted as an inevitable part of learning.

Passively accepting the status quo of any culture is inconsistent with multicultural education; simply substituting one myth for another contradicts its basic assumptions because no group is inherently superior or more heroic than any other. At this level, students not only "celebrate" diversity, but they reflect on it and confront it as well. As expressed by Kalantzis and Cope, "Multicultural education, to be effective, needs to be more active. It needs to consider not just the pleasure of diversity but more fundamental issues that arise as different groups negotiate community and the basic issues of material life in the same space—a process that equally might generate conflict and pain." [10]

Multicultural education without critique implies that cultural understanding remains at the romantic or exotic stage. If we are unable to transcend our own cultural experience through reflection and critique, then we cannot hope to understand and critique that of others. For students, this process begins with a strong sense of solidarity with others who are different from themselves. When based on this kind of deep respect, critique is not only necessary, but in fact healthy.

Without critique, the danger that multicultural education might be used to glorify reality into static truth is very real. Thus there has been vigorous criticism of the way multicultural education has been conceptualized and implemented in the past: "The celebration of ethnicity in intercultural education can . . . in fact function both as a new more sophisticated type of control mechanism and as a pacifier, to divert attention from social and economic inequality." [11] This criticism by Skutnabb-Kangas points out how diversity often skirts the issue of racism and discrimination. In some schools, *diversity* is a more euphemistic substitute for dealing with the very real issues of exclusion that many students face. Racism needs to be confronted head-on, and no softening of terms will help. However, when *diversity* is understood in the more comprehensive way described above, it can lead to inclusion and support of all people. A powerful example of this can be found in the inspiring and moving account by Greeley and Mizell of two schools' experiences in addressing racism and making it explicit in the curriculum. [12]

In the school, affirmation, solidarity, and critique mean using the culture and language of all students in a consistent, critical, comprehensive, and inclusive way. This goes beyond creating ethnic enclaves that can become exclusionary and selective, although for disenfranchised communities, this might certainly be a step in the process. It means developing *multicultural* settings in which all students feel reflected and visible, for example, through two-way

Table 1–1. Levels of Multicultural Education

	Monocultural Education	**Tolerance**
Antiracist/Antidiscriminatory	Racism is unacknowledged. Policies and practices that support discrimination are left in place. These include low expectations and refusal to use students' natural resources (such as language and culture) in instruction. Only a sanitized and "safe" curriculum is in place.	Policies and practices that challenge racism and discrimination are initiated. No overt signs of discrimination are acceptable (e.g., name-calling, graffiti, blatantly racist and sexist textbooks or curriculum). ESL programs are in place for students who speak other languages.
Basic	Defines education as the 3 R's and the "canon." "Cultural literacy" is understood within a monocultural framework. All important knowledge is essentially European American. This Eurocentric view is reflected throughout the curriculum, instructional strategies, and environment for learning.	Education is defined more expansively and includes attention to some important information about other groups.
Pervasive	No attention is paid to student diversity.	A multicultural perspective is evident in some activities, such as Black History Month and Cinco de Mayo, and in some curriculum and materials. There may be an itinerant "multicultural teacher."
Important for All Students	Ethnic and/or women's studies, if available, are only for students from that group. This is a frill that is not important for other students to know.	Ethnic and women's studies are only offered as isolated courses.
Education for Social Justice	Education supports the status quo. Thinking and acting are separate.	Education is somewhat, although tenuously, linked to community projects and activities.
Process	Education is primarily content: who, what, where, when. The "great White men" version of history is propagated. Education is static.	Education is both content and process. "Why" and "how" questions are tentatively broached.
Critical Pedagogy	Education is domesticating. Reality is represented as static, finished, and flat.	Students and teachers begin to question the status quo.

Characteristics of Multicultural Education

Acceptance	Respect	Affirmation, Solidarity, and Critique
Policies and practices that acknowledge differences are in place. Textbooks reflect some diversity. Transitional bilingual programs are available. Curriculum is more inclusive of the histories and perspectives of a broader range of people.	Policies and practices that respect diversity are more evident, including maintenance bilingual education. Ability grouping is not permitted. Curriculum is more explicitly antiracist and honest. It is "safe" to talk about racism, sexism, and discrimination.	Policies and practices that affirm diversity and challenge racism are developed. There are high expectations for all students: students' language and culture are used in instruction and curriculum. Two-way bilingual programs are in place wherever possible. Everyone takes responsibility for racism and other forms of discrimination.
The diversity of lifestyles and values of groups other than the dominant one are acknowledged in some content, as can be seen in some courses and school activities.	Education is defined as knowledge that is necessary for living in a complex and pluralistic society. As such, it includes much content that is multicultural. *Additive multiculturalism* is the goal.	Basic education is multicultural education. All students learn to speak a second language and are familiar with a broad range of knowledge.
Student diversity is acknowledged, as can be seen not only in "Holidays and Heroes" but also in consideration of different learning styles, values, and languages. A "multicultural program" may be in place.	The learning environment is imbued with multicultural education. It can be seen in classroom interactions, materials, and the subculture of the school.	Multicultural education pervades the curriculum; instructional strategies; and interactions among teachers, students, and the community. It can be seen everywhere: bulletin boards, the lunchroom, assemblies.
Many students are expected to take part in curriculum that stresses diversity. A variety of languages are taught.	All students take part in courses that reflect diversity. Teachers are involved in overhauling the curriculum to be more open to such diversity.	All courses are completely multicultural in essence. The curriculum for all students is enriched. "Marginal students" no longer exist.
The role of the schools in social change is acknowledged. Some changes that reflect this attitude begin to be felt: Students take part in community service.	Students take part in community activities that reflect their social concerns.	The curriculum and instructional techniques are based on an understanding of social justice as central to education. Reflection and action are important components of learning.
Education is both content and process. "Why" and "how" questions are stressed more. Sensitivity and understanding of teachers toward their students are more evident.	Education is both content and process. Students and teachers begin to ask. "What if?" Teachers empathize with students and their families.	Education is an equal mix of content and process. It is dynamic. Teachers and students are empowered. Everyone in the school is becoming a multicultural person.
Students and teachers are beginning a dialogue. Students' experiences, cultures, and languages are used as one source of their learning.	Students and teachers use critical dialogue as the primary basis for their education. They see and understand different perspectives.	Students and teachers are involved in a "subversive activity." Decision-making and social action skills are the basis of the curriculum.

bilingual programs in which the languages of all students are used and maintained meaningfully in the academic setting. The curriculum would be characterized by multicultural sensitivity and inclusiveness, offering a wide variety of content and perspectives. Teachers' attitudes and behaviors would reflect only the very highest expectations for all students, although they would understand that students might express their abilities in very different ways. Instructional strategies would also reflect this multicultural perspective and would include a wide variety of means to teach students. Parents would be welcomed and supported in the school as students' first and most important teachers. Their experiences, viewpoints, and suggestions would be sought out and incorporated into classroom and school programs and activities. They, in turn, would be exposed to a variety of experiences and viewpoints different from their own, which would help them expand their horizons.

Other ways in which these four levels might be developed in schools are listed in Table 1–1. Of course, multicultural education cannot be categorized as neatly as this chart would suggest. This model simply represents a theoretical way of understanding how different levels of multicultural education might be visible in a school. It also highlights how pervasive a philosophy it must be. Although any level of multicultural education is preferable to the education offered by a monocultural perspective, each level challenges with more vigor a monolithic and ethnocentric view of society and education. As such, the fourth level is clearly the highest expression of multicultural education.

The fourth level is also the most difficult to achieve for some of the reasons mentioned previously, including the lack of models of multicultural education in our own schooling and experiences. It is here that we are most challenged by values and life-styles different from our own, and with situations that severely test the limits of our tolerance. For instance, dealing with people who are different from us in hygienic practices, food preferences, and religious rites can be trying. It is also extremely difficult and at times impossible to accept and understand cultural practices that run counter to our most deeply held beliefs. For example, if we believe strongly in equality of the sexes and have in our classroom children whose families value males more highly than females, or if we need to deal with parents who believe that education is a frill and not suitable for their children, or if we have children in our classes whose religion forbids them to take part in any school activities except academics—all of these situations test our capacity for affirmation and solidarity. And well they should, for we are all the product of our cultures and thus have learned to view reality from the vantage point of the values they have taught us.

Culture is not static; nor is it necessarily positive or negative. The cultural values and practices of a group of people represent their best strategies, at a particular historical moment, for negotiating their environment and circumstances. What some groups have worked out as appropriate strategies may be considered unsuitable or even barbaric and uncivilized by others. Because each cultural group proceeds from a different context, we can never reach total agreement on the best or most appropriate ways in which to lead our lives. In this sense, culture needs to be approached with a relativistic framework, not as something absolute.

Nevertheless, it should also be stressed that above and beyond all cultures there are human and civil rights that need to be valued and maintained by all people. These rights guarantee that all human beings are treated with dignity, respect, and equality. Sometimes the values and behaviors of a group so seriously challenge these values that we are faced with a real dilemma, but if the values we as human beings hold most dear are ultimately based on extending rights rather than negating them, we must decide on the side of those more universal values.

Multicultural education is not easy; if it were, everyone would be doing it. Similarly, resolving conflicts about cultural differences is difficult, sometimes impossible. For one, the extent to which our particular cultural lenses may keep us from appreciating differences can be very great. For another, some values may be irreconcilable. Usually, however, accommodations that respect both cultural values and basic human rights can be found. Because societies have generally resolved such conflicts in only one way, that is, favoring the dominant culture, few avenues for negotiating differences have been in place. Multicultural education, although at times extremely difficult, painful, and time-consuming, can help provide one way of attempting such negotiations.

Notes

1. I am grateful to Susan Barrett for this wonderful example.

2. See, for example, Molefi Asanti, *Afrocentricity: The Theory of Social Change* (Trenton, NJ: Africa World Press, 1988).

3. Carol Ascher, *School Programs for African American Male Students* (New York: ERIC Clearinghouse for Urban Education, Teachers College, Columbia University, May 1991).

4. Gloria Ladson-Billings and Annette Henry, "Blurring the Borders: Voices of African Liberatory Pedagogy in the United States and Canada," *Journal of Education,* 172, 2 (1990), 86.

5. Cornel West, *Race Matters* (Boston: Beacon Press, 1993).

6. For an important analysis of the multicultural debate and how cultures interact, see Joel Spring, *The Intersection of Cultures: Multicultural Education in the United States* (New York: McGraw-Hill, 1995); for a critique of multicultural education from both the left and the right, see Sonia Nieto, "From Brown Heroes and Holidays to Assimilationist Agendas: Reconsidering the Critiques of Multicultural Education." In *Multicultural Education, Critical Pedagogy, and the Politics of Difference,* edited by Christine E. Sleeter and Peter McLaren (Albany: State University of New York Press, 1995).

7. Christine E. Sleeter, *Keepers of the American Dream: A Study of Staff Development and Multicultural Education* (London: Falmer Press, 1992).

8. Wurzel, for instance, maintains that it is necessary to go through seven "stages of the multicultural process," and these range from *monoculturalism* to *multiculturalism.* See Jaime Wurzel, "Multiculturalism and Multicultural Education." In *Toward Multiculturalism: A Reader in Multicultural Education,* edited by Jaime Wurzel (Yarmouth, ME: Intercultural Press, 1988).

9. I have expanded this model in a recent article, providing specific scenarios for each level. See Sonia Nieto, "Affirmation, Solidarity, and Critique: Moving Beyond Tolerance in Multicultural Education," *Multicultural Education,* 1, 4 (Spring 1994), 9–12, 35–38.

10. Mary Kalantzis and Bill Cope, *The Experience of Multicultural Education in Australia: Six Case Studies* (Sydney: Centre for Multicultural Studies, Wollongong University, 1990), 39.

11. Tove Skutnabb-Kangas, "Legitimating or Delegitimating New Forms of Racism."

12. Kathy Greeley and Linda Mizell, "One Step among Many: Affirming Identity in Anti-Racist Schools." In *Freedom's Plow: Teaching in the Multicultural Classroom,* edited by Theresa Perry and James W. Fraser (New York; Routledge, 1993).

2

Life After Death

Critical Pedagogy in an Urban Community

J. Alleyne Johnson

Editors' Notes: Drawing from Freire's work, J. Alleyne Johnson
adapts critical pedagogy to her middle-school classes, emphasizing
the importance of connecting day-to-day realities of urban students
to the syllabus. With her discovery of death as a generative theme in
the lives of her students, Johnson transformed her role as "knowledge giver" to that of a teacher sharing power and making knowledge with her students. Students were invited to express thoughts
and feelings about the deaths of their friends and to use that trou-
bling material for critical thinking. Johnson's methods of incorporating students' knowledge into pedagogy are a lesson for teachers of
all levels.

Recently I saw a dead boy. I don't know for sure if he was dead. He
looked dead. He laid on the ground in fetal position. Blood oozed
from beneath him slowly changing the color of his shirt. I was cran-
ing my neck through the car window to see why there were so many
policemen on Redding Blvd., when I saw him. Four police cars,
lights flashing hysterically, surrounded the stilled body. People were
everywhere. I scanned the crowd for any familiar adolescent faces. I
wanted to get out of the car and gather with the crowd. I wanted to
see if the boy was dead. What happened? Did anyone see? I knew
I'd hear about it tomorrow. My students all lived around here. In the
hood. It could be family, a homey I saw lying on the ground. I hoped
not. It would be hard enough as it was to insist that we get back to
the math problems, world history, and lessons in sentence structure
for English. (Journal entry, April 18, 1993)

33

When I wrote the above, I was a teacher of a combined seventh- and eighth-grade "special" class at Brent Junior High School in Northern California's East Bay area. I taught social studies, math, English, and physical education during the first four periods of each day. My students' experience with violence and death was one of the first insights they shared with me about their realities of living in, around, or near a poor neighborhood, one not unlike many others in urban areas across the United States.

All of my students know someone who was murdered. One recent death was that of a young man who had attended our school two years earlier. The day after his death, everyone was whispering about it. Although only one person in my class was actually related to this young man, the death was felt personally by many of them. Not only was he a former student, this young man was a "homey," that is, someone from the flatland neighborhood where all of my students—and most of the others who attended Brent—lived. Another student in my class had witnessed the actual shooting. After listening a while to their quiet murmuring, I respectfully asked, "Did someone die?" The young people confirmed the death without giving me the details I had gathered from just listening. I then asked, "When was the funeral?" They responded that it would be that afternoon. They asked me, "Why you ask, are you going?" I replied, "Yes." I introduced my lesson after a brief pause. I waited to hear a reaction to my attending the funeral. None came. I was thinking about the colors I had worn to school that day: a black-and-yellow African print blouse with a bright yellow silk skirt. These were not colors that I would normally wear to a funeral. As I looked down and frowned at my attire, the student who was a relative of the deceased quietly said, "It don't matter what you have on. Anybody who want to come, can come." She had answered my unstated question. I nodded, grateful for the reassurance as I began the world history lesson.

Later that day, in English class, we continued the lesson we had started the day before. I was teaching the students about different kinds of narrative paragraphs and assigned students to construct a first-person narrative. Students had to interview each other and write these paragraphs using the information they collected. From past experience, I knew students liked talking into a microphone, so I used a tape recorder and an outside mike to make the interview process more exciting for them and to enhance the interactive process of the assignment.

I had an interview topic prepared, but I told them they could choose their own. As I moved about the room, I noticed, not surprisingly, that in their interview groups a number of students wanted to discuss the recent death. Salima, the eyewitness to the shooting, ended up being interviewed by Tavia, a classmate whose brother had died in a similar incident a year earlier:

Tavia: On the day that Hasan died, what happened?

Salima: It was a large crowd of people. One of the males had a gun. Everybody start running when he pulled it out, except for Hasan 'cause he didn't have no reason to run. Me and my cousin ran across the street and we watch the shooting of Hasan. He got shot in the stomach and he got up start walking. Then the man shot him in the chest. He got back up start walking. He shot him on the side of the head. He got up start walking. And the man finally shot him in the back of the head and Hasan just laid his coat down like a pillow and he laid his head down on it. He started saying 'bye to everybody cause he knew he was gon' die.

But [then] I didn't hear nothing about it. The story was not printed in the newspaper. Hasan's funeral is October 7, 1992. It was a sad tragedy for a lot of people. I felt bad about it because he was a cool person. He was cool with me.

Tavia: After it happen, did it take long for the ambulance to come?

Salima: Well the police showed first. Then the ambulance come. I'll tell you like this: I felt like whupping them police A—, you know what. They just stood there you know, they just stood there for a little while watching him. If it was me, if it was me being a police officer I'd be trying to put him in my police car and try to get him to the hospital so he wouldn't die. He was just a cool person. I don't know why this man shot him and this man got life in jail. If that was me, the judge or the jury, I would kill that M—. You know what? I would kill him 'cause he don't have no reason to take nobody life. 'cause if he got that gall to take somebody life, I'd take his.

Tavia: But don't you think that if he get killed, if we just kill him, if we kill the people that killing other people, that's all they gon' do is rest in peace, because they asking God for his forgiveness, we don't know if God gon' forgive them, but all he gon' do is rest in peace like everybody else resting in peace. 'Cause when the world end that's all God gon' look at, is our good side and our bad side. The guy who shot Hasan or whoever shot my brother, their good side probably be filled with good things and their bad side probably be filled with less and you know, they might just be resting in peace. It's good that he is suffering in jail and he gon' think about all what he did. I don't know.

We love him [Hasan] very much and you know we sorry for him to be dead. That's why we making this article like today, cause the damn newspaper people ain't doing nothing about it, so you know, we feel real sad about it, you know. We just love him. He gonna rest in peace.

Salima and Tavia finished their interview, but I did not immediately ask for the tape recorder's return. Later, Tavia spoke alone on the interview tape, recording some of her own thoughts about death and dying:

I just feel real sad that he's gone cause everybody's leaving like this. Because my brother died. Like A.B. that went to Harris Junior High. Like my cousin Shawn, Hario. Everybody's just dying like this. I just wish that I could be there for my cousin and everybody else that's gone. But he's going to be resting in peace now and we gon' let him go on and rest in peace. Because we do love him.

A year after the brutal death of her brother, Tavia still misses him and is struggling with the loss of an important influence in her life. Of her own volition, Tavia decided to give personal testimony about the frequency of death in her family and in her neighborhood. I did not know she had done this until I listened to the tape later that day.

Nationwide, nearly 7,000 people between the ages of ten and twenty-four died of gunshot wounds in 1991 ("Bleeding Colors," 1993). People, mostly men, specifically Black men, are being murdered.[1] This rising homicide rate is frequently mentioned in the news, and is usually followed by a more general report on violence, poverty, crime, unsafe neighborhoods. Occasionally, one hears about racism and the political, economic, social, and moral implications of these deaths. Rarely is it reported that someone's father or mother, son or daughter, brother or sister, aunt or uncle has been killed, or that the death has had a traumatic effect on the immediate and extended families. A family's trauma is especially silenced when the dead person was a "wrongdoer," someone who broke the law. Whether someone was a "gangsta" killed by cohorts or police usually receives more attention than whether someone was a "homey"—a friend, a loved one.

This 1993 release by the rap group GETO BOYZ acknowledges the death of all the homies:

> Another homey got smoked but it's no surprise/ Everybody's trippin' cause the boy was too young to die/ A sad sight to see my homey take his last breath/ Everybody's trippin' 'cause they can't accept my homey's death/ Another killing was reported on the evening news/ Somebody's brother got killed behind a pair of shoes/ In the midst of all this shit I think about myself/ Wondering when somebody's gon' try to take me off the shelf. (© 1993 N-the-Water, Inc., ASCAP; Straight Cash BMI)

The song reiterates the death and familial loss embedded in rising homicide rates in urban areas. It notes the mindless killing that takes place, and the trauma that family members suffer in the wake of personal tragedies. It also notes the questions faced by those in the midst of the violence about their own mortality. Death is at home, in the news, in the culture at large. And death is unquestionably in our schools.

Education: A Matter of Life and Death

> Education as the practice of freedom—as opposed to education as the practice of domination—denies that man is abstract, isolated, independent, and unattached to the world; it also denies that the world exists as a reality apart from men. (Freire, 1989, p. 69)

The purpose of this article is to assert the need to make connections between the day-to-day realities of students' lives and the day-to-day process of teaching and learning that takes place in urban public schools across the United States. In the small city where I lived, we had twenty-one homicides by the middle of 1993. I realized that this homicide rate had an impact on my students' lives and also spoke to societal issues of power and oppression. As such, the need for a critical pedagogy is vital. Henry Giroux (1992) describes critical pedagogy as an educational process that integrates issues of power, history, self-identity, and the possibility of collective agency and struggle. In this article, I tell the story of one classroom community in which teacher-student interactions formally addressed and acknowledged death as an important issue in the lives of the students. This acknowledgment enabled the teacher (me) and students together to find power for ourselves in disempowering circumstances through the employment of critical pedagogy. I describe my journey as I came to realize that connecting school knowledge with the students' real-life issues is essential in my classroom.

This article evolves from my concurrent experiences as an urban middle school teacher in Northern California and a graduate student at the University of California at Berkeley. The privilege of having time to write about my teaching is the result of my experience as a graduate student. In my writing, I struggle to combine several "languages": the language of my students, the language of secondary education teachers and schools, and the language of teachers and writers within the academy. The process of combining and balancing these languages as producers of different but equally important sets of knowledge is integral to my work, and represents the formation of my own critical pedagogy. Giroux (1992) points out that

> critical pedagogy needs a language that allows for competing solidarities and
> political vocabularies that do not reduce the issues of power, justice, struggle,
> and inequality to a single script, a master narrative that suppresses the con-
> tingent, the historical and the everyday as serious objects of study. (p. 75)

My struggle to combine these languages is also my struggle not to subsume the important issues related to my work. Issues such as the politics of authority and power (between, for example, university researchers and classroom teachers, teachers and students, etc.), class, and the "re-presentation" of race occupy my mind as I write this article.[2] Thus, I have carefully developed a language or re-presentation—written and spoken—that mirrors those languages utilized by my students and the teachers about whom I write. As Ngugi Wa Thiongo (1986) asserts, "From a word, a group of words, a sentence and even a name, one can glean the social norms, attitudes and values of a people" (p. 8).[3] The insistence, pervasive in university settings, on finding one voice, one definitive writing style is problematic in the face of my varied experience. I claim the languages of all those with whom I teach and work and study as a part of my own ethos and in my formation of a critical pedagogy.

Each of these languages speaks volumes on the state of U.S. schools, but unfortunately, conversations combining all three languages are rare. Across the nation, students who are failing or have "failed" at school can tell anyone who will listen why schools "didn't teach them anything." The "failing" students I have met and their parents are apt to point out the school's failure to educate all of its children. Practitioners struggle with the frantic rhythm of classrooms, which leaves little time to acknowledge or to record fleeting reflections on the act of teaching. In addition, in universities across the country, graduate teacher researchers like myself struggle to translate solutions often hidden in convoluted academic writings into daily practice. I hope that this article will illustrate the power found in merging the conversations of the students, of teachers and schools, and of the academy.

Death in U.S. Society

Until recently, most discussions of death in the literature were of an existential nature; death was discussed only in relation to aging, terminal illnesses, or war, as opposed to death as a more general part of life, an everyday occurrence that threatens one's human existence. These limited discussions of death come, in part, from a fear of the inevitability of death (Corr & McNeil, 1986; Kubler-Ross, 1969; Schowalter, 1987). Partly as a way of coping, people subsume the impact of death in rhetoric about ageism, illness, violence, and moral issues. The view of death as oppositional to life, instead of as part of an inevitable, natural progression, makes it a difficult issue to discuss.

Discussions of adolescent death are even more complex and problematic. One significant factor is that the most common causes of adolescent death— suicide, accidents, and homicide—all occur unexpectedly (Schowalter, 1987). In addition to the shock of a loss, surviving adolescents often contend with the inability of the adults around them to discuss death. Audrey Gordon (1986) expands on this idea. She writes that

> at the point where the teen has a personal experience with the death of a significant person, all the [mainstream American] cultural messages about death as distant, violent or beautiful are challenged. Nothing in previous experience has prepared the youth for the feelings of rage, loneliness, guilt and disbelief that accompany a personal loss. (p. 22)

For young African American adolescents, the difficulties of dealing with death are even further complicated by the brutal nature of homicide, which is the main cause of Black adolescent death. Furthermore, the literature and media have generated certain perceptions of African American homicide. For instance, newspaper headlines scream: "MAN GUNNED DOWN IN . . . "— a headline that could describe an event in a poor neighborhood in any major U.S. city. Television shows like *Cops, Crime Stories,* and *Hunter* sensationalize such acts of violence. The music industry commodifies the "romance" of violence, frequently, but not only, in rap music.[4]

The response to the increase in deaths by homicide has been a public out-cry for increased police surveillance, weaponry, and manpower, as well as prison construction. Embedded in this response is what many scholars identify as a racist notion; that is, that the violence occurring in Black, low-income neigh-borhoods is entirely the fault of the people in those neighborhoods (Baldwin, 1985; Blackwell, 1985; Brown, 1988; Jordan, 1977; Wilson, 1990; Wright, 1987). Amos Wilson (1990) provides a rich discussion of the racist underpin-nings in perceptions of crime and violence in Black communities. He locates this bias in many aspects of crime and violence reporting, from FBI reports to general attitudes and responses toward "crime in the streets," as "an African-American monopoly" (p. 19). Wilson views criminal justice statistics as hav-ing much less to do with accurate reports of crime in the United States than with what he sees as a generally held belief about the violence-prone nature of Blacks. He quotes Evan Stark:

> [The] alternative view [to blacks being more violent-prone] is supported by national surveys of crime victims, a far more accurate source of information about crimes committed than arrest reports. According to the FBI, for ex-ample, the proportion of blacks arrested for aggravated assault in 1987 was more than three times greater than the proportion for whites. But the National Crime Survey, based on victim interviews, found that the actual proportion of blacks and whites committing aggravated assault in 1987 was virtually iden-tical: 32 per 1,000 for blacks; 31 per 1,000 for whites. (Stark, 1990, quoted in Wilson, 1990, p. 25)

The tragedy of homicides among Blacks is negated in this suggested framework of crime and violence. Violence becomes the word that both sub-sumes one event (the tragedy of the victim's death) and qualifies another action (a brutal homicide). In addition, this framework defines the actors as potential menaces to society, thereby undermining any sympathy when lives are taken by an act of violence. As a result, the public feels a macabre sense of relief when it is reported that the "menaces" kill each other.

Death framed as violence begs the question, "Where is the tragedy?" This framework leaves no room to mourn a family member lost to a brutal death. On an even more insidious level, the "violent" framing of African American homi-cide incriminates both the assassin and the deceased. Looking at death only through a lens of violence generates silence around the issue of this death as loss. Thus, the tragedy and overall impact of death felt by surviving African American adolescents is hidden by mainstream society's inability and unwill-ingness to deal with the issue of death or with the brutal way most Black ado-lescents encounter death.

In this harsh light and harsher silence stands the African American ado-lescent whose friend or loved one was gunned down. There are too few spaces where Salima and Tavia, the students quoted earlier, could deal with their emo-tions about witnessing a killing of a "cool person" or losing a sibling. Few are the spaces where Tavia could admit that she "just feel real sad that he's [her brother] gone 'cause everybody's leaving like this." Few are the spaces where the two young people can discuss different views of the tragedy. Salima's anger at her friend's death is directed at the policemen—their seeming lack of interest and their failure to act swiftly to save a life. She also expresses anger at the assassin and argues for his death. Tavia sympathizes with her friend, but responds to Salima's wish for vengeance by reminding her that "if we kill the people that killing other people, that's all they gon' do is rest in peace."

Tavia's and Salima's experiences with death reflect those of many African American students from low-income families living in poor neighborhoods across the country. The students at Brent are among these; therefore, I will examine how death entered my classroom. I am not referring to the rise in school crime and violence, but rather the long-term effects of experiencing frequent deaths on teaching and learning in urban classrooms.[5] I will show how I transformed the notions of teacher authority and legitimated knowledge within my classroom. Through my approach to teaching and learning, I acknowledged one of the most traumatic life experiences survived by my students—the trauma of death.

Cluster Academy: Another Kind of Death

Brent Junior High School has a population of approximately nine hundred students. In the 1992–1993 school year, 62 percent of the students at Brent were African American. Some of these students are bussed from poor neighborhoods of the city to the middle- and upper-class neighborhood where Brent Junior High is located. As these minority students, mostly African Americans, leave the flatlands and come up the hill to the school, they yell greetings, friend to friend, that formerly blended with the morning rhythms of their neighborhoods, but sound harsh in the quiet neighborhood surrounding the school. Nothing affirms their presence in the hill neighborhood, not even their roles as students at the school. As a Black woman ascending the hill, I too feel some sense of displacement, but, unlike them, I ascend the hill to a position of relative power. I am a teacher there.

In the 1992–1993 school year, the school district received Chapter One funding. With these federal dollars, they created Cluster Academies, which are classes that provide prevention/intervention services for students who have been promoted based on their age or retained in grades seven, eight, or nine. Each junior high school in the district had at least one Cluster Academy class. These classes are allowed to have a maximum of twenty-five students. Brent had only one Cluster class, which I taught. Twenty-one of my students were Black, two were Asian, and one was Mexican.

The general perception at Brent Junior High is that Cluster Academy is "a classroom for bad students" who are labeled "at risk," "learning disabled," "violent," "disruptive," and other debilitating terms, even by their own schoolmates. The general feeling around the school was that students who were placed in Cluster Academy could not function in regular classes, mainly because of "behavioral" problems, secondarily because of academics. My students were, in fact, the ones with the most reported disciplinary and behavioral problems in the school. Prior to being placed in Cluster, the best of these students averaged a C on their report cards, and many had received straight F's. By all of the school's indicators, any attempt to educate these students was hopeless. The Cluster teacher was not expected to make much headway with these students, and the students themselves were very aware of this. I once asked my students to write their perceptions of the school's view of Cluster Academy, and combined their individual responses into the following essay:

How People View Cluster

People look at Cluster as though we do not do anything, we are doomed, all we ever do is play, and we are bad all the time. That's how people look at Cluster. People say that Cluster kids are stupid. It's a class for dummies. Some people think that we are just dumb and just bad. I bet if we let someone from regular classes in for a day they would be shocked. Even a teacher. We do more work than in regular classes. People always pass judgment on each other and for what? Just to put someone down. To me it does not make any sense. Some people talk about the Cluster Kids every day, probably not just students. Maybe teachers. Maybe even the principal talk about us too.

People make it seem like we're those terrible kids. Every time we get sent out of class, they suspend us or give us SAC [suspension alternative class]. Some kids in regular classes are cutting classes and all they get is a note to get back to class. They don't even give the Cluster class a chance in the office. One time [counselor X] suspended me without hearing my side of the story. I think it's because I'm in Cluster class. This counselor didn't used to act like that when I was in regular classes.

I think they look over us like we are bums in the street. I'll let them know how I feel about being looked over. I'm not saying that everybody looks over us. I'm saying that its people like [Mr. X (a teacher)] and a whole bunch of kids. I don't like when they say that Cluster is dumb. I get mad and curse and say "You dumb!" but I don't really mean it. I just get mad.[6]

Initially, the call for classes like Cluster Academy came from a desire of policy makers, school officials, and concerned parents to aid educationally disadvantaged students (Fine, 1991; Levin, 1971; Minow, 1990; Ravitch, 1983). However, clearly the euphemistic title of the class did not impress the students and did not hide the reality of their being framed as a certain type of student by being placed in Cluster Academy class. By perceiving the negative label and the subsequent negative treatment, Cluster students experienced another reality, one that contradicted the original intent of the formation of the class.

It was my challenge, then, to change the Cluster students' negative self-perceptions of the Cluster Academy class and to liberate them from their images as Cluster students. I began to reflect on how other parts of their lives might impact the roles they see for themselves as students. Although there were many times when my students would criticize the way the school community viewed them, their critique was difficult for them to maintain in light of so few school experiences that affirmed their abilities and competencies as students.

It was true that a number of students experienced difficulty in reading and math; difficulties that I now believe were exacerbated by the way teachers "taught" the subjects. For example, I started the year with skills and drills in math because I, to some degree, also bought into the view that students' difficulties were due to their lack of math ability, as opposed to a range of causes, not the least of which might be my presentation of the material and the teaching method. I noticed, however, math in operation on the P.E. field, when students were playing baseball, setting up teams, and keeping score; I saw it in money and candy exchanges and bartering. I decided, therefore, to risk seeing how much of their difficulty with math was contextual and situational, or presentational and procedural, according to classroom norms. I let them take one of the Friday math tests in groups of four students. Some of the test questions were created by the students themselves, submitted in advance. I also included an applied math problem I'd found about setting up a basketball tournament schedule. The students responded well to making up the test questions, and to having a problem on a familiar topic that they were interested in.

After this experience, I reflected on how well the students responded to acting as agents in their own learning process. This reflection was the avenue through which the issue of death entered our classroom and the advent of my attempts to transform the structure of education in our classroom. In the process of being "students," these young people might also find power in being themselves: who they were outside the classroom and away from the school.

Death

I first realized how much death was on the minds of these young people when I let them draw during a "rained-out" physical education period. I encouraged them to draw whatever they wanted. I noticed that the letters "R.I.P" were in almost every drawing. In some, "R.I.P" and the name of the person or persons who died comprised the drawing. In others, the words were located in corners or at the bottom of the drawing.

When I looked at my students' artwork earlier in the year, the drawings didn't appear to me to have anything to do with death or resting in peace. One picture that especially impressed me was a detailed drawing of the artist's neighborhood. In the picture were two tall buildings, each with eighteen squares representing windows. A brick wall adjoined the second building. "R.I.P XIV" was drawn on the wall along with other graffiti. A "gangsta," wearing a XIV's hat ("XIV" is the name of a neighborhood gang), high-top sneakers, and a t-shirt with a marijuana plant on it, sat on the wall. An old car, its tires flat and the back window broken, was parked in front of the wall. Another homey, giving the peace sign, stood in front of the car. I was so impressed by the drawing's detail and depth that "R.I.P" initially seemed like only another detail. Yet as time passed, I noted that "R.I.P" was frequently scratched into the desks, and appeared in the young people's art and on their hats and t-shirts. I then began to acknowledge the presence of death in the classroom.

Later in the semester, my interactions with the students around the death of the former Brent student made it clear that I had to address the issue of death with my students. Something that mattered this much to them and was so prevalent in their thoughts could not be ignored. My challenge was to find a way to deal with death in the classroom.

Paulo Freire's (1989) work offered me ideas to begin the process of negotiating the issue of death in the classroom. Freire's "banking concept" of education critiques teacher-student relationships. The banking concept is the idea that "knowledge is a gift bestowed by those who consider themselves knowledgeable upon those whom they consider to know nothing" (p. 57). He describes the character of the teacher-student relationship as it traditionally operates in public schooling: "This relationship involves a narrative subject (the teacher) and patient, listening objects (the students)" (p. 57). As a person new to the role of teacher, I quickly realized that the burden of conveying specific information to the students is placed on teachers by the structure of the schooling process. In California, for example, there are restrictive curriculum guidelines for every grade level in public schools. Covering all of the topics dictated by the guidelines is virtually impossible, considering the many interruptions that occur daily during school, where students exit and enter the classroom continuously. Neither administrators nor teachers logically expect to complete all of the requirements, yet students are held accountable based on state guidelines as they move from one grade level to the next. The goal of having the students present every day to receive this "gift" of knowledge seems an even more insurmountable task if one acknowledges the many outside disruptions, including those caused by the prevalence of death, in students' lives.

Moreover, Freire questions the relevance of the gift of knowledge to the lives of students. He notes that in using the "banking concept" of education "the contents, whether values or empirical dimensions of reality, tend to become lifeless and petrified. Education is suffering from narrative sickness" (p. 57). The symptom of this sickness in my classroom was the students' response to lifeless, disengaging material, their blank faces staring back as I lectured. No learning was taking place. It became obvious that the superficial nature of teacher as the "giver of knowledge," and students as the "patient," listening receptors needed to be transformed.

At one point, in a desperate attempt to ignite some excitement in my students, I stopped "teaching" and started to talk about possible field trips that might bring to life the importance of the material I presented. The shutters of disinterest on students' faces lifted momentarily. I went on about where we would go, what we would do, and how we would do it. As I paused to catch my breath and reign in my own excitement, one student packed a powerful punch, asking loudly, "Did you ask us?" I was stunned into silence and had no reply. I realized that, as hard as I had tried not to, I had fallen back into the trap of teacher as authoritative knowledge-giver. I had not engaged the students, or asked what they might like to do with my idea. I merely brainstormed in front of them about what *I* thought *they* would find interesting without asking for their input. Not only did I realize my failure to engage students with my curriculum, I also realized that I was ignoring other issues that were occupying their thoughts—such as death and dying—as shown clearly in their art and in the earlier taped interview.

I began to see that education, real education, as Freire states, must begin with a solution to the teacher-student contradiction—where the teacher is the only conveyer of knowledge and the knowledge brought into the classroom by students is unrecognized and negated—by reconciling the poles so that both are simultaneously teachers and students. Once again, my awareness of the importance of death to my students returned to me, but I had no idea where to start: How could I broach the subject? What part of the discussion might be culturally taboo? In what lesson would the discussion fit? How would I grade it? How would I make up the time I would lose in covering "school knowledge" (the curriculum) if I used class time to discuss death? The conflict between teaching a prescribed curriculum and wanting to respond to students' realities became unbearable—and so I sought their help.

Renegotiating Death in the Classroom

We were halfway through the school year, and things were becoming really stale in the classroom. In despair, I wrote and read a letter to my students. The following is an abridged version of the letter:

> Something's happened to me. What happened is that I lost it. I get discouraged trying to teach you. I get caught up in the everyday—giving out referrals, teaching at you, forgetting that I had a bigger picture when I came into the room. There's a certain number of black kids (and the number is growing) that come into schools and just don't make it the way the schools say that you should. They make it in other ways but the school and the teachers do not care. So these kids get placed in classes like Cluster and Opportunity. That's why I chose to teach Cluster. I felt that I could turn things around, that I could prove the school wrong about these kids.
>
> But then I get down here and I get discouraged but this is where I went wrong. I think I know what's best. I bring in all the ideas and just expect you to do them. I stopped asking you what you want to do, what you want to be taught. What do you think will help you the most in the long run? . . . Anyway I propose or put to you that we think of a project or something to end the semester with. My idea is to first get each of you to write about what troubles

you the most about your life that you would like to change and then we decide as a class what out of those things we can try to start changing before the semester ends. But we must make a plan *together*. It will take time but I believe that we can do it. Some of the things I thought about are: going to high school next year, dying, getting shot, clothes, sex, parents, brothers and sisters, the police, the hood, gangstas. But I don't know that any of these things are the most important. Whatever we decide, we must also think up a plan.

That was my idea but I truly want to hear yours so that we are doing this together. I recently read this essay that a black student at Clark High wrote. She wrote that one of her teachers "wallowed over the class like a bowl of jelly." I don't want to do that. I want to interact with you. I won't take people playing the fool, but I want to be sure I let everyone have a say in their education.

Thank you for listening.

The young people did not comment on the letter, except to ask me to read it a second time for the latecomers, and again the next day for the people who had been absent. At first, I thought they only wanted to hear it again because the word "shit" was in it (original version), but then I saw other reasons: I asked for their input, and I acknowledged that I, too, got tired of school every day the way it was.

The process to become a community where knowledge is expected from and acknowledged by all members, although trying at times, is one from which my students and I hoped to extract some value. I was attempting to undo or at least challenge a multiplicity of hegemonic processes in the classroom simultaneously. In the weeks after I read my letter to the students, I allotted two English class periods per week to discuss the end-of-semester project. There was a lot of classroom conversation that did not necessarily include me, and I eventually had to "join" with the various groups to have a voice in the discussions.

The class eventually voted to create a newspaper. Students decided that anyone could write as many articles in as many sections as they wanted. I arranged time in one of the school's computer rooms so that students could type in their contributions. The students read and critiqued each others' writing for spelling and grammar. I did not impose any spelling or grammatical rules, but checked with individuals to verify that their use of other than standard English was a personal, informed choice. The first paper took about four weeks to complete, taking up all of their class periods in the last week for final editing changes and production.

The students became very involved in the process; everything started to matter, from how many pages the newspaper would be, to what color paper to use, to how it would be distributed. During the process of constructing the newspaper, I noticed that the students became less afraid of being vulnerable with me and with each other and of challenges they were initially hesitant to face. The writings for the "Special Memories" section brought out a lot of personal and sad exchanges in the classroom. I learned a lot about coping with the stresses of day-to-day living from these young people. They also showed me humor in the worst situations. A camaraderie grew between me and my students that extended into other class periods when we were not working on the paper.

This interaction resulted in the creation of the *Cluster Chronic*. The students decided to share their newspaper with the rest of the school community. In the first year, we distributed two editions and completed a third that was distributed only to members of the class. Creating this newspaper was powerful on many levels. First, I saw a change in how my students felt about Cluster Academy. For example, they decided to include the collaborative essay, "How People View Cluster," adding the following ending paragraph:

> It's alright being in Cluster. Some teachers, they woo [say] "Cluster is so nice. They do all their work." This makes me feel very happy. People look at Cluster like its a messed up class but its not. It's a good class for me. Who puts on all the shows and do newspapers? Cluster kids are getting talked about because we made a newspaper and no one else did. We did a concert. I don't feel we get enough props [validation] for the things we do at Brent School and that's all I have to say.

Second was the response of the rest of the school community to the newspaper. Cluster students distributed the newspaper during their lunch break to students in the rest of the school. Teachers received any copies that remained. The following excerpts from my field notes illustrate the magic of the moment of distributing the first edition:

> We distributed the newspaper 4th & 5th period lunch to the students of the school. I announced it over the intercom that we were going to be doing this. It was great! The students were reading it. Some had it on their laps, reading it while they ate their lunch. Some were in the lunch line reading it while they waited to go in. GP [a security guard] sat down and read the whole thing. I did not see any papers thrown anywhere although D [the custodian] said that he picked up a few. Ms. M. [a teacher] came into the class for a copy. She said "the kids are all reading it." Ms. S. asked for a copy. Ms. H. [the vice principal] asked for 2 copies to take to the district office.
>
> My kids were walking tall when they distributed the newspaper. At first I kept a few copies for the teachers but the kids kept asking for them to give to other students. I ended up with only two copies for the teachers' room. M. immediately took one up as I put them down.
>
> One English teacher stopped me and told me how she enjoyed the paper. She said that she was an English teacher and she agonized about letting the kids write slang words. She said, "the kids would put slang words into the computer and the spell check would go crazy!" Because she was an "English Teacher" the slang words worried her so much. Yet she recognized and appreciated the emotion, the realness in the kids' writing. (Journal entry, April 1993)

The act of creating a newspaper that was widely read by their peers in the school was empowering for the young people.

Finally, the most powerful experience for all of us in writing the newspaper was while revisiting the topic of death. To give respectful mention and remembrance to their loved ones who had died, the young people created a "Special Memories" section in the first edition of the newspaper. There were six articles in this section. In addition, the "Street Life" section, which included opinions on events that occur in students' neighborhoods, had two articles about death. In all, eight contributions in the *Cluster Chronic* discussed death in the young people's lives. Below are three of the eight:

SPECIAL MEMORIES

In Loving Memories

I love my cousin Trevel Jamison
He was one of the best
R.I.P. David Rogan and Hasan Bess
To all the birds we have to feed
Rest in peace Andre Reed
And all the ways we have to go
R.I.P. Gizmo

written by Sabrina Brown

James Roberts—Dec. 10, 1974 to Aug. 29, 1991

In loving memories of James Roberts. He attended Clarke and Brent Middle Schools and Sojourner High School. He loved to go fishing and riding around in his car. He was 18 years old when he died. He left us his beloved kids James Jr. and Jamilah. He loved football. He departed this life August 29, 1991. I really do miss him. We had our ups and downs but he still told me what was right from wrong,

I was hurt when my brother left me because he was my mother's only son. Now I don't have a big brother but its going to be all good, because he's going to see me again in the next life. We really do miss him.

written by Tavia Keller

STREET LIFE

My Opinion

There are more than two-hundred people getting killed because of gun wars. People are getting shot by mistake. More people should start a crime watch in their neighborhood. Some people are being killed over a word. Sometimes there are fights but mostly threats. A man was beaten to death with a baseball bat because of the part of town he lived in. I think this stuff is wrong because brothers are killing each other and by the year 2000 there will not be enough black men to communicate with.

written by Willis Irwin

On the day of the first edition, I made the following field note: "We talked about dying and family. Rodney, me, Damon, and some others said we did not know what we would do if our Moms died" (Journal entry, April 1993). I asked no questions about death, but instead shared my feelings about the subject. This enhanced my relationship with my students, as we acknowledged our whole selves, not only the roles of "student" and "teacher." It was also a relationship where knowledge was not mine alone; everyone gave and everyone received.

As I struggled to deal with death in the classroom, I gained clarity from another teacher's experience, which was less successful than mine. The following tells of this teacher's attempt to negotiate the issue of death without changing the operating norms and behaviors in her classroom, and emphasizes the difficulty of this endeavor as well as its necessity.

Critical Pedagogy: No Teaching as Usual

The day after the funeral of the student mentioned at the beginning of this article, I made copies of the funeral program for the students who had known the deceased but had not attended the service. Another of my students' teachers took one of the funeral programs and copied only the picture of the deceased. The following day, she handed out copies of this picture to her class, asking students to write a letter of condolence to the mother of the deceased.

The young people's reaction was swift. The girl who was related to the deceased screamed obscenities at the teacher, burst into tears, and ran out of the class. Other girls also cursed the teacher as tears fell from their eyes. Paralyzed with confusion, this well-meaning teacher dropped the subject and barely managed to get through the rest of the period. She was still shaken by the experience as she related it to me the next day.

Later, feeling more comfortable with the students after working with them on the first issue of the *Cluster Chronic,* I ventured to ask them what had occurred that day with the other teacher. Their indignation was still apparent in their responses:

> She had the nerve to copy his picture on a ditto!

> Coral ask her "why you put his picture on a ditto and ask us to write his momma a letter when his momma is having a hard time as it is, you stupid-ass b-t-h?!"

> A school ditto! A school activity!

> Don't nobody wanna keep feeling those memories!

> It's like she making his death a joke.

It seemed that this teacher had assumed she had to "teach" the students how to cope with death. She had assumed the role of "knowledge-giver," and these students were not about to be "told" how to handle death. They coped with death on an almost daily basis. They and their communities were already coping the best way they knew how. These students were not about to compromise a lived experience to the banking concept of knowledge transference. The students' response was passionate, with the intent to hurt and insult the teacher the way they'd perceived themselves to be hurt and insulted. This well-intentioned teacher omitted an important part of the negotiation. She didn't ask them.

Conclusion

Death is one example of students' life experiences that enters the classroom whether a teacher chooses to acknowledge it or not. It is also one of many student experiences that debunk the notion of classroom teaching and education as neutral spaces or endeavors. It is important to find a way, with the help of the young people, to connect teaching in the school with life outside of school and, as Freire suggests, to find space for the emergence of teacher-students and student-teachers.

Although the classroom I share with the young people has come a long way, there are still days when education suffers from "narrative sickness," but now there are twenty-six of us acting as doctors on call, so diagnosis is possible. Cuban and Tyack (1989), who wrote a historical perspective on schools and the students who don't fit them, make two suggestions for policy reform relevant to this discussion. They state that "as hard as it may be to change the school to match the students of an 'imperiled generation,' it is a more promising strategy than trying to fit the student to the school" (p. 29). They propose further "to undertake comprehensive changes that take no features of schools for granted" (p. 29).

Our classroom is now an exciting place where learning and teaching takes place, bringing life to a usually lifeless curriculum. We've become a community of student-teachers and a teacher-student. We are a community of learners. Students have opinions about what they would like to get from their education. I have found that it is important to start from where they are. I ask them.

In this article, I attempted to demonstrate how our class moved from traditional one-way teaching to an interactive teaching and learning environment. I no longer want to acknowledge students only to the extent of how well they fulfill my expectations or their response to a prescribed, petrified curriculum. I believe that it is not effective or responsible to teach on a day-to-day basis as though nothing that happens outside of the school building impacts on the act of teaching. My students were empowered through the acknowledgement of knowledge acquired as a consequence of their lived experiences. They also taught teachers the benefits of respecting and incorporating students' knowledge into their classroom pedagogy. Whether we as teachers choose to address it or not, students' lives come with them to school, death and other aspects of students' realities come into our classrooms. Instead of wishing for other students, let us gear our work towards the students we have.

Appendix

Following are the three other articles from the *Cluster Chronic* that deal with death:

In Loving Memories of Omont L. Wilson

Omont was a proud young man. He stayed in J.F.K manor. Omont had two brothers by the names of Marvin Wilson and Kiniko Wilson. Omont departed this life a few days after Christmas. He left behind loving memories of what he and his family used to do together. He left behind good and helpful friends that hang inside of "Easter Hill" on South 26th Street. Omont liked to ride bikes with me, Ree-Love, Ghetto "o", and other friends. Omont is badly missed by family and friends. May He Rest In Peace.

writern by RJ Johnson

In Loving Memories Willie L. Bowie

On March 20, 1991 Willie L. Bowie departed this life leaving behind two little boys of his own by the names of Kamari and Larry Bowie. His family was badly hurt when they found out this tragedy. R.I.P. B-40.

written by RJ Johnson

In Loving Memories—Dameion D. West

In loving memories of Dameion. I love him from the bottom of my heart. He means something to me more than some of the other people I know. I know and you know that Dameion was a young, Black, intelligent teenager. Before he got laid in his grave he came over to my house and kissed my momma and everything, and then the next day his first cousin came over to my house and told my momma that Dameion just got killed. He said that he was out there fighting with his friend and his friend got beat up. After the fight was over the boy told Dameion that he was going to get killed. At the time Dameion wasn't tripping, because as I said before, Dameion was a young, loving Black boy. That boy just looked back and shot him. I'm glad that Dameion didn't have any kids because now they would be without a father and that's not what we want. Everyone needs a father, especially these little kids nowadays that don't have a mother, so you know they need a father.

written by Coral Wilson

Notes

1. See Wideman and Wideman (1984); McCall (1991); Blackwell (1985).

2. The writing of "re-presentation" in this way is a political act—creating an awareness of the politics of identity formation, particularly with regard to race, in the U.S. social context.

3. Ngugi's (1986) comment refers specifically to African culture, but language as the most powerful bearer of a culture has been posited by social scientists for centuries.

See DuBois (1961); hooks (1989); Smitherman (1986); Sanchez (1970); and Bernstein (1971).

4. Rappers like Ice Cube, Too Short, Ice-T, and NWA (Niggas with a Attitude) made their mark on the music industry with a particular discourse of violence in their music. The irony of death in the African American community is sometimes played out in different songs from the same album. For instance, the GETO BOYZ's poignant rendering of death as a loss of a life in "Six Feet Deep" is followed by a rap tale justifying the murder of a Black woman.

5. For a critique of the impact of school crime and violence in urban schools, see Comer (1980).

6. The students who wrote this essay are Sabrina Brown, Kevin Henderson, James Porter, Danny Simpson, Coral Wilson, Rodney Walker, Stacey Willis, RJ Johnson ("Rodney" in the text), and Damon Marshall.

References

Baldwin, J. 1985. *The evidence of things not seen.* New York: Henry Holt.

Bernstein, B. 1971. *Class, codes and control.* New York: Schocken Press.

Bleeding Colors. 1993: *West County Times* Special Report (September 26): pp. 1–18.

Blackwell, J. E. 1985. *The Black community: Diversity and unity.* New York: Harper & Row.

Brown, R. L. 1988. *The state of Black America.* New York: National Urban League.

Comer, J. 1980. *School power: Implications of an intervention project.* New York: Free Press.

Corr, C. A., & McNeil, J. N., eds. 1986. *Adolescence and death.* New York: Springer.

Cuban, L., & Tyack, D. 1989. *Mismatch: Historical perspectives on schools and students that don't fit them.* Unpublished manuscript.

DuBois, W. E. B. 1961. *Souls of Black folk.* Greenwich, CT: Fawcett.

Fine, M. 1991. *Framing dropouts: Notes on the politics of an urban public high school.* Albany: State University of New York Press.

Freire, P. 1989. *Pedagogy of the oppressed.* New York: Continuum.

Giroux, H. A. 1992. *Border crossings: Cultural workers and the politics of education.* New York: Routledge.

Gordon, A. K. 1986. The tattered cloak of immortality. In C. A. Corr & J. N. McNeil (Eds.), *Adolescence and death* (pp. 16–31). New York: Springer.

hooks, b. 1989. *Talking back: Thinking feminist, thinking Black.* Boston: South End Press.

Jordan, W. D. 1977. *White over Black: American attitudes toward the Negro, 1550–1812.* Chapel Hill: University of North Carolina Press.

Kubler-Ross, E. 1969. *On death and dying.* New York: Macmillan.

Levin, H. 1971. A decade of policy developments in improving education and training for low-income populations. In R. Herman (Ed.), *A decade of federal anti-poverty programs* (pp. 123–188). New York: Academic Press.

McCall, N. 1991. Dispatches from a dying generation. *Washington Post,* 13 January, p. C1.

Minow, M. 1990. *Making all the difference: Inclusion, exclusion and American law.* New York: Cornell University Press.

Ngugi, W. T. 1986. *Decolonising the mind: The politics of language in African literature.* London: James Currey.

Ravitch, D. 1983. *The troubled crusade: American education 1945–1980.* New York: Basic Books.

Schowalter, J. E. 1987. Adolescents' concepts of death and how these can kill them. In J. E. Schowalter, P. Bushman, P. R. Patterson, A. H. Kutscher, M. Tallmer, & R. G. Stevenson (Eds.), *Children and death: Perspectives from birth through adolescence.* New York: Praeger.

Smitherman, G. 1986. *Talkin and testifyin: The language of Black America.* Detroit: Wayne State University Press.

Wideman, J. E., & Wideman, R. D. 1984. *Brothers and keepers.* New York: Henry Holt.

Wilson, A. N. 1990. *Black-on-Black violence: The psychodynamics of Black self-annihilation in service of White domination.* New York: Afrikan World Infosystems.

Wright, J. B. 1987. *Black robes, White justice.* Secaucus, NJ: L. Stuart.

3

Empowerment Education

Freire's Ideas Adapted to Health Education

Nina Wallerstein and Edward Bernstein

Editors' Notes: In this chapter, medical educators Nina Wallerstein and Edward Bernstein provide an overview of Freire's philosophy and its application to health education. They offer an extensive case study of the Alcohol and Substance Abuse Prevention (ASAP) program at the University of New Mexico. This program is designed to empower youth to make healthier choices in their lives and effect positive social changes. It emphasizes the problem-posing process of dialogue, critical reflection, and social action, to reach Native American youths and their communities. The authors also illustrate how to take Freire's ideas beyond the classroom to community organizing.

Introduction

Empowerment education is an effective health education and prevention model for personal and social change. This article explores the strategy of empowering education: its impact on health, its underlying philosophy as inspired by Brazilian educator Paulo Freire, and its differences with traditional health education. The model is demonstrated through a case study of an adolescent substance abuse prevention program in New Mexico.

In much of the literature, empowerment has been defined largely by its absence leading to: alienation,[1-3] victim-blaming,[4] learned helplessness,[5] or powerlessness.[6-7] This article adopts the opposite approach, defining empowerment as a social action process that promotes participation of people, organizations, and communities in gaining control over their lives in their community and larger society. With this perspective, empowerment is not characterized

53

as achieving power to dominate others, but rather power to act with others to effect change.

Empowerment education, as developed from Paulo Freire's writings, involves people in group efforts to identify their problems, to critically assess social and historical roots of problems, to envision a healthier society, and to develop strategies to overcome obstacles in achieving their goals. Through community participation, people develop new beliefs in their ability to influence their personal and social spheres. An empowering health education effort therefore involves much more than improving self-esteem, self-efficacy or other health behaviors that are independent from environmental or community change; the targets are individual, group and structural change. Empowerment embodies a broad process that encompasses prevention as well as other goals of community connectedness, self-development, improved quality of life, and social justice.[8]

Health Rationale

Considerable research documents the effects of lack of control or powerlessness in disease causation or, conversely, of empowerment in health enhancement. The literature in social epidemiology and social psychology examines lack of control over one's life as a risk factor, stemming from overburden of life demands without adequate resources to meet the demands.[9] Other literature—social networks and support, community organizing, and new health promotion approaches—examines gaining control as a strategy for health.

Social epidemiological research has long documented that lower socioeconomic status is related to increased morbidity and mortality, from such risks as improper sanitation, hazardous jobs, malnutrition, poor education or minority status.[10-13] Recent research however has begun to examine an underlying susceptibility to disease from the risks of lack of control and disempowerment as confounders of the specific risk factors.[14-18] Occupational research in particular has identified lack of control as a risk for coronary heart disease, measured by position in the job hierarchy[19,20] or having low decision-authority with high demands, typically in low-status jobs.[21,22]

The argument that lack of control over one's environment affects health is bolstered by social-psychological research among the elderly. Nursing home residents given some life control develop better mental and physical health indicators, than people given the game intervention but without choice or decision-making power.[23-25] Other more limited social-psychological definitions of control have proven important in prevention and treatment compliance: social competence in negotiating the world,[26,27] adolescent life competency training[28] and self-efficacy.[29,30]

Recent social network interventions suggest that the dimension of control may be an important component of the preventive effects of social support.[31,32] By training natural helpers[33,34] or by developing community empowerment problem-solving programs,[35] social support and community participation increase and in turn enable greater control in community life. One weakness with natural helper programs that ignore empowerment is that communities may evolve better helping mechanisms within their borders, but still not have the power or level of organization to have an impact on poverty or environmental stressors.[36]

Community organizing is a field that overlaps substantially with empowering education. Successful organizing in the Alinsky tradition directly reduces socioeconomic or environmental health risks by promoting job development or toxic waste cleanup.[37–41] Health is affected indirectly through enhancing social competence, social support, and community debate, such as seatbelt coalitions that raise awareness as they lobby for legislation. Historically, however, community organizing has differed from empowering education in its emphasis on winnable goals rather than on a participatory process that engages people in critical analysis of root causes as the basis for social action. An exception is the Highlander Center that best demonstrates how education can work with organizing to empower local people to help themselves.[42,43]

Health promotion approaches increasingly include community norm and institutional policy change to enable and reinforce healthy behavior choices.[44] Much of health promotion, including community-wide interventions, however, has targeted individual behaviors, rather than social or environmental risks.[45] Health promotion programs have also least reached poor and minority peoples who face broad risk factors, including lack of control, that take precedence over behavioral risks. A new generation of health promotion theorists, many with the World Health Organization, recognize the role of control and social action in health:[46]

> Health promotion is the process of enabling individuals and communities *to increase control over the determinants* of health and thereby improve their health. Such a process requires the direct involvement of individuals and communities in the achievement of change, combined with political action directed towards the creation of an environment conducive to health.[47] (emphasis added)

In practice, this statement means targeting all levels of health problems, including socioeconomic risks, over and beyond individual behavior risks. In addition to outcomes, it also means focusing on the process of empowerment that addresses lack of control through community participation and critical thinking.

Empowering Education: The Freire Approach

> Education should have as one of its main tasks to invite people to believe in themselves. It should invite people to believe they have the knowledge.[48]

Brazilian educator Paulo Freire offers major theoretical writing on empowering education. In the late 1950s, Freire initiated a successful literacy and political consciousness program for shantytown dwellers and peasants in Brazil.[49] In the last three decades, Freire's ideas of democratic or empowering education have been a catalyst for worldwide programs in: literacy,[50,51] English as a Second Language,[52,53] peace education,[54] health education,[55,56] teenage school discipline,[57] youth centers,[58] adult education and college level,[59,60] and community development.[61]

Freire's central premise is that education is not neutral and takes place in the context of peoples' lives. About this context, Freire asks, who does education serve and for what purpose? Does education socialize people to be objects and accept their limited roles within the status quo, or does it encourage people to question critical issues of the day and fully participate in the social and political life of society?

To Freire, the purpose of education should be human liberation so that learners can be subjects and actors in their own lives and in society. To promote this role, Freire proposes a dialogue approach in which everyone participates as equals and colearners to create social knowledge. The goal of group dialogue is critical thinking by posing problems in such a way as to have participants uncover root causes of their place in society—the socioeconomic, political, cultural, and historical context of personal lives. But critical thinking continues beyond perception—towards the actions that people take to move beyond powerlessness and gain control over their lives.

In many ways, Freire's ideas are similar to health education's guiding principles: to start from the problems of the community, to use active learning methods, and to engage participants in determining their own needs and priorities.[62-64]

Despite these similarities, Freire's approach complements and substantially extends traditional health education. On the surface, Freire's philosophy of learner-as-subject may appear similar to health education's emphasis on people's responsibility for their own health decisions. On closer examination, a Freirian approach diverges significantly. While health education assumes that individuals can make healthy decisions with enough information, skills, and reinforcement, Freire assumes that knowledge does not come from experts inculcating their information. His emphasis is on the collective knowledge that emerges from a group sharing experiences and understanding the social influences that affect individual lives.

To Freire, the health educator's role is to contribute information after the group raises its themes for mutual reflection. Rather than impose their own cultural values, educators should enter into "authentic dialogue" so people emerge from their cultural silence and self-blame to redefine their own social reality.[65,66]

In addition to group dialogue and understanding the social dimensions of problems, Freire diverges in his view that true learning requires acting in the world. Unlike many health education programs which end in a classroom, a

Freirian program emphasizes action and subsequent reflection as keys to the learning process. Because the group process uncovers the personal and socio-political dimensions of problems, Freirian change strategies are broader. For example, rather than only using a predetermined curriculum, such as resisting peer pressure, a Freirian program would encourage group members to derive their own curriculum and actions that address the problems of alcohol abuse in their lives and community.

Freire offers a three-stage methodology that forms the basis of an empow-ering education program. The first step is listening to understand the felt issues or themes of the community. Step two is participatory dialogue about the in-vestigated issues using a problem-posing methodology. Step three is action or the positive changes that people envision during their dialogue.

In a Freirian approach, the listening stage is conducted in equal partner-ship with community members to identify problems and determine priorities. This community team with decision-making authority differs from the tradi-tional health educator who may make independent decisions after a community needs assessment. Despite the ideal of the community setting priorities, fund-ing restrictions often dictate programs. Even with a prefunded issue, such as suicide prevention, listening with community members can tailor programs to local needs. To Freire, listening is a continual process that extends beyond ini-tial needs assessments; community members therefore become active in all program stages and are more likely to continue organizing after funding ends.

The stage two dialogue process is key to understanding Freire's approach. Using issues identified during the listening process, Freire proposes creat-ing discussion objects called "codifications" or "codes" to structure problem-posing dialogue about these issues.

A "code" is a concrete physical representation of an identified commu-nity issue in any form: role-plays, stories, slides, photographs, songs, etc. Each code re-presents the community reality back to discussion participants and enables them to project their emotional and social responses into the object for a focused discussion. An effective code shows a problematic situation that is many-sided, familiar to participants, and open-ended without solutions.

Although codes present open-ended situations, critical thinking about is-sues does not occur spontaneously. Facilitators provide group leadership by using a five-step questioning strategy that moves discussion from the personal to the social analysis and action level. People are asked to (1) describe what they see and feel (2) as a group, define the many levels of the problem (3) share similar experiences from their lives (4) question why this problem exists and (5) develop action plans to address the problem. Codes can generate this dis-cussion progression with a small core team or with large community groups to broaden community dialogue and action. This process is elaborated in the case study which follows.

After the initial listening and dialogue stage, the third stage of action emerges directly from the problem-posing discussion. As people test out their analyses in the real world, they begin a deeper cycle of reflection that includes input from their new experiential base. This recurrent spiral of action-reflection-action enables people to learn from their collective attempts at change and to become more deeply involved to surmount the cultural, social, or historic barriers.

Because of its multiple targets of change, it is deceptive to consider this process problem-*solving*. Most often, the changes people seek in their lives and communities do not have immediate solutions. Even lifestyle change takes concerted effort to adjust habits; cultural or policy change in a community can take even longer. This process is therefore called problem-*posing* (rather than solving), recognizing the complexity and time needed for solutions with individuals and communities. Although change may evolve slowly, problem-posing can be a nurturing process with people exploring visions as they work on problems.

The Alcohol Substance Abuse Prevention (ASAP) Program

The ASAP Program is an Emergency Center community- and school-based participatory prevention program that seeks to reduce excess morbidity and mortality among multi-ethnic middle and high school students. Operating since 1982 through the University of New Mexico School of Medicine, ASAP seeks to empower youth from high-risk populations to make healthier choices in their own lives, to play active political and social roles in their communities and society, and, as community participants, to effect positive changes.

As a result of the risks of poverty (New Mexico is the 46th lowest state in per capita income), rural living, and high percentage of minorities, New Mexican youth are over-represented in national mortality rates. Compared to the U.S. all race injury mortality rate of 83/100,000 for 15–24 year olds, New Mexican Indian youth have a rate of 233/100,000, Hispanics 115/100,000, and Anglos 93/100,000.[67]

The standardized mortality ratio (SMR) reveals an excess motor vehicle crash mortality (above a national baseline of 100) as 460 for Native Americans, 171 for Hispanics, and 148 for Anglos. Alcoholism mortality is the most dramatic. The SMR for Indians is 2800, 900 for Hispanics, and 373 for Anglos.[68] The minority group over-representation in these health statistics has its roots in historic conflicts, years of internalized powerlessness, and present life conditions. These have included limited access to jobs, education, decent housing, and health care; the suppression of cultural values and languages; and the loss of Native American and Hispanic land, water, and mineral rights. Because New Mexican Anglos have shared economic underdevelopment and isolated rural life, they also show excess mortality above national rates.

These limited opportunities and conflicts for youth suggest that prevention programs must comprehensively address behaviors, personality, immediate peers, and family environment, as well as the negative social conditions under which youth live. To challenge feelings of powerlessness, strategies must also build concretely on positive attributes within the individual, family, and environment, such as youth's desire for excitement (falsely promised through alcohol advertisements) and autonomy, or people's cultural values of community cooperation.[69]

ASAP Program Description

The ASAP program brings small groups of middle and high school volunteer students from predominantly minority high-risk communities for four visits to the University Hospital Emergency Center and County Detention Center in Albuquerque. At these sites, students interact with patients, their families, and jail residents who have alcohol and drug-related problems. Medical, nursing, and health education students and faculty are trained as volunteer facilitators to lead the teenage groups.[70] Since 1982, ASAP has involved several hundred teenage students, more than a hundred health professional students, and teachers and teen center coordinators from over 15 schools in Albuquerque, Native American pueblos, and Hispanic rural towns.

During their visits to the emergency center and jail, ASAP youth interview patients and jail residents and participate in a curriculum[71] that incorporates methods from other adolescent health programs: social learning and resistance to peer pressure[72-74]; life skills competencies and decision-making about alternative choices[75-77]; peer education strategies[78]; and analysis of media and policies that influence consumption, such as New Mexico's drive-up liquor windows. After the four sessions, the youth receive additional training to become peer educators in their schools, younger-age feeder schools, and in community settings.

ASAP's underlying educational philosophy has been inspired by Freire's ideas which include: participation of young people as colearners with health professionals and patients; the value of students' experience as contributing to social knowledge about substance abuse; critical thinking with students asking their own questions of patients and themselves; and group dialogue to explore root causes and motivate students to engage in creative actions that address problems in their communities and society as a whole. This philosophy recognizes the dynamic interaction between personal growth, and participation in community change.

ASAP also draws from other influences: the worldwide movement to transform education in the 1960s towards student-centered experiential learning and social involvement,[79-81] and Jessor's work on youth's covarying problem behaviors that require both distal and proximal interventions.[82,83]

By adopting a Freirian perspective, ASAP distinguishes itself from other program models such as "just say no" and "scared straight." Both of these approaches take place in a punitive environment where youth are treated as objects to be controlled through shame or fear. Just say no programs isolate students from their peer group and ignore the larger social-economic realities that contribute to alcohol and drug abuse. Just saying no has become the panacea to a social problem whose solution is in fact far beyond individual willpower.

Although ASAP may appear to be similar to a scared straight model by showing the real-life consequences of substance abuse, ASAP differs in its emphasis on youth empathy and sharing experiences in a safe group environment. Instead of being preached to, youth become subjects of their own learning as they ask questions, explore the many levels of the problem, make decisions for their own choices, and share the seriousness of substance abuse with friends and their communities. Although youth learn through discussion that individuals have not created the epidemic problem of substance abuse, ASAP believes individual youth have an important role in societal change. Saying no to substance abuse for ASAP participants becomes a self-affirmation and is only the beginning of broader responsible action.

On a programmatic level, ASAP implements Freire's three-stage methodology of listening, dialogue, and action. Listening is promoted at every level of the ASAP program. At the emergency center, the experience that the youth bring with them is validated by empathetic listening of the group. In brainstorming sessions, youth formulate their own questions to ask patients and jail residents. They role play active listening, open and closed questioning methods and explore their prejudices prior to visiting with patients and their families. The patients or residents interviewed (often treated as objects themselves) who share their life pain often experience some healing, as documented in video footage. Through take home projects in between sessions, students interview family members and community leaders to listen and learn more about their community problems. The facilitators also participate in colearning by discussing content after students raise their own questions and learning issues.

On the organizational level, listening is critical. Program evaluation and policy are formulated through student written feedback after each session, weekly meetings with facilitators, biannual staff and facilitator retreats, and an annual event for all program participants including parents. Local sites often set their own policies. For example, in the selection process, some schools select leadership students, while others randomly select students to enter the experimental design and to counter elitism within the student body.

The dialogue problem-posing process is also built into all components of the program through small group discussion, sharing of life experiences and use of discussion "codes" (as described earlier). In the hospital, the most dynamic code is the patient life story which students discuss after leaving the patient's room. Other codes include newspaper articles, slides, collages, songs, and two short video films developed by the program. By definition, codes provoke discussion of deeply-felt issues that may be threatening or painful. The value of codes is that they enable people to engage in positive dialogue about an experience or object that is initially removed from them. Despite the high drama, the emergency center and patients' lives often serve as a safer code than student's own families. Careful discussion about the codes can help people work through their own life pain and transform feelings towards actions.

An example of this dialogue process is the use of two "trigger" videos (to trigger discussion). Produced with the teenagers, the ASAP videos show emotional vignettes of students interviewing patients about alcoholism and drunk driving. They contain questions for peer educators to lead discussions in their communities about these problems and preventive actions based on local needs.[84]

One of the trigger films concerns an Indian woman in her late twenties who came into the emergency center drunk and who had been raped. She talked with the youth for over an hour about her alcoholism. The four-minute concentrated trigger, "No One To Turn To," movingly captures her life story of losing her mother when young, being raised by siblings who drank in front of her and paid her with beer for babysitting. As she says, "that's all they thought I was worth, you know." She discusses her loneliness and her dependence on alcohol over her Indian religion.

In leading discussions on this film with their peers, the youth use Freire's questioning strategy, easily remembered through the acronym SHOWED: naming the problem, or what do we "See" here; defining the many levels, or what's really "Happening" to her, to her feelings; sharing similar experiences, or how does her story relate to "Our" lives, how do we feel about it; questioning the root causes of this problem, or "Why" has she become an alcoholic on an individual, family, and societal level; exploring how we can become "Empowered" with our new social understanding; and finally, what can we "Do" about these problems in our own lives.[85]

The final step is the culmination of the problem-posing process as it places responsibility on discussion participants to take some action. Using this film in peer teaching with younger grades, the youth ask: How can she get help? What would you do if your family gave you beer? What are better ways for you to handle your own loneliness? What can we do to improve self-esteem? What can we do about advertising? How can we prevent community problems and improve community self-esteem?

Although the ASAP program has always included a community perspective at the hospital and jail, only in the last years has ASAP developed enough of a working relationship with a few sites to pilot community outreach and organizing. An example of community involvement is ASAP's work over the last three years in a combined middle and high school on an Indian reservation, one hour drive from Albuquerque. In 1985, ASAP was invited into the community by the school-based Teen Center after one student was killed and another paralyzed in a drunk driving crash. The school serves 400 students from two reservations totalling several thousand inhabitants. In addition to alcohol problems, the youth face an estimated unemployment rate of 75 percent on one reservation due to the closing of a uranium mine a few years ago.

True to community organizing principles, ASAP's program was facilitated by the Teen Center (which provides clinical, educational, and counselling services) and a newly created Students Against Drunk Driving (SADD) chapter.[86] ASAP initially only brought students through the hospital and jail experience. It took two years for ASAP's peer educator and leadership training to become a joint effort between ASAP, SADD, and teen center theater club students.

Program Evaluation

For the last five years, ASAP has conducted quantitative assessments at a few willing Albuquerque schools. In addition, facilitator and teenager evaluation forms are filled out after each session. Over the last year, interview and observation research has been conducted into the conditions and indicators of empowerment. In preliminary findings from the qualitative data, the ASAP program has begun to identify new variables that would make the quantitative assessment tool more sensitive to program effects.

Some of these variables can best be seen in interview comments from the reservation students. Youth have said they have a greater awareness of the consequences of their own partying and drinking and driving behavior; instead of just taking the next drink without thinking, the memory surfaces of a patient's alcohol-related car crash, even a year later. Students have said they have more confidence in talking about difficult issues with their friends and in groups. They talk about asking questions of patients, then of themselves, and ultimately with others as they become peer educators and leaders. In peer teaching, they demonstrate the empathy they have developed in the Emergency Center. As one student said:

> Talking to these people at the hospital really got me to think, wow just think, some of these people around my neighborhood might just want to talk . . . These people really had feelings and they really wanted to have someone to care about them, because they were hurting and that's why they drink so much, and they wanted to be needed and accepted . . . Maybe if I just talk to them and tell them I did care about you (them) maybe that would make an impression in their lives.

In their peer teaching, the Indian youth have expressed a sense of responsibility and caring for others. "If you're ever at a party, don't let them drive. Keep them there. You don't want to be in the ER (Emergency Room/Center), that hurts too much. I've lived through it." Rather than preach about drinking, they have told other kids not to use alcohol to avoid problems. Instead, the youth have put themselves in a leadership position, telling others to come to them at anytime for help.

At the reservation school, the students have conducted peer teaching in groups of four or five. Not only does group peer teaching provide mutual support, but it also enables more students (even the shy ones) to develop self-affirming helper roles, and stresses connections with others rather than leadership or alienation above others.

Though students easily talk about changes in themselves and in their relations to peers—especially through the peer teaching, the impact on family has been difficult to judge. Many students have expressed frustration with not being able to change family members. Some students suggest an increased communication within the family, even crying and working through their grief when they've told their parents about a patient. In contrast, they've said they have not been able to talk about the death of one of their own family. Because of their youth and the enabling patterns of family members towards alcoholics, ASAP seeks to avoid rescue fantasies for families. The emphasis is on assuming responsibility for their own behavior and on working with friends to effect community change.

The direct impact on the school and community is much harder to gauge than personal changes, even when ASAP has concentrated on outreach. After three years in the reservation school, there is a beginning level of critical mass to change school norms with over 50 students having participated in ASAP, in addition to other Teen Center programs. The SADD chapter with ASAP members has recently attracted the "partiers" who openly still drink, but say they don't drink and drive.

On a community level, students have begun to make their voice heard. Last year, the Teen Center sponsored presentations by ASAP students at village meetings and at the two Tribal Councils; normally girls are not permitted to attend the village meetings. In 1987, one of the tribal councils voted to empower an action committee to plan a drug and alcohol campaign for the Pueblo; several youth were invited to participate. Making the problem visible has been identified as especially important for community prevention programs on reservations.[87]

In the quantitative evaluation in Albuquerque schools, students are randomly selected and assigned into control and experimental groups with neither group identifiably at higher risk. ASAP administers a pretest and posttest at one-month and eight-month follow-up, with questions on attitudes towards substance abuse, self-reported behavior change, riskiness perception, and ability to influence others and control their own lives. (Questions on communication changes, empathy, leadership, and specific efficacies in influencing others are to be included.)

Using a repeated measure design with the current instrument, the results in one Albuquerque midschool have shown a statistically significant increase in self-reported perception of riskiness of drinking, drugs and driving for the intervention group at the eight-month follow-up. In contrast, the control group showed a significant drop in riskiness perception.[88] This decline has been recognized in normal adolescent development, particularly in this age group.[89] The program's effects of significantly increasing perception of risk and countering normal development patterns, is particularly important because lack of riskiness perception (or invulnerability) has been identified as a contributor to health damaging behaviors.[90]

Limitations and Future Directions

In the last few years, expectations have grown for prevention programs to have immediate result, for example counting how many kids make public statements to say no to drugs. The dilemmas are many for this short-term approach. For adolescents and adults, individual behaviors are inherently difficult to change in the face of health-damaging environments, such as media influences, unemployment, and cultural identity conflicts. To a large degree, these objective conditions are intractable to immediate solutions and require long-term and broad-based policy and social changes.

Evaluation therefore must look at empowerment as a long-term process with many steps along the way, such as building self-esteem or participation in community organizing efforts. The ASAP program has begun to identify steps that appear important for empowering changes in the population it serves: establishing trust and building on natural empathy for friends to consolidate a support network (also indicated in other programs)[91] communicating experiences and feelings in a safe environment; promoting ability to present their ideas to peers and adults; participating in cooperative actions so individuals don't feel the burden of the problem alone; and fostering critical thinking about the consequences of risk-taking actions and about youth's role in society.

Conditions for change are also important to assess. Community organizing theory recognizes the importance of coalitions with local programs and of long-term commitment for trust to be established about an outside program's motives. Although the interaction between programs may prohibit the direct attribution of program effects on a community, an empowerment model—as embodied by ASAP—can only exist through working with the reality and resources of a community.

Being responsive to the needs of local sites is positive, yet it can also create challenges. In ASAP, for example, many local sites have been unwilling to participate in the experimental research design. These sites have preferred to send leadership students through the program to have more influence when they return to the school, rather than participate in the randomized selection and assignment process necessary to assess individual student changes.

One of the inherent difficulties for ASAP in reporting community change is that youth cannot assume full responsibility for creating a healthy environment. Not only do students pick up messages depending on individual needs (some apply the learning to their own life choices, whereas others blossom into successful leaders), but adults need to contribute leadership for institutional and environmental change. ASAP, however, demonstrates that youth can and should be involved in a problem-posing and community action process. At the reservation school, students have clearly expanded the educational dialogue and made visible their concern for alcohol abuse.

Some issues still need to be addressed in how empowerment strategies can have an impact on the community: the role of leadership between the outside concerned professional and community leaders; a better understanding of the action-reflection-action spiral that produces change; and the creation of a sense of community and commitment that enables people to keep participating despite the setbacks, inevitable in any community.

An empowerment model acknowledges the role of outside leadership to provide resources and experience, but the question remains how to engender dialogue and collective work with community members (i.e., teens, parents, teachers) so shared visions and community-based leadership emerge. The empowering step or bridge between reflection and action means creating a supportive community that can analyze successes and failures, identify obstacles, yet still maintain goals and motivation to address the root causes of powerlessness and disease.

The need for a supportive community was tragically demonstrated in the spring of 1987 when a former ASAP student was killed by a drunk driver as she was walking beside the road. In a memorial gathering, students from all ASAP schools remembered her for the very qualities that ASAP hopes to engender: her caring, her laughter, and her leadership. The service became a time for reaffirming who she was, expressing grief, and renewing dedication to working on the problems.

Conclusion

In conclusion, the ASAP model has the following affective, cognitive, behavioral, and social components as inspired by Freire:

1. ASAP is participant-centered with the *youth taking responsibility* for asking questions and contributing their personal experiences, feelings, and thoughts about strategies for change.

2. ASAP is *small group-centered* with knowledge socially generated from dialogue about the patients and their own lives.

3. ASAP promotes *active learning on an emotional level.* Patient stories become a code to work through their feelings of sadness, empathy, and anger at the patient and at their own harsh lives, and to emerge with a sense of expanded opportunities.

4. ASAP promotes active learning on a *cognitive level, using the problem-posing methodology.* Students identify the problems they see in the emergency center and jail, share their own family and community experiences, analyze the root causes, and pose alternatives for themselves, their peers, and communities.

5. ASAP promotes active learning on a *behavioral* (and cognitive) level, with assertiveness and communication techniques, role-plays, and decision-making activities.

6. ASAP promotes *connectedness and social support* with others, building on natural empathy and values of community cooperation through small groups at the hospital, small group peer teaching, and annual recognition parties and ASAP/SADD chapters.

7. ASAP promotes a *sense of self-achievement* by engaging youth in assertiveness training, and peer teaching.

8. ASAP promotes *socially responsible leadership and transfer of decision-making* by supporting youth in peer teaching and in choosing their own arenas for action such as school-wide campaigns against drinking and driving.

Together the components of this model incorporate Freire's underlying philosophy of personal and social transformation with people who often experience societal inequalities, cultural conflicts, or lack of control. For health professionals, Freire's ideas offer guidelines in how to work with communities which are often very different from the professionals' own culture. Through this approach, mutual growth and change can occur on both sides.

At the same time, ASAP has contributed to a deepening of the Freirian approach by emphasizing feelings, empathy, group connection, and individual emotional growth as a motivator for youth to assume an active role in society. The ASAP program has also demonstrated how Freire's ideas can be taken beyond the classroom, by integrating the educational philosophy of problem-posing dialogue with community organizing.

Empowerment education with its dual focus on participatory reflection and action should be incorporated into the other prevention strategies of health promotion, disease prevention, and health protection. By becoming incorporated into current prevention approaches, empowerment education can enhance changes in personal growth, social support, community organizing, policy and environmental changes, and other indicators of increased control over one's life in society.

Notes

1. Seeman, M: On the meaning of alienation. *American Sociological Review* 24:783–791, 1959.

2. Sennett R, Cobb J: *The Hidden Injuries of Class.* New York, Vintage Books, 1972.

3. Jessor R, Graves T, Hanson R, Jessor S: *Society Personality and Deviant Behavior: A Study of a Tri-ethnic Community.* Huntington NY, Robert Krieger Publishing Co., 1975.

4. Ryan W: *Blaming the Victim.* New York, Vintage Books revised edition, 1976.

5. Maier S, Seligman M: Learned helplessness: Theory and evidence. *Journal of Experimental Psychology: General* 105(1):3–46, 1976.

6. Gaventa J: *Power and Powerlessness*. Chicago, University of Illinois Press, 1980.

7. Joffe JM, Albee GW (eds): *Prevention through Political Action and Social Change*. Hanover and London: University Press of New England, 1981.

8. Rappaport, J: In Praise of Paradox: A social policy of empowerment over prevention. *American Journal of Community Psychology* 9(1):1–24, 1981.

9. Syme SL: Strategies for health promotion. *Preventive Medicine* 15: 492–507, 1986.

10. Antonovsky A: Social class, life expectancy and overall morbidity. *Milbank Memorial Fund Quarterly* 45:31–73, 1967.

11. Kitagawa E, Hauser P: *Differential Mortality in the United States*. Cambridge, Harvard University Press, 1973.

12. Syme SL, Berkman L: Social class, susceptibility, and sickness. *American Journal of Epidemiology* 104:1–8, 1976.

13. USDHHS, Secretary's Task Force: *Report on Black and Minority Health, Volume 1: Executive Summary,* August 1985.

14. Dayal H, Power R, Chiu C: Race and socioeconomic status in survival from breast cancer. *Journal of Chronic Disease* 35(8):675–683, 1982.

15. Tyroler HA, Knowles MG, Wing SB, Logue EE, Davis CE, Reiss G, Heyden S, Hames CG: Ischemic heart disease risk factors and twenty-year mortality in middle-age Evans County black males. *American Heart Journal* 108:738–746, 1984.

16. Haan M, Kaplan G: *Contribution of Socioeconomic Position to Minority Health.* Human Population Laboratory. California Department of Health Services, Report to NIH Task Force on Black and Minority Health, Jan. 1985.

17. Haan M, Kaplan G, Camacho-Dickey T: Poverty and health: A prospective study of Alameda County residents. *American Journal of Epidemiology.*

18. Haan M, Kaplan G, Minkler M, Miszcynski M, Syme SL: Socioeconomic Status and Health, in Amler and Dull (eds): *Closing the Gap: The Burden of Unnecessary Illness.* New York, Oxford University Press, 1987.

19. Marmot MG, Rose G, Shipley M, Hamilton PJS: Employment grade and coronary heart disease in British civil servants. *Journal of Epidemiology and Community Health* 3:244–249, 1978.

20. Lee R, Schneider R: Hypertension and arteriosclerosis in executive and non-executive personnel. *JAMA* 167:1447–1450, 1958.

21. Karasek R, Baker D, Marxer F, Ahlbom A, Theorell T: Job decision latitude, job demands, and cardiovascular disease: A prospective study of Swedish men. *American Journal of Public Health* 71:694–705, 1981.

22. Alfredsson L, Karasek R, Theorell T: Myocardial infarction risk and psychosocial work environment: An analysis of the male Swedish working force. *Social Science and Medicine* 16:463–476, 1982.

23. Langer E, Rodin J: The effects of choice and enhanced personal responsibility for the aged: A field experiment in an institutional setting. *Journal of Personality and Social Psychology* 34:191–198, 1976.

24. Rodin J: Aging and health: Effects of the sense of control. *Science* 233: 1271–1276, Sept. 19, 1986.

25. Schultz R: Aging and Control, in Garber and Seligman (eds): *Human Helplessness: Theory and Applications,* New York, Academic Press, 1980.

26. *Journal of Primary Prevention* 6(3):168–180, 1986.

27. Albee George W: Preventing psychopathology and promoting human potential. *American Psychologist* 37(9):1043–1050, 1982.

28. Botvin GJ, Baker E, Botvin EM, Filazzola AD, Millman RB: Prevention of alcohol misuse through the development of personal and social competence: A pilot study. *Journal of Studies on Alcohol* 45(6):550–552, 1984.

29. Bandura A: Chapter 9: Self-Efficacy, in *Social Foundations of Thought and Action: A Social Cognitive Theory,* New Jersey, Prentice Hall, 1986.

30. O'Leary A: Self-Efficacy and Health, in *Advances in Behavior Research and Therapy.*

31. Cohen S, Syme SL (eds): *Social Support and Health.* Orlando, Florida, Academic Press, 1985.

32. Gottlieb BH, (eds): *Social Networks and Social Support.* Volume 4, Sage Studies in Community Mental Health, Beverly Hills CA, Sage Publications, 1981.

33. Young C, Giles DE Jr, Plantz MC: Natural networks: Help-giving and help-seeking in two rural communities. *American Journal of Community Psychology* 10(4):457–469, 1982.

34. D'Augelli A, Vallance TR, Danish S, Young C, Gerdes J: The community helpers project: A description of a prevention strategy for rural communities. *Journal of Prevention* 1(4):209–224, 1981.

35. Pilisuk M, Parks S, Kelly J, Turner E: The helping network approach: Community promotion of mental health. *Journal of Primary Prevention* 3(2):116–132, 1982.

36. Israel B: Social networks and social support: Implications for natural helper and community level interventions. *Health Education Quarterly* 65–80, Spring 1985.

37. Alinsky S: *Reveille for Radicals.* New York, Random House, 1946.

38. Staples L: *Roots to Power, A Manual for Grassroots Organizing.* New York, Praeger Publishers, 1984.

39. Reitzes DC, Reitzes DC: Alinsky reconsidered: A reluctant community theorist. *Social Science Quarterly* 63(2):265–279, 1982.

40. McKnight J, Kretzmann J: Community organizing in the 80's: Toward a post-Alinsky agenda. *Social Policy* 15–23, 1984.

41. Freudenberg N: *Not in Our Backyards!* New York, Monthly Review Press, 1984.

42. Adams F: *Unearthing Seeds of Fire: The Idea of Highlander.* Winston-Salem, NC, John Blair Press, 1975.

43. Tjerandsen C: *Education for Citizenship: A Foundation's Experience.* Santa Cruz, CA, Emil Schwarzhaupt Foundation, Inc., 1980.

44. Green L: Modifying and developing health behavior. *Annual Review Public Health* 5:215–236, 1984.

45. Farquhar JW, Fortmann SP, Maccoby N, Wood P, Haskell WL, Taylor CB, Flora JA, Solomon DS, Rogers T, Adler E, Breitrose P, Weiner L: Chapter 84: The Stanford Five City Project: An Overview in Matarazzo et al. (eds): *Behavioral Health: A Handbook of Health Enhancement and Disease Prevention.* Silver Spring, Maryland, John Wiley and Sons, 1154–1165, 1984.

46. Epp J: *Achieving Health for All: A Framework for Health Promotion.* Canada, 1986, (unpublished).

47. Health Promotion in Action: Practical ideas on programme implementation. *Health Promotion* 1(2):187, 1986.

48. Freire P: By learning they can teach. *Convergence* (1) 1973.

49. Freire P: *Education for Critical Consciousness.* New York, Seabury Press, 1973; Continuum Press, 1983.

50. Kozol J: *Illiterate America.* Garden City, New York, Anchor Press/Doubleday, 1985.

51. Elsasser N, John-Steiner V: An interactionist approach to advancing literacy. *Harvard Educational Review* 47(3), 1977.

52. Wallerstein N: *Language and Culture in Conflict: Problem Posing in the ESL Classroom.* Reading, Massachusetts, Addison-Wesley, 1983.

53. Auerbach E, Wallerstein N: *ESL for Action: Problem-Posing at Work.* Reading, Massachusetts, Addison-Wesley, 1987.

54. Moriarty P: *Codifications in Freire's Pedagogy: A North American Application.* San Francisco State University Master's Thesis, 1984.

55. Minkler M, Cox K: Creating critical consciousness in health: Applications of Freire's philosophy and methods to the health care setting. *International Journal of Health Services* 10(2):311–322, 1980.

56. Werner D, Bower B: *Helping Workers Learn.* Palo Alto, CA, The Hesperian Foundation, 1982.

57. Alschuler AS: *School Discipline: A Socially Literate Solution.* New York, McGraw Hill, 1980.

58. Reed D: *Education for Building a People's Movement.* Boston, South End Press, 1981.

59. Shor I (ed): *Freire for the Classroom: A Sourcebook for Liberatory Teaching.* New Hampshire, Boynton/Cook, 1987.

60. Shor I: *Critical Teaching and Everyday Life.* Boston, South End Press, 1980.

61. Hope A, Timmel S, Hodzi C: *Training for Transformation: A Handbook for Community Workers.* Gweru, Zimbabwe, Mambo Press, Vol. 1–3, 1984.

62. Delbecq, Vanderven, Gustafson: *Group Techniques for Program Planning.* Illinois, Scott, Foresman and Co., 1975.

63. Lewin K: *Field Theory in Social Science.* New York, Harper & Brothers, 1951.

64. Blum HL: *Planning for Health Development and Application of Social Change Theory.* New York, Human Sciences Press, 1974.

65. Freire P: *Pedagogy in Process: The Letters from Guinea Bissau.* New York, Seabury Press, 1978.

66. Mackie R: *Literacy & Revolution: The Pedagogy of Paulo Freire.* New York, Continuum Press, 1981.

67. *Selected Health Statistics, New Mexico 1982–1983.* Health and Environment Department, Health Services Division, Vital Statistics Section, Santa Fe, New Mexico, p. 44.

68. *Selected Health Statistics, New Mexico 1982–1983.* op. cit. p. 81.

69. Bernstein E, Wallerstein N: A.S.A.P.: A prevention program developed for adolescents in New Mexico, *Journal of Border Health.*

70. Daube D, Bernstein E, Wallerstein N: The alcohol and substance abuse program: Its impact on medical students. *Substance Abuse. AMERSA Journal* 8(4):16–26, 1987.

71. *ASAP Emergency Center and Detention Center Curriculum.* Department of Family, Community, and Emergency Medicine, University of New Mexico, Albuquerque, 1988.

72. Telch MJ, Killen JD, McAlister AL, et al.: Long-term follow-up of a pilot project on smoking prevention with adolescents. *Journal of Behavioral Medicine* 5(1):1–8, 1982.

73. Englander-Golden P, Elconin J, Satir V: Assertive/leveling communication and empathy in adolescent drug abuse prevention. *Journal of Primary Prevention* 6(4): 231–243, Summer 1986,

74. Collins LR, Marlett GA: Social modeling as a determinant of drinking behavior: Implications for prevention and treatment. *Addictive Behavior* 6:233–239, 1981.

75. Botvin GJ, Eng A: The efficacy of a multicomponent approach to the prevention cigarette smoking. *Preventative Medicine* 11:199–211, 1982.

76. Botvin GJ: *Life-Skills Training: Teacher's Manual.* New York, Smithfield Press, 1983.

77. Perry C, Murray D: Enhancing the transition years: The challenge of adolescent health promotion. *The Journal of School Health:* 307–311, May 1982.

78. Perry C, Jessor R: The concept of health promotion and the prevention of adolescent drug abuse. *Health Education Quarterly* 12(2):169–184, 1985.

79. Kaufman A (ed): *Implementing Problem-Based Medical Education.* New York, Springer Publishing Company, 1985.

80. Rogers C: *A Way of Being.* Boston, Houghton-Mifflin, 1980.

81. Horn J: *Away with All Pests.* New York, Monthly Review Press, 1971.

82. Jessor R, Graves T, Hanson R, Jessor S: *Society Personality and Deviant Behavior: A Study of a Tri-ethnic Community.* Huntington, New York, Robert Krieger Publishing Co., 1975.

83. Jessor R, Jessor SL: Toward a social-psychological perspective on the prevention of alcohol abuse. Reprint NIAAA: *Normative approaches to the prevention of*

alcohol abuse and alcoholism. Research Monograph No. 3. Washington, D.C., U.S. Government Printing Office, pp. 37–46, 1980.

84. ASAP: *Discussion Trigger Films: Drinking and Driving and Alcoholism.* Video and Brochure, Department of Family, Community, and Emergency Medicine, University of New Mexico, Albuquerque, 1987.

85. Shaffer R: *Beyond the Dispensary.* Nairobi, Kenya, AMREF, 1983.

86. Davis S, Hunt K, Kitzes J: An emergency approach to improving the health of Indian adolescents and youth: A public health demonstration project initially implemented for two Pueblos and a Navajo community, 1987.

87. Beauvais F, Laboueff S: Drug and alcohol abuse intervention in American Indian communities. *The International Journal of the Addictions* 20(1):139–171, 1985.

88. Bernstein E, Woodall G: Changing perceptions of riskiness in drinking, drugs and driving: An emergency department-based alcohol and substance abuse prevention program. *Annals of Emergency Medicine* 16(12):1350–1354, December, 1987.

89. Finn P, Brown J: Risks entailed in teenage intoxication as perceived by junior and senior high school students. *Journal Youth and Adolescence* 10(1):61–76, 1981.

90. Bragg BWE, Finn P: *Young Driver Risk-Taking Research: Technical Report of Experimental Study.* U.S. Dept. of Transportation, National Highway Traffic Safety Administration, DOT HS-806-375, July 1982.

91. Minkler M: Building Supportive Ties and Sense of Community among the Inner-City Elderly: The tenderloin senior outreach project. *Health Education Quarterly* 12(4):303–314, 1985.

4

A Gay-Themed Lesson
in an Ethnic Literature Curriculum

Tenth Graders' Responses to "Dear Anita"

Steven Z. Athanases

In this article, Steven Athanases describes the responses of a multi-ethnic class of tenth graders to a lesson dealing with gay and lesbian experiences. The teacher of a course entitled "The Ethnic Experience in Literature" chose to introduce her class to Brian McNaught's essay "Dear Anita: Late Night Thoughts of an Irish Catholic Homosexual." Athanases describes the teacher's goals for the course, her curriculum, and student activities to support her goals. He then describes how the lesson itself unfolded, analyzing the essay that introduced the issue and the students' responses to it. Athanases shows how a careful selection of text, a classroom climate that welcomes thoughtful discussion of diversity, and sensitive treatment of gay and lesbian concerns can deepen students' understanding about identities and oppression, which, in the context of an ethnic literature curriculum, can help students develop a deeper understanding of the common ground that oppressed groups divided by difference share.

Beginning early in the school year, I watched Reiko Liu engage her students in literature study through discussions that required thinking about, and invited exploration of, such issues as cultural identity, subculture/dominant culture tensions, and ethnocentrism.* The works students read in her course, "The Ethnic Experience in Literature," also raised the difficult issues of cultural domination, racism, sexism, lynching, and rape. Reiko's class norms enabled

---

* The names of students, teachers, and the school have all been changed.

her tenth graders to respond with curiosity, candor, and, at times, anger. Generally, however, they responded with sensitivity and maturity, despite the potential for awkwardness, tensions, and divisiveness that can occur when such issues arise in multiethnic urban public high school classrooms where racial and other tensions often run high.

In January, however, most of the class responded with little empathy to Marguerite, the character who struggles with her sexual identity in Maya Angelou's *I Know Why the Caged Bird Sings* (1969). Students remarked that being a lesbian is not normal, that gays choose to be gay and too often "go around talking about it." As with the entire curriculum, Reiko's goals for a unit on Ethnic Short Stories and Essays, to follow Angelou's book, included not only explorations of difference, but also recognition of common ground. She hoped her students would, as she put it, "take with them an understanding that people they thought were strange or different are not that strange or different after all." In that spirit, Reiko chose to "get gutsy" and include a piece dealing with gay experience. With the assistance of her best friend on the faculty, a gay man, she searched for readings, deciding on the essay, "Dear Anita: Late Night Thoughts of an Irish Catholic Homosexual," by Brian McNaught (1988a), a counselor and speaker on gay issues. For a workshop she later conducted, Reiko composed these notes on "Dear Anita":

> This article is addressed to Anita Bryant, who campaigned against the rights of gay people to teach in Dade County schools. McNaught discusses how he, like Anita, was raised to believe stereotypical notions of homosexuality as a sin and a mental disorder and of gay men as sexually interested in children. He effectively argues against each of these points and relates the painfulness of living in a society that denies him his human rights.

Reiko's purpose in the "Dear Anita" lesson fit her goals of teaching sensitivity to diversity and seeking common ground across marginalized groups. She told me she wanted her students to understand

> how it feels to be different, in this case as a gay person, how the whole world tells you that you're sinful, that you're a shame to the whole society, that you're a child molester, all these negative things. I want especially some of the more homophobic members of our class to understand where this person is coming from. And I want them to make a transition to how that's not too unlike having people tell you you're ignorant or you're stupid because of your racial background. These kids will probably say that being gay is different from being a member of an ethnic group. They've voiced that already. But I want them to understand that the effect on the person is not all that different.

What follows is background information detailing the inclusion of issues of sexual orientation in curriculum; an account of how the "Dear Anita" lesson unfolded; an analysis of the essay, the lesson, and the students' responses to these; and a close look at one student's role in the process. My analysis focuses on ways Reiko stimulated thoughtful discussions of literature and diversity and examines students' responses to such work.

Background

Calls for more inclusive literature curricula from the English Coalition Conference (Lloyd-Jones & Lunsford 1989), the Task Force on Racism and Bias (1986) for the National Council of Teachers of English, and other groups serving English and language arts teachers argue that "content integration" (Banks 1993) can help insure that all students learn of the pluralistic nature of the United States, of contributions from all groups to U.S. culture and letters, and of the realities of racism and oppression lived by many in this country. To encourage inclusiveness and to work against stereotype formation, thoughtful educators can select texts by and about groups defined by not only race and ethnicity, but also gender, sexual orientation, religion, and other significant definitions of cultural and social group (Banks & Banks 1993; Stotsky 1994).

Despite the inclusion of sexual orientation in the language of some literature on diversified curricula, teachers, particularly in K–12 classrooms, seldom provide positive representations of gay and lesbian characters or address issues of sexual orientation or homophobia when they arise in lessons. Reasons for the dearth of such work in the classroom are numerous and varied. For example, the larger sociopolitical context within which schools operate has generally marginalized contributions of people of color and women, and concealed or avoided revealing the sexual orientation of prominent gays and lesbians. As a result, texts selected for class use have remained almost exclusively those authored by White men (Applebee 1993); when authors are gay, this fact is generally repressed.

The deliberately limited use by teachers of gay and lesbian authors has been partially due to a lack of information and resources on diverse selections, although other reasons figure in this picture as well. Many teachers, for example, feel uncomfortable dealing with issues of sexual orientation, are not convinced it is a topic appropriate for study, or are themselves homophobic. Even when teachers are convinced of the importance of exploring gay and lesbian experiences in literature, they often still fear that community members will view such study as promoting homosexuality, thus instigating a backlash. For gay or lesbian teachers not out at school, such a backlash could lead to being "outed" or, for teachers already out, it could lead to accusations of "recruiting." In addition, some administrators who are unwilling to take risks censor their own teachers' efforts toward such inclusiveness (e.g., Hammett 1992), while others use threats of dismissal to censor teachers. For example, a teacher in New Hampshire faced job loss because her twelfth graders were reading E. M. Forster's *Maurice* and May Sarton's *The Education of Harriet Hatfield*, which have, respectively, gay and lesbian protagonists (McVicar 1995).

Other factors contribute to the lack of inclusion of gay and lesbian lives in curricula. Many teachers may avoid such issues as racism in schools that are fraught with racial tensions. In a similar way, some teachers fear responses to gay and lesbian issues by youth who are in the process of sexual identity formation. Some teachers may worry that male students in particular will resist such lessons, finding them objectionable or disturbing.

Finally, few published works describe ways teachers have managed such work and how students have responded, although essays in recent collections (e.g., Garber 1994; Harbeck 1992; Jennings 1994) include mention of such work, and recent narratives describe the teaching of Rita Mae Brown's *Rubyfruit Jungle* (Boutilier 1994) and Alice Walker's *The Color Purple* (Lankewish 1992) in high schools. Additionally, the teaching of queer issues in Mexican American literature (Gonzalez 1994) and of homophobia in writing courses in college settings (Hart & Parmeter 1992) have been described. Harris (1990) also offered strategies for studying gay- and lesbian-themed literature at the secondary level. However, despite these efforts, descriptions of what occurs when lessons unfold and analyses of how students respond to and co-construct this work are still needed to aid in building theories of successful pedagogy in the teaching of gay- and lesbian-themed literature.

What follows is an account of a study that asked two questions. First, when a teacher working in a multiethnic setting includes a lesson on gay and lesbian experiences and homophobia in the context of an ethnic literature curriculum, how do students respond to the text and the lesson? Second, to what can those responses be attributed?

Framing the Study

Reiko Liu, Her Curriculum, Her Students

My study of the "Dear Anita" lesson is part of a year-long ethnography in which I observed two tenth-grade English classes in two different urban public schools. In each case, the teachers worked to make text selections more diverse by using newly designed ethnic literature curricula, supported by instruction grounded in the elicitation of students' own literary responses rather than the pursuit of canonical interpretations, and by classroom discourse supportive of exploratory thinking rather than mere recitation of facts (Athanases 1993b). I visited the sites two or more times weekly during the school year. My field notes were supported by audiotapes and videotapes of full-group and small-group discussions, student surveys and writing samples, and school and classroom artifacts. In total, I interviewed more than sixty teachers, students, parents, and other school personnel. Two years later, I returned to the school where Reiko taught and conducted a retrospective survey. I led a pair of group discussion interviews with all but three students from the original class, focusing on their reflections on the class from the distance of two years. I also conducted

Table 4–1. Reiko's students by ethnic identification

African American	Alycia Cassandra Demar LeTonia Richard Tanisha Tyrone	European American Filipino American	Andrea Celeste Mark Alberto Cristina Ferdy Robert
Chinese American	Genevieve Irene Li Vanessa Vicki Vivian Yong		

periodic informal follow-up interviews with both teachers in the two years following the focal study year. This discussion features Reiko's "Dear Anita" lesson, but draws on the larger study for elaboration and support.

Having immigrated to the United States from Japan as a teenager, Reiko experienced culture clash as an immigrant and later in marriage to a Chinese American. Seeing herself as a child of the sixties who had a vision of social change, Reiko remained committed to social justice and to public education as "the vehicle for equality and for participation in a democratic society." During her eighteen years of teaching, Reiko developed "freewheeling discussions" to enable her high school students to explore social issues arising from literature. She helped shape the district's new tenth-grade course on "The Ethnic Experience in Literature." In her first year of implementation, Reiko exposed her students to literature by and about people of a range of ethnicities and socialized students into discussions of diversity with the care that is her hallmark.

Richards High School where Reiko taught is a moderate sized school of grades 9–12 serving children of primarily middle- to low-income families. Reiko's tenth-grade English class was representative of the student body — of the twenty-one students, one-third were African American, one-third Chinese American, and the remaining third of Filipino and European ancestries (see Table 4–1). Despite the name of the course, Reiko's Honors English class included students at various academic levels.

While overt hostility or violence rarely occurred at the school, most students characterized the interethnic climate as one of avoidance and, at best, tolerance. Few at Richards reported appreciation among students for cultural difference, and, as attested to by letters to the editor in the school newspaper and comments by teachers, counselors, and students, some tensions existed between groups, particularly African Americans and Asian Americans. All of Reiko's students of color wrote of experiences with racial injustice.

Community Influences

All students shared two influences originating from the community—a strong religious presence and exposure to gay and lesbian life. In the predominantly African American neighborhood surrounding Richards, a large number of Baptist churches are set among small residences and businesses. All the churches operate out of small converted corner buildings, except for one large, traditional-looking church. For Chinese American students, the other large ethnic group at Richards, many of whom bus to school from Chinatown, the Catholic Church is as present in their neighborhoods as the Baptist Church is near Richards. Religion plays a central role in the lives of many Richards students, evidenced by remarks about church-going, stories of church activities, and, in the case of five of Reiko's students, firm devotion to the school's gospel choir.

Many of Richards' students have seen at least media images of gays and lesbians since they live in the San Francisco Bay Area, where lesbians and gays are relatively visible and hold some political power. In the school itself, one teacher, Ms. Salzman, came out five years earlier and keeps a photo of her partner on her desk. On the first day of school each year, she comes out so that students wanting to make schedule changes might do so (none ever did), and, as she puts it, to clear the air "so we [can] get on with the business of the class, which [is] learning history." It was clear to me that most students considered Ms. Salzman and Mr. Kendall (another out gay teacher and Reiko's best friend on the faculty) among the most effective and most caring teachers at Richards. Ms. Salzman sponsored safe, underground, district-supported, student gatherings for gay and lesbian students, made known through posters on corridor walls and announcements in daily bulletins. When Ms. Salzman's daughter was born to her and her partner, the principal posted a banner in the office. When Ms. Salzman and her partner chaperoned the prom, the principal remarked, "This has got to be a first for the district!"

Despite a strong gay and lesbian presence in local news and among educators, and despite the beginning of a school support group and some support from the principal, homophobia persisted at Richards. Rarely did students hear about the support group. In the early stages of the group's formation, the principal did not include announcements of the group in the school bulletin; when this changed, many teachers ignored or refused to read the announcements. Posters announcing the group were typically torn down. In addition, gay and lesbian students were sometimes harassed by peers, and a faculty member tore down the banner in the office that announced the birth of Ms. Salzman's daughter. A student, before graduation, told Ms. Salzman that if she prayed hard enough she could recover from being a lesbian. These community influences and school-life realities frame students' responses to Reiko's lesson.

The "Dear Anita" Lesson

The Ethnic Short Stories and Essays Unit

Unable to locate an adequate anthology, Reiko searched libraries, bookstores, and friends' collections to assemble short prose works and excerpts for a five-week unit scheduled to begin in February (Table 4–2).

Reiko began the unit with a chapter from Martin Luther King Jr.'s book, *Stride Toward Freedom* (1958), noting that, "It sets a positive tone for more heated discussions that may arise later." Reiko wrote for her district teacher workshop:

> King relates his search for a method of coping with injustice that would be both moral and effective. He gives a compelling rationale for the use of non-violence and brings to life the age-old notions of love as a unifying force, of hating the sin but not the sinner.

During the five weeks, students read, discussed, and wrote about each text, including "Dear Anita," Brian McNaught's essay.

The Lesson

The lesson Reiko designed for "Dear Anita" covered two to three class periods. On the first day, she distributed the essay as homework and provided background, specifically Anita Bryant's efforts during the 1970s to ban gay and lesbian teachers from classrooms. On the second day, after a full-class discussion, Reiko asked students to do the following: "Write a 'Dear Brian' letter in response to the 'Dear Anita' article that you have read. Respond to each of the major points [the author] raises and tell whether or not he effectively addresses Anita's concerns. (Min. 300 words)." On a quiz at the end of the unit two weeks later, students wrote paragraphs on two of four questions, one dealing with "Dear Anita": "If Martin Luther King were to express his view on the plight of gay people as mentioned in the 'Dear Anita' article, what might he say, based on what you know of his philosophy?"

Analysis of "Dear Anita"

In his eleven-page essay, McNaught speaks to Bryant using language that masks how deliberately he has structured the work to teach and persuade. McNaught uses all three of what rhetoricians identify as Aristotle's persuasion

Table 4–2. Reiko's Unit of Ethnic Short Stories and Essays

Author's Ethnicity	Literary Title and Author
African American	"A Pilgrimage to Nonviolence," from *Stride Toward Freedom,* Martin Luther King Jr.
	"How I Started Writing Poetry," Reginald Lockett
Chinese	"Four Directions," from *The Joy Luck Club,* Amy Tan
	"Boy Crazy," Wendy Ho Iwata
European/ Euro-American	"The Lift That Went Down into Hell," Par Lagerkwist
(Jewish)	"The Magic Barrel," Bernard Malamud
(Gay)	"Dear Anita: Late Night Thoughts of an Irish Catholic Homosexual," Brian McNaught
Filipino	From *America Is in the Heart,* Carlos Bulosan
	"A Scent of Apples," Bienvenido N. Santos
Japanese	From *No-No Boy,* John Okada
Native American	"Chee's Daughter," Juanita Platero and Siyowin Miller

categories: ethos (ethics of the speaker or writer), logos (logic or reasoning), and pathos (emotional appeals). Narrating his journey from childhood to adulthood, McNaught first establishes an ethos of a family-loving, religious, ethical citizen who Bryant would value "playing and praying" with if she did not know he were gay (McNaught 1988a, 5). Next, as Table 4–3 demonstrates, one by one, McNaught logically refutes myths common in debates about homosexuality, many of which Bryant perpetuated in her anti-gay campaign. Most of these myths he spells out explicitly, some are implied, all are refuted.

Having established a credible ethos and having logically addressed myths in debates on homosexuality, McNaught then creates a scenario in which Bryant's thirteen-year-old son, Bob Jr., discovers he is gay. With this hypothetical story, McNaught itemizes each challenge a young gay man faces (Table 4–4).

In the process, McNaught creates strong emotional appeal, sharing his own painful journey through a suicide attempt, and noting that "Some people in this country, as we both know, would prefer I hadn't changed my mind [about taking his own life]. But not you, Anita" (13). His persistent use of the direct address (appealing directly to Bryant throughout the essay) and his construction of her as a sensible and caring citizen and mother maintains the appeal that builds in the end to emotionally charged language about the "psychological terror" of being gay and the "primal scream" of the gay civil rights movement

Table 4–3. Myths in Debates about Homosexuals
and McNaught's Refutations in "Dear Anita"

Myths in Debates about Gays	Refutations
Come from bad backgrounds	McNaught, like many other gays, had strong family and religious upbringing
Psychologically imbalanced	Merely living in a hostile world
Promiscuous	His sexual encounters were late, tentative
Have shameful values	Often share same values with straights
Gays are a freakish few	Ten percent of U.S. population: 22 million
Sex is for procreation only	Many straights marry for reasons other than childbearing; human need for touch
God hates homosexuals	Easy to abuse Scripture
Good religion means literal reading of Scripture	Bible must be understood in cultural context
Cross-dressing is widespread	Most transvestites are heterosexual males
Gays and lesbians hate members of opposite sex	Must distinguish between friendships and object of desire for mates
Gays are child-molesters	Pederasts are rarely gay
Gay teachers will corrupt	Good teaching is good teaching
Gay pride is flaunting a lifestyle	Expression of self and culture are important to all individuals and in many groups
Homosexuality is a choice	It's an orientation, often "constitutional"
Gays want special rights	Gay civil rights are human civil rights

"pleading to straight society to refrain from forcing us to live in shadows of self-hate" (14).

Having used ethos, logos, and pathos to persuade, McNaught closes firmly: "Gay civil rights are human civil rights" (14) and no one has the right to interfere with another's development of "the wholeness of our being . . . unless it truly interferes with the rights of others" (15). To challenge someone's right to life, liberty, and the pursuit of happiness, he argues, is to challenge both "the cornerstone of this country" and "the very fiber of our faith which we both claim to follow" (15). In this way, McNaught closes by suggesting that if Bryant persists in her campaign against gays and lesbians, she is not a hero but someone who is anti-democracy and anti-faith.

Table 4–4. Challenges Bob Bryant Jr. Would Face
as a Gay Man, in McNaught's Scenario

Difficulty understanding confusing feelings

Fear of losing parents' love

Being alone, with no one to talk to (not minister nor teacher)

Trying to be heterosexual but failing

Hearing and participating in anti-gay epithets and jokes
(internalized homophobia)

Coping with family expectations of settling down with woman
and having children

Contemplation of suicide and possible suicide attempt

Deciding: marry and hide, remain celibate, or seek same-sex companion

Coping with parents' failure to come out, their tolerating anti-gay
epithets in the home

Data Analysis

Data for the present study included an audiotape and a videotape of class discussion of "Dear Anita"; three audiotaped interviews with Reiko (before the lesson, immediately after the lesson, and on the following day); the "Dear Brian" writings; the set of unit quizzes; audiotaped interviews with eight case study students selected from the larger study as a varied and representative class sample in terms of gender, ethnicity, and writing and speaking performance; two sets of surveys, one administered at the end of the unit, one two years later; and audiotapes of discussions conducted two years and three months after the lesson, just before the students graduated.

For analysis of the "Dear Anita" discussion, I transcribed the talk from audiotape, adding behavioral descriptions from the accompanying videotape. I used speaker turn (each time someone audibly took the floor) as the unit of analysis to analyze the talk structure and turn-taking patterns. I tracked the discussion content, charting topics, how they began, and who initiated them, and analyzed questions for who raised them, the functions they served, and what they yielded. I coded Reiko's questions and her other comments to analyze roles she played in shaping discussion. I examined the discourse for knowledge sources used during discussion to determine evidence speakers used to authenticate claims.

One student, Tanisha, took far more turns than any other student and played an enormous role in discussion. I pulled out all of her turns at talk and constructed a performance script, identifying a verb to clarify the verbal action (Long & Hopkins 1982) of each of Tanisha's turns at talk (e.g., critiques, challenges, inquires, cites, reinforces). With the full transcript contextualizing her turns, I then used this script to describe patterns in Tanisha's discussion performance.

In my analysis of the "Dear Brian" essays, a broad set of themes emerged across them. I similarly identified themes in student quizzes, two sets of surveys, transcripts from case study interviews, and transcripts from the retrospective discussion. In addition to analyzing patterns in students' responses *within* each of these sets of data, I analyzed response patterns of case study students *across* data sets (i.e., each student's responses in writings, in discussions, in interviews). Also, I analyzed patterns of response across the various individual analyses.

Finally, analyses from the full ethnography were used to elaborate or provide comparison and contrast to those in the present study. The longitudinal nature of the study allowed for an investigation of patterns of language use and an examination of how teaching and learning evolved. Claims were strengthened by gaining multiple views of what occurred, including teacher and student perspectives, multiple student perspectives, and perspectives of a diverse group of case study students in terms of gender, ethnicity, academic preparedness, and frequency of participation in discussion.

Students' Responses to the Lesson

The Discussion of "Dear Anita"

Structure of the discussion.   From the third-floor classroom, its walls adorned with student poetry and Renaissance newscast posters from an earlier *Othello* unit, occasional shrieks could be heard through the open window from the P.E. class on the blacktop below. In class, as usual, students sat in a circle with Reiko and spoke without raising hands. Of eighteen students present, fifteen participated in discussion, fourteen of their own volition and one at Reiko's invitation. Conversation was fast paced and highly engaging. Many students took numerous short turns in a volleying manner, rather than few longer turns. This reflected in part the class norm of co-constructing interpretations, and in part the controversial nature of the topics. Nine of the eighteen students took ten or more turns during the discussion. As in other discussions during the year, Reiko asked questions but rarely evaluated students' responses, letting students respond to each other, build on each other's remarks, and challenge each other's ideas. As a result, students often engaged in long runs of talk without Reiko's intervention. Eight times during the discussion, students took more than ten consecutive turns without comment from Reiko, and three of these times, students continued for twenty-five turns or more without teacher remark. The videotape shows Reiko watching students closely, shaping discussion in a variety of ways. Of forty-four turns she took, exactly half were questions, half statements. For example, fourteen of Reiko's turns aided comprehension of the text by contextualizing it with cultural and background information and clarifying meaning. Six turns, mostly questions, worked toward interpretation, five challenged students to sharpen or elaborate claims, and seven were process-oriented turns to launch and guide discussion. Ten of Reiko's turns addressed the issue of empathy. Her questions pressed students to imagine struggles of gays and lesbians (e.g., "How can it be to be such a person . . . having the whole world telling you that you're sick and deranged and sinful?"), and, using textual details, she reminded students of McNaught's perspective on the plight of gays (e.g., when she said, "You tried your best to do what's expected of you. You try to be the best student, the best athlete, winner of all these trophies, and swimming and all this, playing the part of the All-American male, and yet inside, you know you're different."). In these ways, Reiko worked to move the discussion toward her goals.

Content of the discussion.   Reiko began with a discussion of McNaught's Irish heritage and Catholic upbringing; specifically, she asked how these may have shaped his attitudes and sense of self, particularly given the view of homosexuality in Catholicism. Reiko pointed out the impact of cultural expectations, particularly to marry and raise a large family. Next, the class addressed the issue that inspired Bryant's movement, whether gay and lesbian teachers should be permitted to teach. The class easily reached an accord, agreeing that one's freedom to teach should be determined by competence in the classroom and not by sexual orientation. Ferdy, who is active in discussions, offered, "There should be no doubt about it that they should be in school. If they fit the qualifications, you know, then they should have the right to teach." Richard then raised a concern, which Tyrone and Tanisha challenged:

Richard: If they start likin' one of their students, then they're like too far gone, it's gettin' personal.

Tyrone: But if you were to think about it, a straight teacher could be eyein' a student just as well as a homosexual. Like male teachers, with a girl comin' to class.

Richard: But I'm talkin' about with the same sex.

Tyrone: I know, but I'm sayin' that it hurt your ego and your pride, but it's the same THING. A grown man lookin' at you just like a woman doin' it. But if it's a woman you gonna—

Tanisha: Yeah, you're gonna say, "Oh yeah!"

Richard: But you're talkin' about—

Reiko: But Tyrone is saying either way is wrong.

Fifteen minutes into discussion, Richard asked if sexual orientation is a choice. He added that it seemed that Brian could have chosen to stay with women like when he dated them in high school. A few students joined him, and

Reiko and Tanisha both challenged them repeatedly with questions like this one from Tanisha: "Why would he CHOOSE to do something that he KNEW was going to cause him a lot of grief and all of his family and a lot of people most likely and everybody around him a lot of grief?" Reiko later referred to this stretch as being "hung up on the element of choice." The class then discussed development of Brian's sexual identity, including his exploration of intimacy with women, and Cassandra asked if that made McNaught bisexual. Students named pop singers they thought were bisexual (Boy George, Prince), but Tyrone and Tanisha said these singers were in fact heterosexual. Reiko returned to the essay, asking how they would feel in Brian's shoes. Cassandra responded, "It would make you not want to be," and Tanisha added loudly and intensely, "That's why he tried to commit suicide!" Demar added, "It should turn you around." Before anyone could respond to Tanisha's remark or Tanisha could contest Demar's, Reiko had a question on the floor.

She asked the class the degree to which McNaught dispelled the myths of homosexuality, which was a goal of his essay. Students argued that he successfully countered gay stereotypes, especially the notion of gay men as pedophiles. Tanisha pointed out that McNaught refuted this myth by saying the majority of child molestation is committed by heterosexual males; she added that such acts are about abuse of power and not about sex, anyway. Richard returned to his earlier question about choice, asking Reiko, "Didn't he sort of like CHOOSE to be with the guys? So didn't he make that choice?" Tanisha argued that the only choice was about not hiding being gay, and Robert added that Brian was learning to accept his homosexuality: "Sometimes you gotta go where people will accept you and won't make fun of you." Tyrone added, "Where people aren't gonna try to kill you." They agreed that choice is, as Robert put it, "about where you want to live, but not about being gay."

After having her hand up for awhile, LaTonia asked about the impact on the child of a lesbian couple: "What do you think the chances are of the child growing up being a homosexual or lesbian or whatever?" The topic was not in the essay, but Reiko told me after class that she let the students explore it since there was intense interest. Six students, three male, three female, argued that the child of, say, Ms. Salzman and her partner would be unfairly hurt by peer pressure and therefore confused. Tanisha offered reasoned responses to these arguments: their daughter likes their male friends, they'll explain things to her, she'll be able to handle it if she can be strong. Five of the students (three male, two female), all African American like Tanisha, faced-off with Tanisha, pointing at her and arguing with increasing intensity that a child needs to know that she came from a mother and father. Tanisha stood her ground and gained intensity, too, as she appeared to align herself with Ms. Salzman and her partner. Things reached a crescendo when Tanisha finally dramatized the point that having two parents does not guarantee emotional health. She disclosed that after her parents were divorced she lived for five years with a stepmother who was jealous of her, who called her stupid, and who "beat me with a vacuum, with lots of stuff" that left scars all over her body. "I am really insecure about it," she went on. "Like when someone tells me to shut up, it REALLY hurts my feelings. I mean if somebody told you to shut up, I mean you're like, NO, don't tell me to shut up." Tyrone added, "I'll say, 'Your mama!'" Demar, a member of the group challenging Tanisha, said, "That's child abuse. This is entirely different." Tanisha could not find the words in that moment to explain how her emotional narrative supported her implied argument that having two heterosexual parents in the home does not ensure emotional well-being.

Ferdy then asked, "If a student came into our classroom and all of a sudden we broke out with a discussion like this, and that person was that girl we were talking about, how would SHE feel?" Demar responded, "She'd feel like dirt." Reiko used that moment to remind the class that 10 percent of the population is gay, and "There might be somebody here that might be suffering because you guys laugh and joke . . . doesn't this article say that gay teenagers have a really hard time, that the suicide rate is very high?" Her return to the core issues, away from the gay parenting topic that had occupied 20 percent of the discussion, appealed for empathy, in this case not just for Brian and other gays and lesbians "out there," but also for those at school and perhaps in this very class.

In response, the discussion closed with strong testimonials from three students on behalf of gay people, two of whom had objected to gay parenting. Tyrone argued, "If you wanna be gay, you know, that's fine, you know, it should be accepted as THAT, not as, 'You gay? I don't want to have anything to do with you.'" Robert addressed the myth of gay promiscuity, ending with, "The degree of desire is the same, but with *who* it's different." And Cassandra, who had challenged gay parenting, closed the discussion, pounding her fist dramatically on her desk for emphasis as she exclaimed each sexual orientation label: "Whether you're a lesbian, homosexual, heterosexual, or bisexual, you're a person, and you have the right to do whatever you want to do." As students filed out, Tyrone called from the door, "That was a very intelligent discussion we had." Celeste, however, lingered after the bell to reiterate her point: Ms. Salzman's daughter will be insecure "because her peers will never accept her parents."

Tanisha in discussion.   Just as some students drew on their experiences as members of ethnic groups to better understand literature studied during the year in Reiko's class, Tanisha may have drawn strength for her convictions on gay issues from her personal experiences and feelings. In her senior year, one and a half years after the "Dear Anita" discussion, Tanisha came out as a lesbian and met with other gay and lesbian students in Ms. Salzman's group. Although Tanisha had generally been a frequent participant in discussions all year, her involvement increased during the "Dear Anita" discussion, in which she took sixty-five turns, or 27 percent of all student turns in the discussion. Other students often counted on Tanisha to simplify complexities in the readings, and her turns particularly served that purpose during this lesson. Additionally, her

interactions refuted myths of homosexuality, and challenged both her peers and
Anita Bryant. She expressed incredulity that anyone could believe a person
would choose to be part of an oppressed group. She challenged her peers' prob-
lematizing of gay parenting with reasoned responses, and as classmates pointed
at her and raised their voices, Tanisha held her ground. Throughout the discussion, she aligned herself with Ms. Salzman and her partner, and through them,
all gays and lesbians interested in parenting. Finally she used her own story of
a painful family life as support for her stand, though there is little evidence that
her peers grasped the gist of this.

Tanisha, well-read and often articulate in class discussions, challenged the
group to stay focused on the issues raised by the essay rather than utter remarks that perpetuated stereotypes. Nicknamed "Ms. Equality" by her mother,
Tanisha often was a voice of justice. On issues of race and gender, she raged
against unfairness and now she similarly challenged homophobia.

Themes in Student Writings

Moving beyond myths of homosexuality.   The "Dear Anita" lesson helped
break stereotypes and myths (many from Table 4–3) the students had held
about gays and lesbians. In the "Dear Brian" letters, the most frequently cited
stereotype was of gays as child molesters. Just as the class reached easy accord
on this issue in discussion, students wrote of their appreciation for McNaught's
clarification. Two girls pointed out that they used to think of homosexual men
as a bad influence on children, but they both directly attributed a change in understanding of this issue to the essay. Cassandra also told Brian in her letter that
she used to think of gays as child molesters, and "If you had not clarified that,
I would have had a different attitude toward homosexuals because of my strong
feelings for children" (she hoped to some day become a child psychologist).
Two others cited experiences as reinforcement of McNaught's dispelling of
this myth: Vanessa recalled a gay guest speaker in Family Living "who did not
look at male students any different from females." Alicia said she used to think
of gays as child molesters until she came to know a wonderful gay teacher at
her previous school about whom she stated, "I loved [him] with all my heart,
he was one of my best teachers, a good friend and confidant."

A second stereotype some students said the lesson dispelled was that of
gay men as promiscuous. In addition to the remarks about McNaught's late-
blooming sexuality and about "gay" meaning much more than sex, some students wrote in their letters to Brian that they now understood that homosexuality can also be about what Ferdy called "the company of another" and what
Vanessa referred to as "feelings, love, understanding, and trust one feels for another." Students reported that the lesson refuted other myths. Vanessa came to
understand that homosexuality is not a psychological disorder to be treated.
She told me afterward that as she listened to the disagreement in the discussion

about whether gays should get therapy to change or whether these are feelings that can't change, "I decided they can't change the feelings. It's not like a *disease* or something." She felt her one contribution to the discussion helped: "Homosexuals are just like normal people, just like us. It's just that their outlook on things is different." Some students noted that they understood now that notions of gays coming from bad backgrounds and holding shameful values were stereotypes, too. They were struck by McNaught's upbringing as a model child and teen, an athlete, a God-loving and family-oriented person. Demar wrote about Brian's stable childhood, saying, "Hell, you grew up better than I did." He continued, "For Anita to call your values shameful would almost be a sin. A matter of fact, if you and I met somewhere we would probably be pretty good friends."

Finally, in their writing, students reinforced other remarks about myths dispelled in their earlier talk. Demar argued for the importance of teachers' doing their jobs well, not their sexual orientation, as what truly matters: "I've had gay teachers and I and all the rest of the students turned out absolutely fine." Cassandra acknowledged that before reading McNaught's letter she thought that gays and lesbians all hated members of the opposite sex. Similarly, Vanessa used personal experience, recalling how the gay speaker in Family Living said he has women friends, something Tanisha echoed in an interview a few days later: "I know a lot of homosexuals. And they all have friends who are women. So if you're not a misogynist, well, of course you like women. It doesn't mean you have to jump in bed with them."

Developing empathy for gays and lesbians.   In addition to changed understandings of the nature of homosexuality, some students wrote of empathy they now felt for lesbians and gay men. Five students referred in their writings as well as in the discussion to suicide attempts by gays and lesbians as something truly terrible. Yong said of Brian's attempted suicide, "Thank God you changed your mind after you drank the bottle of paint thinner." Three students reported feeling guilty for the prejudices they had felt toward gays. One apologized to Brian and hoped he would forgive her. Vicki said, "It was people like me that forced you to commit suicide. Your life means more than anything in the world." A few students wrote about Brian's early confusion over his sexual feelings and his struggle to try to conform to a heterosexual standard. One commented that sexuality is a gift and that she felt for Brian since so many people cannot accept homosexuality as natural. Robert remarked that he understood now how gays might fear ridicule based on religious beliefs. Vanessa summed up, saying, "Anyone with half a heart should have been moved or should have changed their stereotyped opinions when he/she read this article."

Equality and justice.   The theme of equality and justice for gays and lesbians persisted in students' responses, especially in their responses to the quiz question. A fairly consistent response emerged in papers of students who chose to answer the question of how Martin Luther King Jr. would respond to the plight of gays and lesbians. Essentially, they argued that if King were alive today, he would support acceptance of and equality for gays and lesbians. All but two students, Richard and Celeste, whose responses are discussed later, stated that other than loving someone of their own gender, gays are no different and deserve support. Vivian, for example, argued that:

> No matter the situation, M. L. King will still practice his theory of agape. . . . He has expressed his point of view about many groups of people with different ideas and principles. Why should these . . . change towards people whose sexual preferences are different than that of the majority in the world? . . . Martin Luther King is against negative thoughts or feelings to even our enemies. He does not practice any form of hatred. . . . I'm sure this also applies to people who choose partners of their own sex.

Alberto argued for embracing gays beyond just tolerance, "God made all men and women equal, no matter what creed, religion, sex, or lifestyle, and . . . because God wants man happy." Alberto felt King would encourage people to "treat gays as part of society" and try to make friends with them and "learn about their lifestyle." A number of students mentioned that King would endorse equal rights for gays and lesbians, and that he would encourage gays to fight for these rights as he fought discrimination. Two students added that King would have disagreed with Anita Bryant's efforts since, as Genevieve put it, "She is trying to teach exactly the opposite of what he believes in—equal rights for all." Tanisha went one step further in her response, envisioning King in a proactive role, staging sit-ins with gay and lesbian groups and building coalitions between anti-racism and anti-homophobia groups.

Cassandra and LaTonia, both Baptists and active in the school's gospel choir, whose responses shared some similarities with others' responses, nonetheless left the door slightly open for disapproval. Cassandra suggested that "God may not approve," and LaTonia stated that some religions or cultures may view homosexuality as sinful. Still, both felt King would support and accept gay rights. Mark, in contrast, offered a unique and sobering possibility, that King would offer gays support at best but would probably remain neutral: "[He] probably would not be any major mover for civil rights for homosexuals . . . since his religion probably would have forbidden it."

Identification and validation.   Two students expressed feelings of identification and validation in their "Dear Brian" letters. Cristina, raised a Catholic, began her letter, "I am a fifteen year old girl who once questioned myself about my sexuality. . . . I share your [McNaught's] values and beliefs." Elaborating on ways society restricts and condemns people, particularly gays and lesbians, Cristina closed, saying,

> The worst thing that a homosexual person can do is hide his or her true identity. I chose to try to discover myself. In the process, I realized that I am a con-

fused, young and naive person. Unlike the person I want to be, deep inside, I feel that I will eventually find happiness with the person that I all ready am. A friend, Cristina.

Reiko wrote on Cristina's letter, "I think you will, too, Cristina. Your letter is quite moving because it reaches out to another person as an equal." The essay struck a chord for Cristina, who identified with the struggle for sexual identity and self-definition.

A second student who may have found validation in the lesson was Tanisha. While she did not explicitly identify with Brian, Tanisha positioned herself with the oppressed groups in her alignment with him, Ms. Salzman, and other gays and lesbians. Part of this was due to Tanisha's sensitivity to the oppressed, her sense that "everybody seemed to be against" homosexuality. Tanisha referred to her earlier argument that people need "not be so narrow-minded. . . . You need to open up and think how other people feel, don't just go with what you feel and everybody else." In her writing, Tanisha critiqued Celeste's position on sin as "that old crock about how they don't condemn *you* but your sin." She continued, "If you think about it, it's just as bad, so you're really condemning the person. I mean it [homosexuality] comes from the person's being." Tanisha's capacity for empathy was evident throughout the year; she took on her peers directly in discussions of gay issues and continued as if speaking to them in her writings. She wrote, "Why should it matter if you love a woman and are a woman or if you love a man and are a man? If there is love there and it's pure, why should the form matter?" In a follow-up interview when she was a senior, she recalled how important the "Dear Anita" lesson was in her education about people considered "unnormal," a lesson that may have helped provide her with courage to be out and strong while still in high school, despite negative responses from peers. Ms. Salzman recalled this courage: after posters announcing the gay and lesbian support group were torn down, the group got a six-foot ladder, and Tanisha stood on it to hang posters out of reach of those wanting to destroy them.

Resistance based in religious teachings.   The two students unmoved by McNaught's essay remained committed to the belief that homosexuality is sinful and, therefore, wrong. Richard, who argued in discussion that gays choose to be gay and argued against gay parenting, said in his letter to Brian that he should have "tried harder not to be gay" and that he should have gotten "more help and kept seeing a psychiatrist." While the main thrust of his argument is rooted in his religious beliefs, Richard also misread McNaught's rejection of his Catholic upbringing: "You say that you believe God condemns homosexuality but you are homosexual. And at that you are a Catholic homosexual. How can you live with that?" McNaught's remarks about such condemnation were in the context of the beliefs he was raised with, which he rejected and then refuted in the essay. Moreover, Richard either did not agree with or ignored

McNaught's argument that scripture must be understood in historical context if rigid interpretations are to be avoided.

Celeste, a practicing Catholic who entered the class mid-year, steadfastly maintained that "homosexuality is an abomination before God." Following Martin Luther King Jr.'s stance toward racists, she argued that she could justifiably condemn the sin and not the sinner. She told Brian he must read scripture literally and stop trying to change his Catholic faith to justify his sin. Too many today, she, explained, have

> accepted their sinful lives as a good way of life. . . . This is not only homosexuals, but adulterers, murderers, the power hungry, and the greed of those who seek only self-gratification. All of the above I would not want teaching my children because it does not promote life.

In the margin Reiko wrote, "This is rough company for anyone to be put in."

Like Richard, Celeste ignored or misunderstood portions of McNaught's essay. She wrote, "All through the whole entire thing, he's still having this like argument in his mind: 'Am I or am I not?' And he never really chooses at the end if he is." McNaught is, however, quite clear in the essay that he is gay; the subtitle for the essay, "Late night thoughts of an Irish Catholic homosexual," clarifies this. Celeste continued, "gay civil rights, according to you, are more important of an issue instead of the Civil Rights for all living in the United States." However, McNaught is also clear on this point: In response to Bryant's threat to remove gay teachers from schools, he argues, "Gay civil rights are human civil rights. Competent people should not be denied jobs because of what they do as consenting adults in the privacy of their homes" (McNaught 1988a, 14).

Celeste's response may have been due, in part, to the fact that as an Irish Catholic she shares McNaught's ethnicity and religion. Celeste felt McNaught's essay painted Irish Catholics as inflexible and unloving, since this is how she judged McNaught, and she resented this and told Reiko so in an addendum to her essay. After responding to Celeste's letter, Reiko wrote to her that she saw McNaught as

> thoughtful and loving, not inflexible and unloving as you see him. My intent in having students read this article is to have them think about the issues and draw conclusions of right or wrong on their own. And, please understand, I in no way want to attack anyone's nationality or religion. That is the farthest thing from my mind! The author's being Irish Catholic just means that he faced religious and cultural prohibitions against the kind of lifestyle he leads.

In the retrospective discussions two years later, Tanisha reported her appreciation for Celeste's courage in standing up to outspoken peers, even when she did not appreciate Celeste's sometimes unpopular opinions. Celeste had only been in the tenth-grade class three weeks when the "Dear Anita" lesson occurred, and already she had enraged peers who found her insensitive and Eurocentric. On one occasion, when she protested Black History month ("I don't get an Irish History month"), one African American girl in class stood and exclaimed, "After four hundred years of oppression, you'd begrudge us one lousy month?!" She told Brian in her letter that his idea of living in a hostile world is ridiculous, that "we all live in a hostile world." Here she minimized oppression, flattened it out into something everyone feels in an imperfect world, perhaps, in part, a function of her lack of experience with the racism and injustice most of her peers knew first-hand. She also told Brian, "All sinners want their sins to be justified by others so they will continue to persist in actions towards gay rights, or any civil rights." Her claim that those who struggle for civil rights want their sins justified by others flies in the face of the community-building that occurred for five months in Reiko's class before Celeste entered. Nonetheless, Reiko addressed Celeste's issues head on in her response to her essay, handling her feelings sensitively. This was particularly important since Celeste's major support for her opinions came from her understanding of and faith in her religion, belief systems tied to her own sense of family and culture.

Students' Reflections on the Lesson

The effects of the "Dear Anita" lesson lasted beyond the unit. In a survey I conducted later that spring, seven students, a third of the class, described the "Dear Anita" discussion and lesson as memorable. Although one student criticized how the class got off the subject "discussing homosexuals but not relating to the story," others recalled the discussion as highly engaging and informative. One said he "learned much about gay stereotypes, gay fact and fiction." Another recalled the debate on choice and realized "you can't tell a person to change what they feel because it's impossible." In case study interviews in which I asked students to reflect on the unit and the full school year, most spoke of the impact of the "Dear Anita" lesson. Vivian thought King's chapter and McNaught's essay were the most interesting pieces from the unit. Cassandra remarked:

> Before I thought in the *Bible* it says when two people of the same sex come together it's earthquakes and the world's coming to an end. I was against it. But then I read "Dear Anita" and they have rights, too. . . . I was confused at first. Are they good people or bad people? But I came to realize they're just people, too.

Alberto, who is Filipino, remarked, "I'm a Catholic and the Catholic Church is supposed to be against it, and how could you be against a person when it says in the *Bible* you're supposed to love your neighbor as yourself?" He told me he had whispered to Mark during the discussion the question he eventually raised to the class: "If you have sex with a man does that make you gay, or is there more to it?" He said he spoke with his mother and wants to learn more about homosexuality.

In the survey I conducted two years and three months later, eighteen students reflected on the works of greatest impact from their tenth-grade year.

Citing reasons such as identification and exposure to learning about difference, students selected Maya Angelou's (1969) autobiography and an excerpt from Amy Tan's *The Joy Luck Club* (1989) as particularly memorable. Three students selected "Dear Anita," which Genevieve called "an eye-opener" that made her feel she was "wrong in condemning them. I felt really bad. It has changed me a whole lot in my perception of homosexuals." Robert said, "I really had to rethink my feelings on homosexuality. . . . [It] really made me stop judging homosexuals by the ignorant opinions and stereotypes that were going around." During the accompanying retrospective discussions, students reflected on changed attitudes and new perceptions due to Reiko's class. Robert recalled the study of "Dear Anita":

> At first I was always calling gay people queers and stuff but then we kept talk-ing about it and then like my homophobia just started to go away because whenever we talked about gay people it was just throwing stereotypes around, right? And then junior year and now . . . it's like, you start to see that all people are just like everyone else and you get to interact with them, and all that stuff just melts away, all those old fears and prejudices.

Clearly, the "Dear Anita" lesson had a strong impact on most of Reiko's stu-dents and may have had a lasting effect. To what can we attribute these results? A complex set of conditions made the impact of this lesson possible.

How Curriculum and Instruction
Shaped Students' Responses
Importance of Text Selection

As my analysis of McNaught's essay demonstrates, by sensitively describing his own story, McNaught's piece helps readers move beyond stereotypes (Tables 4–3 and 4–4). While some might critique McNaught as a gay apolo-gist who asks, "Accept us because we're just like you," Reiko's choice of "Dear Anita" showed sensitivity to her students. Rather than deny her students' reli-gious backgrounds, Reiko chose a work written from a religious perspective by a devout Catholic and loving, family-oriented man. This religious connection provided many students with a firm ground for identification as they grappled with the issues McNaught presents.

Reiko's choice of text followed principles articulated in the multicultural literature. First, the essay—about gay experiences—was written by a gay man, or "cultural insider," which made it more possible to achieve "cultural ac-curacy" (Bishop 1992; Yokota 1993). Students responded to this feature of the work, finding it a credible "inside view" of what it means to be gay. Second, the essay presented sociological perspectives on homosexuality, as important here as in treatment of racism and other atrocities in U.S. history, providing an analysis of institutional structures that have caused and continue to contribute to social inequities (Gibson 1984; Hilliard 1974; Mura 1988). Reiko's lesson explored some of this, dealing with the oppression McNaught and other gays and lesbians experience, particularly through the use of Martin Luther King Jr.'s chapter as a way of invoking the issue of civil rights. Third, the essay showed a protagonist from a marginalized group in an empowered state, what is called in the literature "beyond victimization" (Greene 1993; Pace 1992). McNaught reports his suffering, but his convictions regarding human rights come through strongly in the end, and students responded to this strength of voice. Finally, effective multicultural education avoids perpetuation of "othering" that results from study of marginalized groups as purely different (Gibson 1984). Thoughtful educators attend both to difference and to common ground across groups. Here again, invoking King in consideration of McNaught served this purpose well.

A Safe Environment for Explorations of Diversity

Reiko's students had practiced for months various strategies of openly exploring diversity. When students had questions about a culture different from their own, for example, they knew they could comfortably raise these questions without fear of either ridicule for their ignorance or accusations of insensitivity. Reiko frequently modeled this practice and invited students to share cultural knowledge that might shed light on issues under consideration.

In a discussion of an excerpt from Amy Tan's *The Joy Luck Club* (1989), for example, African American students asked Chinese American students about words and cultural norms they did not understand when reading the selection. Reiko used Tan's treatment of mother-child conflict as an opportunity for building common ground, by inviting students to engage in cross-cultural exchange of mother and grandmother tales (Athanases 1993a). Such classroom practices made it easier for Reiko's students to ask candid questions, without embarrassment or criticism, about "choice" for homosexuals, the place of sex in sexual orientation, and the impact on children of gay parenting. While some of the students at times parroted myths and lines they had no doubt heard spoken by their elders or in the media, the videotape showed a group of students generally trying to understand the issues at hand and responding to Reiko's prompts for greater empathy. This was one goal of the entire curriculum, and was not new to them. They respected empathy as a worthy goal set by a teacher they respected highly and often looked to for clarity about complex cultural issues.

Discussion and Writing as Vehicles for Thinking and Feeling

Though Reiko had goals for her students that included enhanced empathy for gays and lesbians, her lesson invited thinking and not mere recitation of fact. Questions were generally authentic ones for which prespecified answers were not available. She raised "why" questions that invited thinking and perspective-taking on hypothetical questions that invited empathy. Nine students asked questions during the "Dear Anita" discussion, which is unusual for public school classrooms generally dominated by teacher-controlled talk with a strict pattern of teacher initiating talk with a question, student responding, and teacher evaluating (Cazden 1986; Mehan 1985). Important to this thinking climate is the use of evidence for support. Beyond the text, which Reiko and her students repeatedly cited for support, students used other sources for evidence and confirmation in their talk and writing: gay and lesbian teachers (Ms. Salzman, Mr. Kendall, a teacher from another school); media portrayals of gay lives (*A Current Affair* and another television show); a guest speaker in Family Living class; and personal encounters with gays and lesbians. Students tapped other literary works, making the intertextual connection Reiko fostered (such as the Martin Luther King-McNaught link) a way to reason through the issues of diversity. Finally, these students, most of whom had felt the pain of racism, tapped experiences of this pain in the language they used to reason with confidence that gays and lesbians deserve equality and a quality life. Demar, for example, wrote to Brian:

> It reminds me of racism. Like some incidents in racism when the qualifications are perfect. You walk in the office, he sees you're black, you're thrown out on your butt. So Brian I see where you are coming from, and you are right.

Cassandra used a civil rights oratorical style as she pounded her desk during her proclamation of rights for gays that closed the discussion. Finally, Reiko's use of a "Dear Brian" letter made the author and his struggle real as students addressed McNaught directly. This humanizing device aided the work to develop empathy that Reiko held as a goal for the lesson and for her entire curriculum.

Discussion

This study provides evidence that a teacher can successfully integrate a gay-themed lesson into a curriculum of diverse literary works. Across data strands, students reported having myths of homosexuality dispelled, an emerging empathy for gays and lesbians, and a clear sense of the rights of gays and lesbians to be who they are without fearing the loss of their jobs, or harm. The students genuinely attempted to work through some of the issues. The study examined just one lesson in one small class of fairly motivated students, and to what degree such successes could occur in other classes is unclear. Still, the study demonstrates that even students at the point of early adolescence can discuss issues of sexual orientation and homophobia with candor, curiosity, and maturity when prompted by an appropriate text, a safe and structured climate for exploration of diversity, discussions and writing that invite thinking, and invitations for empathy.

The Need for Repeated Emphasis

While literature study can enable students to begin to alter their stereotyped notions of others, the realignment of beliefs based on preconceived notions is a slow process (Ramsey 1987, 1992). Generally, repeated emphasis on such concerns is essential. Despite the overwhelming impact of McNaught's essay and Reiko's lesson on her students and their stated beliefs, Celeste resisted McNaught's reasoning and the lesson. Three months later, she and Tanisha, who disagreed strongly on gay issues, became sisters in outrage over the treatment of Native Americans as depicted in three novels they read for a Book Club assignment. For this assignment, students worked in groups to read and plan presentations on full-length literary works by ethnically diverse authors. Two years later, Celeste identified one of these, N. Scott Momaday's *House Made of Dawn* (1989), as the most memorable work from Reiko's class "because it showed me how much the government destroys a people['s] traditions, heritage. And how stubborn and stupid people are because they stick to stereotypes instead of finding out the truth." Clearly, Celeste was capable of enormous empathy, though not yet toward gays and lesbians in her tenth-grade year. And although I do not know where Celeste stood on gay/lesbian issues two years later, during the retrospective discussion, Celeste sat with her friend Tanisha, now an out lesbian, and laughed with Alycia and others as she recalled their tensions in the tenth grade over such issues as Black History Month.

For other students in Reiko's class who supported McNaught's refutations of myths about homosexuality, there were myths not yet dispelled that warranted further conversation and study. The notion of an orientation as something larger than sexual activity is one Alberto imagined to be true but could not yet grasp. Though three students refuted the myth of homosexuality as a choice, the class struggled to find language to distinguish between choosing to be gay and choosing an uncloseted life. Finally, while outside the purview of McNaught's essay, gay parenting aroused concern of a number of students.

The Need for Role Models

Despite evidence of homophobia in the worlds outside and inside school, Reiko's students had been exposed to positive models of lesbians and gay men and, as reported in anecdotes and studies (Sears & Williams 1997), such exposure minimizes homophobia. As students read McNaught's essay and explored issues, they had positive examples to support this evolving empathy for gays and lesbians: beloved and respected gay and lesbian teachers, guest speakers, and media images. This gay presence enabled students to draw on a wider range of knowledge sources to sort through issues. This reinforces the importance of lesbian and gay role models in educating young people about difference, particularly for those who hear other messages from media, peers, adults, and those who rigidly interpret religious teachings. Even in the San Francisco Bay Area,

which has a large population of out lesbians and gays, it was the personal relationships with gays and lesbians that students at Richards needed to draw on as
support for McNaught's refuting of myths of homosexuality.

Importance of Literary Depictions of Gays and Lesbians

Literature curricula need to include works that explore the gay and lesbian
experience, since little evidence exists that sex education dispels myths of homosexuality. Few counselors offer gay youth the support they need, which per-
petuates their potentially dangerous isolation (Sears 1992). Bringing gay and
lesbian themed literature into the students' "orbit of attention" helps to ensure
the cultural reproduction of such works (Smith 1983) and their availability
for all students, who can learn from and find validation in them. Inspired by
McNaught's essay, Tanisha's discussion performance (aligning herself with the
gay author, the lesbian teacher, all gays and lesbians, and challenging myths
and homophobia expressed by her peers) prefigured her act of coming out two
years later. McNaught notes in another essay, "I would guess that on an average day, the majority of gay men and lesbians are called upon to be courageous
about their sexual orientation at least five times" (1988b, 72). Just as the course
invited Tanisha to use her knowledge as a person of color and a young woman,
and to voice feelings about these identities, it may have also allowed her early
opportunities to claim voice on behalf of gays and to rehearse her own lesbian
identity. Although she felt at odds with her peers in the discussion, the class
provided her with the text, the structure, the forum, and the safety to voice what
she did and to help educate her peers.

The Need for Coalition Building

Some educators fear that including sexual orientation and homophobia in a
multicultural curriculum dilutes the focus on race and ethnicity that belongs at
the heart of the multicultural agenda. Reiko's lesson shows that a lesson on gay
and lesbian concerns need not detract from these issues but can, in fact, deepen
students' understanding about identities and oppression and the ways in which
marginal groups both share features and differ. Among the goals of a strong program in diversity is a deepened understanding of common ground for groups
divided by difference, something Reiko's lesson achieved for many participants.
Of the lesson, Robert said simply, "I learned that people are people are people.
One must judge all people in the same way, and that is by who they are inside."

This search for common ground addressed the need many educators find
in schools with students so often divided down lines defined by ethnicity, time
of immigration, and class. It also speaks to the essential need for coalition
building in struggles for civil rights and equality. Gates (1993) points out the
folly of establishing "a pecking order of oppression" and identifies at least one

point of common ground between African Americans and gays as groups: Just as Blacks have been portrayed as "sexually uncontrollable beasts . . . a similar vision of the predatory homosexual has been insinuated, often quite subtly, into the defense of the ban on gays in the military" (43). Noting such connections, as Demar and a number of his peers did, is essential to the coalition-building needed to dispel myths about oppressed groups and to ward off hateful forces that would stereotype and bring harm to members of these groups. The same thoughtful principles that hold sensitive treatment of diversity as a central goal can guide the inclusion of stories of gay and lesbian experiences in any literature program, whether the context is a Mexican American literature course primarily for Hispanic university students (Gonzalez 1994), a college course on women's studies (Kitch 1994), or Reiko's course for tenth graders exploring The Ethnic Experience in Literature.

References

Angelou, M. 1969. *I know why the caged bird sings.* New York: Bantam.

Applebee, A. N. 1993. *Literature in the secondary school: Studies of curriculum and instruction in the United States.* Urbana, IL: National Council of Teachers of English.

Athanases, S. Z. 1993a. Cross-cultural swapping of mother and grandmother tales in a tenth grade discussion of *The Joy Luck Club. Communication Education, 42,* 282–287.

———. 1993b. Discourse about literature and diversity: A study of two urban tenth-grade classes. *Dissertation Abstracts International, 54,* 05-A (Order No. AAD93-26420).

Banks, J. A. 1993. Multicultural education: Characteristics and goals. In J. A. Banks & C. A. McGee Banks (Eds.), *Multicultural education: Issues and perspectives* (pp. 3–28). Boston: Allyn and Bacon.

Banks, J. A., & Banks, C. A. McGee, eds. 1993. *Multicultural education: Issues and perspectives.* Boston: Allyn and Bacon.

Bishop, R. S. 1992. Multicultural literature for children: Making informed choices. In V. J. Harris (Ed.), *Teaching multicultural literature in grades K–8* (pp. 37–53). Norwood, PA: Christopher-Gordon.

Boutilier, N. 1994. Reading, writing, and Rita Mae Brown: Lesbian literature in high school. In L. Garber (Ed.), *Tilting the tower* (pp. 135–141). New York: Routledge.

Cazden, C. B. 1986. Classroom discourse. In M. C. Wittrock (Ed.), *Handbook of research on teaching* (3rd ed., pp. 432–463). New York: Macmillan.

Garber, L., ed. 1994. *Tilting the tower.* New York: Routledge.

Gates, H. L., Jr. 1993. Blacklash? *New Yorker,* May 17, pp. 42–44.

Gibson, M. A. 1984. Approaches to multicultural education in the United States: Some concepts and assumptions. *Anthropology and Education, 15,* 94–119.

Gonzalez, M. C. 1994. Cultural conflict: Introducing the queer in Mexican-American literature class. In L. Garber (Ed.), *Tilting the tower* (pp. 56–62). New York: Routledge.

Greene, M. 1993. The passions of pluralism: Multiculturalism and the expanding community. *Educational Researcher,* 22(1), 13–18.

Hammett, R. F. 1992. A rationale and unit plan for introducing gay and lesbian literature into the grade twelve curriculum. In P. Shannon (Ed.), *Becoming political: Readings and writings in the politics of literacy education* (pp. 250–262). Portsmouth, NH: Heinemann.

Harbeck, K. M., ed. 1992. *Coming out of the classroom closet: Gay and lesbian students, teachers, and curricula.* New York: Harrington Park Press.

Harris, S. 1990. *Lesbian and gay issues in the English classroom: The importance of being honest.* Philadelphia: Open University Press.

Hart, E. L., & Parmeter, S. 1992. "Writings in the margins": A lesbian-and-gay-inclusive course. In C. M. Hurlbert & S. Totten (Eds.) *Social issues in the classroom* (pp. 154–173). Urbana, IL: National Council of Teachers of English.

Hilliard, A. G. 1974. Restructuring teacher education for multicultural imperatives. In W. A. Hunter (Ed.), *Multicultural education through competency-based teacher education* (pp. 38–52). Washington, DC: American Association of Colleges for Teacher Education.

Jennings, K., ed. 1994. *One teacher in ten: Gay and lesbian educators tell their stories.* Boston: Alyson.

King, M. L., Jr. 1958. *Stride toward freedom.* New York: Harper.

Kitch, S. L. 1994. Straight but not narrow: A gynetic approach to the teaching of lesbian literature. In L. Garber (Ed.), *Tilting the tower* (pp. 83–95). New York: Routledge.

Lankewish, V. A. 1992. Breaking the silence: Addressing homophobia with *The color purple.* In C. M. Hurlbert & S. Totten (Eds.), *Social issues in the classroom* (pp. 219–230). Urbana, IL: National Council of Teachers of English.

Lloyd-Jones, R., & Lunsford, A. A., eds. 1989. *The English coalition conference: Democracy through language.* Urbana, IL: National Council of Teachers of English.

Long, B. W., & Hopkins, M. F. 1982. *Performing literature.* Englewood Cliffs, NJ: Prentice-Hall.

McNaught, B. 1988a. Dear Anita: Late night thoughts of an Irish Catholic homosexual. *On being gay: Thoughts on family, faith and love* (pp. 5–14). New York: St. Martin's Press.

———. 1988b. Proud growls and courageous roars. *On being gay: Thoughts on family, faith and love* (pp. 72–75). New York: St. Martin's Press.

McVicar, D. M. 1995. Censored: Job on the line over gay books. *Providence (R.I.) Sunday Journal,* Spetember 3, pp. 3, 16.

Momaday, N. S. 1989. *House made of dawn.* New York: Harper Collins.

Mehan, H. 1985. The structure of classroom discourse. In T. A. Van Dijk (Ed.), *Handbook of discourse analysis, 3* (pp. 142–167). London: Academic Press.

Mura, D. 1988. Strangers in the village. In R. Simonson & S. Walker (Eds.), *The gray-wolf annual five: Multi-cultural literacy* (pp. 135–153). St. Paul, MN: Graywolf Press.

Pace, B. G. 1992. The textbook canon: Genre, gender, and race in U.S. literature anthologies. *English Journal, 81*(5), 33–38.

Ramsey, P. G. 1987. *Teaching and learning in a diverse world: Multicultural education for young children.* New York: Teachers College Press.

———. 1992. *Children's responses to a unit on Native American literature.* Paper presented at the annual meeting of the American Educational Research Association, San Francisco, April.

Sears, J. T. 1992. Educators, homosexuality, and homosexual students: Are personal feelings related to professional beliefs? In K. M. Harbeck (Ed.), *Coming out of the classroom closet: Gay and lesbian students, teachers, and curricula* (pp. 29–79). New York: Harrington Park Press.

Sears, J. T., & Williams, W. 1997. *Overcoming heterosexism and homophobia.* New York: Columbia University Press.

Smith, B. H. 1983. Contingencies of value. *Critical Inquiry, 10,* September, 1–35.

Stotsky, S. 1994. Academic guidelines for selecting multiethnic and multicultural literature. *English Journal, 83*(2), 27–34.

Tan, A. 1989. *The joy luck club.* New York: Ivy Books.

Task Force on Racism and Bias in the Teaching of English. 1986. *Expanding opportunities: Academic success for culturally and linguistically diverse students.* Urbana, IL: National Council of Teachers of English.

Yokota, J. 1993. Issues in selecting multicultural children's literature. *Language Arts, 70*(3), 156–167.

The research reported in this article was funded, in part, by a Spencer Dissertation-Year Fellowship from the Woodrow Wilson Foundation and by a Grant-in-Aid from the National Council of Teachers of English.

5

Discovering Columbus

Rereading the Past

William Bigelow

Editors' Notes: Bill Bigelow, an exceptional teacher and author from Jefferson High School in Portland, Oregon, shares his inventive strategies for a revisionist course of Columbus, one that asks some normally unasked questions. Bigelow invites students to discover what's missing in the Columbus myth, such as the perspective of the Arawaks, the beginning of the slave trade, and Columbus' seizure of already occupied lands. His students critique traditional textbook accounts of Columbus and construct their own meaning. Bigelow invokes Freire for his teaching philosophy; he wants students to be active participants in their own learning and in democratic society. Sweeney's chapter following this one continues the "rethinking" of Columbus.

Most of my students have trouble with the idea that a book—especially a *textbook*—can lie. When I tell them that I want them to argue with, not just read, the printed word they're not sure what I mean. That's why I start my U.S. history class by stealing a student's purse.

As the year opens, my students may not know when the Civil War was fought, what James Madison or Frederick Douglass did, or where the Underground Railroad went, but they do know that a brave fellow named Christopher Columbus discovered America. OK, the Vikings may have actually *discovered* America, but students know it was Columbus who mapped it and *did* something with the place. Indeed, this bit of historical lore may be the only knowledge class members share in common.

What students don't know is that year after year their textbooks have, by omission or otherwise, been lying to them on a grand scale. Some students learned that Columbus sailed on three ships and that his sailors worried whether they would ever see land again. Others know from readings and teachers that when the admiral landed he was greeted by naked, reddish-skinned people whom he called Indians. And still others may know Columbus gave these people little trinkets and returned to Spain with a few of the Indians to show King Ferdinand and Queen Isabella.

All this is true. What is also true is that Columbus took hundreds of Indians slaves and sent them back to Spain where most of them were sold and subsequently died. What is also true is that in his quest for gold Columbus had the hands cut off any Indian who did not return with his or her three-month quota. And what is also true is that on one island alone, Hispaniola, an entire race of people were wiped off the face of the earth in a mere forty years of Spanish administration.

So I begin class by stealing a student's purse. I announce to the class that the purse is mine, obviously, because look who has it. Most students are fair-minded. They saw me take the purse off the desk so they protest: "That's not yours, it's Nikki's. You took it, we saw you." I brush these objections aside and reiterate that it is, too, mine and to prove it I'll show all the things I have inside.

I unzip the bag and remove a brush or a comb, maybe a pair of dark glasses. A tube, or whatever it's called, of lipstick works best: "This is my lipstick," I say. "There, that proves it *is* my purse." They don't buy it and, in fact, are mildly outraged that I would pry into someone's possessions with such utter disregard for her privacy. (I've alerted the student to the demonstration before the class, but no one else knows that.)

It's time to move on: "OK, if it's Nikki's purse, how do you know? Why are you all so positive it's not my purse?" Different answers: We saw you take it; that's her lipstick, we know you don't wear lipstick; there is stuff in there with her name on it. To get the point across, I even offer to help in their effort to prove Nikki's possession: "If we had a test on the contents of the purse who would do better, Nikki or me?" "Whose labor earned the money that bought the things in the purse, mine or Nikki's?" Obvious questions, obvious answers.

I make one last try to keep Nikki's purse: "What if I said I *discovered* this purse, then would it be mine?" A little laughter is my reward, but I don't get any takers; they still think the purse is rightfully Nikki's.

"So," I ask, "Why do we say that Columbus discovered America?" Now they begin to see what I've been leading up to. I ask a series of rhetorical questions that implicitly make the link between Nikki's purse and the Indians' land: Were there people on the land before Columbus arrived? Who had been on the land longer, Columbus or the Indians? Who knew the land better? Who had put their labor into making the land produce? The students see where I'm going—it would be hard not to. "And yet," I continue, "What is the first thing

that Columbus did when he arrived in the New World?" Right: he took possession of it. After all, he had *discovered* the place.

We talk about phrases other than *discovery* that textbooks could use to describe what Columbus did. Students start with the phrases they used to describe
what I did to Nikki's purse: He stole it; he took it; he ripped it off. And others:
He invaded it; he conquered it.

I want students to see that the word *discovery* is loaded. The word itself
carries with it a perspective, a bias; it takes sides. *Discovery* is the phrase of the
supposed discoverers. It's the conquerors', the invaders', masking their theft.
And when the word gets repeated in textbooks those textbooks become, in the
phrase of one historian, "the propaganda of the winners."

To prepare students to examine critically the textbooks of their past we begin with some alternative, and rather unsentimental, explorations of Columbus'
"enterprise," as he called it. The admiral-to-be was not sailing for mere adven-
ture and to prove the world was round, as my fourth-grade teacher had informed her class, but to secure the tremendous profits that were to be made by
reaching the Indies. From the beginning, Columbus' quest was wealth, both for
Spain and for himself personally. He demanded a 10 percent cut of everything
shipped to Spain via the western route—and not just for himself but for all his
heirs in perpetuity. And he insisted he be pronounced governor of any new
lands he found, a title which carried with it dictatorial powers.

Mostly I want the class to think about the human beings Columbus was
to *discover*—and then destroy. I read to students from a letter Columbus wrote
to Lord Raphael Sanchez, treasurer of Aragon and one of his patrons, dated
March 14, 1493, following his return from the first voyage. He reports being
enormously impressed by the indigenous people:

> As soon . . . as they see that they are safe and have laid aside all fear, they are
> very simple and honest and exceedingly liberal with all they have; none of
> them refusing anything he may possess when he is asked for it, but, on the
> contrary, inviting us to ask them. They exhibit great love toward all others in
> preference to themselves. They also give objects of great value for trifles, and
> content themselves with very little or nothing in return . . . I did not find, as
> some of us had expected, any cannibals among them, but, on the contrary,
> men of great deference and kindness. (*Annals of America* 1968, 2, 4)

But, on an ominous note, Columbus writes in his log, "should your Majesties
command it, all the inhabitants could be taken away to Castile [Spain], or made
slaves on the island. With fifty men we could subjugate them all and make them
do whatever we want" (Konig 1976).

I ask students if they remember from elementary school days what it was
Columbus brought back with him from his travels in the New World. Together
students recall that he brought back parrots, plants, some gold, and a few of
the people Columbus had taken to calling "Indians." This was Columbus' first
expedition and it is also where most school textbook accounts of Columbus

end—conveniently. Because the enterprise of Columbus was not to bring back exotic knickknacks, but riches, preferably gold. What about his second voyage?

I read to them a passage from Hans Koning's fine book, *Columbus: His Enterprise:*

> We are now in February 1495. Time was short for sending back a good "dividend" on the supply ships getting ready for the return to Spain. Columbus therefore turned to a massive slave raid as a means for filling up these ships. The brothers [Columbus and his brothers, Bartolome and Diego] rounded up fifteen hundred Arawaks—men, women, and children—and imprisoned them in pens in Isabela, guarded by men and dogs. The ships had room for no more than five hundred, and thus only the best specimens were loaded aboard. The Admiral then told the Spaniards they could help themselves from the remainder to as many slaves as they wanted. Those whom no one chose were simply kicked out of their pens. Such had been the terror of these prisoners that (in the description by Michele de Cuneo, one of the colonists) "they rushed in all directions like lunatics, women dropping and abandoning infants in the rush, running for miles without stopping, fleeing across mountains and rivers."
>
> Of the five hundred slaves, three hundred arrived alive in Spain, where they were put up for sale in Seville by Don Juan de Fonseca, the archdeacon of the town. "As naked as the day they were born," the report of this excellent churchman says, *"but with no more embarrassment than animals . . ."*
>
> The slave trade immediately turned out to be "unprofitable, for the slaves mostly died." Columbus decided to concentrate on gold, although he writes, "Let us *in the name of the Holy Trinity* go on sending all the slaves that can be sold." (Emphasis in Koning; 84–85)

Certainly Columbus' fame should not be limited to the discovery of America: he also deserves credit for initiating the trans-Atlantic slave trade, albeit in the opposite direction than we're used to thinking of it.

Students and I role play a scene from Columbus' second voyage. Slavery is not producing the profits Columbus is seeking. He still believes there is gold in them thar hills and the Indians are selfishly holding out on him. Students play Columbus; I play the Indians: "Chris, we don't have any gold, honest. Can we go back to living our lives now and you can go back to wherever you came from?" I call on several students to respond to the Indians' plea. Columbus thinks the Indians are lying. How can he get his gold? Student responses range from sympathetic to ruthless: OK, we'll go home; please bring us your gold; we'll lock you up in prison if you don't bring us your gold; we'll torture you if you don't fork it over, and so on. After I've pleaded for awhile and the students-as-Columbus have threatened, I read aloud another passage from Koning's book describing the system Columbus arrived at for extracting gold from the Indians:

> Every man and woman, every boy or girl of fourteen or older, in the province of Cibao (of the imaginary gold fields) had to collect gold for the Spaniards.

As their measure, the Spaniards used . . . hawks' bells . . . Every three months, every Indian had to bring to one of the forts a hawks' bell filled with gold dust. The chiefs had to bring in about ten times that amount. In the other provinces of Hispaniola, twenty five pounds of spun cotton took the place of gold.

Copper tokens were manufactured, and when an Indian had brought his or her tribute to an armed post, he or she received such a token, stamped with the month, to be hung around the neck. With that they were safe for another three months while collecting more gold.

Whoever was caught without a token was killed by having his or her hands cut off. There are old Spanish prints . . . that show this being done: the Indians stumble away, staring *with surprise* at their arm stumps pulsing out blood.

There were no gold fields, and thus, once the Indians had handed in whatever they still had in gold ornaments, their only hope was to work all day in the streams, washing out gold dust from the pebbles. It was an impossible task, but those Indians who tried to flee into the mountains were systematically hunted down with dogs and killed, to set an example for the others to keep trying . . .

Thus it was at this time that the mass suicides began: the Arawaks killed themselves with casaba poison.

During those two years of the administration of the brothers Columbus, an estimated one half of the entire population of Hispaniola was killed or killed themselves. The estimates run from one hundred and twenty-five thousand to one-half million. (85–87)

It's important students not be shielded from the horror of what *discovery* meant to its victims. The fuller they understand the consequences of Columbus' invasion of America the better they'll be equipped to critically reexamine the innocent stories their textbooks have offered through the years. The goal is not to titillate or stun, but to force the question: Why wasn't I told this before?

Students' assignment is to find a textbook, preferably one they used in elementary school, but any textbook will suffice, and write a critique of the book's treatment of Columbus and the Indians. I distribute the following handout to students and review the questions aloud. I don't want them to merely answer the questions one by one, but to consider them as guidelines in completing their critiques:

- How factually accurate was the account?

- What was omitted—left out—that in your judgment would be important for a full understanding of Columbus? (For example, his treatment of the Indians; slave taking; his method of getting gold; the overall effect on the Indians.)

- What motives does the book give to Columbus? Compare those with his real motives.

- Who does the book get you to root for, and how do they accomplish that? (For example, are the books horrified at the treatment of Indians or thrilled that Columbus makes it to the New World?)

- What function do pictures in the books play? What do they communicate about Columbus and his "enterprise"?

- In your opinion, why does the book portray the Columbus/Indian encounter the way it does?

- Can you think of any groups in our society who might have an interest in people having an inaccurate view of history?

I tell students that this last question is tough but crucial. Is the continual distortion of Columbus simply an accident, repeated innocently over and over, or are there groups in our society who could benefit from everyone having a false or limited understanding of the past? Whether or not students are able to answer the question effectively, it is still important they struggle with it before our group discussion of their critiques.

The subtext of the assignment is to teach students that text material, indeed all written material, is to be read skeptically. I want students to explore the politics of print, that perspectives on history and social reality underlie the written word and that to read is both to comprehend what is written, but also to question why it is written. My intention is not to encourage an "I-don't-believe-anything" cynicism, but rather to equip students to bring a writer's assumptions and values to the surface so students can decide what is useful and what is not in any particular work.

For practice, we look at some excerpts from a textbook that belonged to my brother in the fourth grade in California, *The Story of American Freedom*, published by Macmillan in 1964. Students and I read aloud and analyze several paragraphs. The arrival of Columbus and crew is especially revealing—and obnoxious. As is true in every book on the "discovery" I've ever encountered, the reader watches events from the Spaniards' point of view. We are told how Columbus and his men "fell upon their knees and gave thanks to God," a passage included in virtually all elementary school accounts of Columbus. "He then took possession of it [the island] in the name of King Ferdinand and Queen Isabella of Spain" (McGuire 1964, 24). No question is raised of what right Columbus had to assume control over a land that was obviously already occupied by people. The account is so adoring, so respectful of the admiral, that students can't help but sense the book is offering approval for what is, quite simply, an act of naked imperialism.

The book keeps us close to God and church throughout its narrative. Upon returning from the New World, Columbus shows off his parrots and Indians (again no question of the propriety of the unequal relationship between "natives" and colonizers), and immediately following the show, "the king and queen lead the way to a near-by church. There a song of praise and thanksgiving is sung" (26). Intended or not, the function of linking church and Columbus is to remove him and his actions still further from question and critique. My job, on the other hand, is to encourage students to pry beneath every phrase and illustration; to begin to train readers who can both understand the word and challenge it.

I give students a week before I ask them to bring in their written critiques. In small groups students share their papers with one another. I ask them to take notes towards what my coteacher, Linda Christensen, and I call the "collective text": What themes seem to recur in the papers and what important differences emerge?

Here are some excerpts from papers written this year by students in the Literature and U.S. History that Linda and I coteach. Maryanne wrote:

> "In 1492 Columbus sailed the ocean blue." He ran into a land mass claiming it in the name of Spain. The next day Columbus went ashore. "Indians," almost naked, greeted Columbus who found them a simple folk who "invite you to share anything they possess." Columbus observed that "fifty Spaniards could subjugate this entire people." Then we are told, "By 1548 the Indians were almost all wiped out"—from a passage in *The Impact of Our Past.*
>
> That story is about as complete as swiss cheese. Columbus and the Spaniards killed off the "Indians," they didn't mystically disappear or die of diphtheria.

Trey wrote his critique as a letter to Allyn and Bacon, publishers of *The American Spirit:*

> I'll just pick one topic to keep it simple. How about Columbus. No, you didn't lie, but saying "though they had a keen interest in the peoples of the Caribbean, Columbus and his crews were never able to live peacefully among them" makes it seem as if Columbus did no wrong. The reason for not being able to live peacefully is that he and his crew took slaves, and killed thousands of Indians for not bringing enough gold . . .
>
> If I were to only know the information given in this book, I would have such a sheltered viewpoint that many of my friends would think I was stupid. Later in life people could capitalize on my ignorance by comparing Columbus' voyage with something similar, but in our time. I wouldn't believe the ugly truths brought up by the opposition because it is just like Columbus, and he did no harm, I've known that since the eighth grade.

Keely chose the same book, which happens to be the text adopted by Portland Public Schools where I teach:

> I found that the facts left in were, in fact, facts. There was nothing made up. Only things left out. There was one sentence in the whole section where Indi-

ans were mentioned. And this was only to say why Columbus called them "Indians." Absolutely nothing was said about slaves or gold . . .

The book, as I said, doesn't mention the Indians really, so of course you're on Christopher's side. They say how he falls to his knees and thanks God for saving him and his crew and for making their voyage successful.

After students have read and discussed their papers in small groups we ask them to reflect on the papers as a whole and write about our collective text: What did they discover about textbook treatments of Columbus? Here are some excerpts. Matthew wrote:

As people read their evaluations the same situations in these textbooks came out. Things were conveniently left out so that you sided with Columbus' quest to "boldly go where no man has gone before" . . . None of the harsh violent reality is confronted in these so-called true accounts.

Gina tried to account for why the books were so consistently rosy:

It seemed to me as if the publishers had just printed up some "glory story" that was supposed to make us feel more patriotic about our country. In our group, we talked about the possibility of the government trying to protect young students from such violence. We soon decided that that was probably one of the farthest things from their minds. They want us to look at our country as great, and powerful, and forever right. They want us to believe Columbus was a real hero. We're being fed lies. We don't question the facts, we just absorb information that is handed to us because we trust the role models that are handing it out.

Rebecca's collective text reflected the general tone of disillusion with the official story of textbooks:

Of course, the writers of the books probably think it's harmless enough— what does it matter who discovered America, really, and besides it makes them feel good about America. But the thought that I have been lied to all my life about this, and who knows what else, really makes me angry.

The reflections on the collective text became the basis for a class discussion of these and other issues. Again and again, students blasted their textbooks for consistently making choices that left readers with inadequate, and ultimately untruthful, understandings. And while we didn't press to arrive at definitive explanations for the omissions and distortions, we did seek to underscore the contemporary abuses of historical ignorance. If the books wax romantic about Columbus planting the flag on island beaches and taking possession of land occupied by naked red-skinned Indians, what do young readers learn from this about today's world? That white people have a right to dominate peoples of color? That might—or wealth—makes right? That it's justified to take people's land if you are more "civilized" or have a "better" religion? Whatever the answers, the textbooks condition students to accept some form of inequality; nowhere do the books suggest that the Indians were, or even should have been, sovereign peoples with a right to control their own lands. And, if Columbus' motives for exploration are mystified or ignored then students are less apt to look beyond today's pious explanations for U.S. involvements in, say, Central America or the Middle East. As Bobby, approaching his registration day for the military draft, pointed out in class: "If people thought they were going off to war to fight for profits maybe they wouldn't fight as well, or maybe they wouldn't go."

It's important to note that some students are left troubled from these myth-popping discussions. One student wrote that she was "left not knowing who to believe." Josh was the most articulate in his skepticism. He had begun to "read" our class from the same critical distance from which we hoped students would approach textbooks:

> I still wonder . . . If we can't believe what our first grade teachers told us why should we believe you? If they lied to us why wouldn't you? If one book is wrong, why isn't another? What is your purpose in telling us about how awful Chris was? What interest do you have in telling us the truth? What is it you want from us?

What indeed? It was a wonderfully probing series of questions and Linda and I responded by reading them (anonymously) to the entire class. We asked students to take a few minutes to write additional questions and comments on the Columbus activities or to try to imagine our response as teachers—what was the point of our lessons?

We hoped students would see that the intent of the unit was to present a whole new way of reading, and ultimately, of experiencing the world. Textbooks fill students with information masquerading as final truth and then ask students to parrot back the information in end of the chapter checkups. The Brazilian educator, Paulo Freire, calls it the "banking method": students are treated as empty vessels waiting for deposits of wisdom from textbooks and teachers (1970). We wanted to assert to students that they shouldn't necessarily trust the "authorities" but instead needed to be active participants in their own learning, peering between lines for unstated assumptions and unasked questions. Meaning is something *they* need to create, individually and collectively.

Josh asked what our "interest" was in this kind of education and it's a fair, even vital, question. Linda and I see teaching as political action: we want to equip students to build a truly democratic society. As Freire (1987) writes, to be an actor for social change one must "read the word and the world." We hope that if a student is able to maintain a critical distance from the written word then it's possible to maintain that same distance from one's society: to stand back, look hard and ask, "Why is it like this, how can I make it better?"

Works Cited

The Annals of America, Volume 1: 1493–1754, Discovering a New World. 1968. Chicago: Encyclopedia Britannica.

de las Casas, Bartolome. [1656] 1972. *The Tears of the Indians.* New York: Oriole Chapbooks. (Originally published in English in London, 1656.)

Freire, Paulo. 1970. *Pedagogy of the Oppressed.* New York: Continuum.

Freire, Paulo, and Donaldo Macedo. 1987. *Literacy: Reading the Word and the World.* Granby, MA: Bergin and Garvey.

Konig, Hans. 1976. *Columbus: His Enterprise.* New York: Monthly Review Press.

McGuire, Edna. 1964. *The Story of American Freedom.* New York: Macmillan.

"Discovering Columbus: Rereading the Past" by William Bigelow originally appeared in Rethinking Schools *4:1 (Fall 1989): 12–13. Reprinted with permission.*

6

Columbus, A Hero?

Rethinking Columbus in an Elementary Classroom

Maria Sweeney

Editors' Notes: In this chapter, Maria Sweeney of Hawes Elementary School in Ridgewood, New Jersey, describes how she teaches Christopher Columbus and the untold story of the Tainos. Sweeney shares research sources and her innovative methods through which students performed skits, role plays, and eventually put together a documentary that influenced the fifth-grade curriculum the following year.

Sweeney's fourth-grade class made news in 1997 when her students' play on sweatshops was banned by the school administration for being inappropriate for young audiences and biased against corporate America. The attention garnered by Evelyn Nieves' report in the *New York Times* led to the play's production on Broadway (Appendix A). Stan Karp traces the history of the theatrical production of Sweeney's class, "Justice, Do It," from the *New York Times* coverage to the media blitz that followed (Appendix B). (See also Bigelow's chapter on sweatshops in this volume.)

Sweeney hopes her students use the skills and knowledge they learn to critique what they're taught, to work for social justice, and to participate in a critical democracy.

Several weeks into a study of Columbus, Victoria, who had been mostly puzzled by and sometimes doubtful of our revisionist view, suddenly lit up and said: "You mean Columbus was greedy and a murderer? I always thought he was a hero. Ms. Sweeney, can I go see what the encyclopedia says about Columbus?" To that, Lauren retorted: "But, Victoria, that's the point! You're not going to read the truth about Columbus in the encyclopedia. They leave out half the story and so do most books. That's why we all thought he was so great."

This exchange reflects changes in my students' thinking during a unit this past spring which I called "The Truth About Columbus." Both Victoria and Lauren began the year believing, as most kids do, that Christopher Columbus was an admirable fellow and that books tell the truth. They, however, ended the year by questioning what they'd always believed about Columbus and, hopefully, all aspects of history.

I teach in a middle- to upper-income suburban school district in northern New Jersey where the student population is about twenty-five percent Asian-American and seventy-five percent European-American. My students take their material and social privileges for granted. I strive to make my students aware of the vast social inequities on which their privilege is based and the historical roots of social inequality in this country. I strongly believe that my students deserve the opportunity to critically examine their society, to begin to understand the causes and consequences of economic disparities and thereby to be able to make informed and ethical choices about how they will live their lives today and in the future.

Throughout the year, I ask my students to consider alternative views of history. I ask them to look for the missing or silenced voices of oppressed groups (women, people of color, the working class, and the poor) and consistently to ask of all that they read, hear, or witness: Is this fair? Is this right? Does this hurt anyone? Is this the whole story? My goal is essentially the same as the one that Linda Christensen expresses so well when talking about her own teaching: "to give students the tools to critique every idea that legitimates social inequality—every idea that teaches them they are incapable of imagining and building a fundamentally equal and just society."[1] I strive to create a classroom atmosphere and curriculum that will prepare my students to forge and participate in a critical democracy. I work to empower my students with the necessary skills and knowledge to critique their world, to unveil injustices and needless suffering, and to work for social transformation. I nurture a strong sense of compassion and caring for those who are oppressed. Moreover, I encourage them to get angry and do something. With the 500th anniversary of Columbus's invasion of the Americas only months away, I took this occasion to help my students reconsider Columbus from the perspective of the people he violated.

How children learn history will ultimately influence how they view the present and judge the actions of their leaders. When students get the message that a particular historical event was right and just, they will view similar current events as justifiable. The Columbus myth is a perfect example. The standard version of the story teaches children to uncritically accept wars and imperialism; it devalues or even erases the rich cultures and struggles of native peoples; and it encourages children to ignore the voices of all those who are dominated. In the words of Bill Bigelow: "The Columbus myth teaches children to accept racism as normal, to believe that powerful, rich, white, Christian countries have the right to dominate people of color in the Third World. It encourages people to listen for the perspectives of the winners, the social elites, and inures them to the historical and literary silences of everybody else."[2]

The story of Columbus is most kids' first history lesson in school and one that they learn repeatedly during their early, impressionable years. By the time my students reach fourth grade the story is "the truth." They believe that Columbus was a brave and intelligent adventurer who proved that the world was round and "discovered" America. They know little or nothing about the Tainos, the Native Americans whose land he invaded, and they have no idea that they only know half of the "Columbus story" and a distorted half at that.

At the start of our critical study of Columbus, I asked my class to tell me the story of Columbus, to tell me all they had read and heard about the man. After listening to several versions, all remarkably similar and predictable, the class composed a collaborative text which I wrote up on chart paper. They all agreed that the class text was basically what had happened. Columbus was a courageous, smart, adventurous, and determined man and the only one who knew the world was round; he got the king and queen of Spain to provide him with three ships so he could find an alternate route to Asia and prove the world was round; on his way he "discovered" America and called the people there Indians, thinking he'd reached the East Indies; the Indians were friendly and naked and gave Columbus gifts; he claimed the land for Spain.

We discussed the sources of their knowledge: biographies of Columbus, teachers, and a filmstrip of the book *Columbus* by D'Aulaire and D'Aulaire shown to all third graders the previous year.[3] In their minds there was no doubt about the validity of these sources.

Once they'd agreed on the "accuracy" of the collaborative Columbus story, I began asking questions: "Whose side of the story is this really?" "What does 'discover' mean?" "Did Columbus really discover America or were there any people living there before he arrived?" Having had the experience earlier in the year of uncovering the silenced voices of women, workers, African Americans, and Japanese Americans during World War II, they knew where I was headed. They agreed that this was Columbus's side of the story and that he couldn't have "discovered" America since people were already living there. I explained that the Tainos had lived on those islands for at least fifteen hundred years before Columbus arrived and that we would spend the next several weeks trying to reconstruct their side of the story.

To emphasize that Columbus didn't discover America, I performed a role play about a "discovered" purse.[4] I grabbed Kacey's backpack and announced that it was mine. "After all," I said, "I *discovered* this backpack so I have a right to claim it as my possession." "NOT! Ms. Sweeney," Andrew protested. "That's Kacey's and you know it." I reminded them of the numerous times when some student had found (discovered) an item in the room such as a pencil or toy and claimed that it was therefore his or hers. They reminded me that through our class meetings we always decided that the discovered item had to be returned to the rightful owner. They understood the analogy. Columbus didn't discover America. He stole it.

We then did an exercise which we do at the start of any unit of study. The students brainstormed all that they knew about the Tainos, which was next to nothing, while I recorded their ideas on chart paper. Then they brainstormed a long list of questions regarding the Tainos and their encounter with Columbus.

We then began exploring alternative views. We read *The Untold Story* by Tina Thomas,[5] a high school student, which is a short critical version of the Columbus story written for children in the voice of a Taino. Thomas introduces most of the crimes and contradictions of Columbus in terms that my fourth graders readily understood:

- Columbus took land that was already inhabited and he took it from a people who believed that land could not be owned.

- Columbus had gold fever and would stop at nothing. He cut off the hands of Tainos who didn't bring him enough gold.

- He kidnapped at least five hundred Tainos and sent them back to Spain to be sold as slaves.

- The Tainos resisted these atrocities, but were overwhelmed by the Europeans' superior weapons.

- Columbus and his men destroyed the ecological balance of a land that had been carefully tended and respected by the Tainos.

The Untold Story immediately sets the kids straight on Columbus's real motives—wealth and power—and it points out how brutally he treated the Tainos. The kids were shocked. They were much more surprised and upset than I had expected. They said things like: "This is so sad." "I feel so sorry for the Tainos." "What made him think he could do that?" Obviously, it's not sufficient for my students just to feel sorry for the Tainos. Not going beyond this point could lead to paternalistic attitudes, but these feelings of sympathy were an appropriate place to begin. I wanted my kids to have compassion for the Tainos and to be upset about their suffering. Rather than study their oppression from a cold, objective, and distant stance, I thought it was important that my students be able to identify with the Tainos and imagine what it felt like to have their land and lives destroyed by these Europeans.

I then divided the class into small groups and asked them to prepare an informal skit based on the story. They were both excited and serious about the task. This wasn't the first time they were acting out the story of a forgotten people, but it was the first time they had something that they had been so sure of turned on its head. Right away one group asked if we could share these skits with the younger grades so they "wouldn't grow up believing that Columbus was a hero." I asked them to hold off on inviting an outside audience because there was much more I wanted them to learn first.

As they presented their skits, I took notes to preserve their lines, knowing that we might want to use them in a later production. This is just a sampling of their initial interpretations:

T.J. introduced his group's skit saying: "Have you ever gotten punched or kicked in a weak spot? This is exactly the kind of thing that Columbus did to the Tainos. He conquered them and took all their gold."

Ibrahim, who was his group's narrator, said: "Many people think that Columbus was a hero, but he was not. Columbus sailed to Bohio [the Taino name for the island of Hispaniola] and tortured the Tainos. He forced them to mine gold and be slaves."

We then studied the untold history of the invasion using primary sources (Columbus's journal, letters, eyewitness accounts) as quoted in *The Conquest of Paradise* and *Columbus: His Enterprise.*[6] As we began reading the words of those who witnessed the conquest, including the words of Columbus himself, we discovered a stark contrast with the sanitized standard version.

We also read parts of *The Tainos: The People Who Welcomed Columbus* by Francine Jacobs and *Columbus and the World Around Him* by Milton Meltzer.[7] Both books, written for upper elementary and middle school students, offer stinging criticisms of Columbus's voyage. My students were completely engaged by the saga and looked forward to each new installment. They grew increasingly angry with Columbus and his men while identifying and sympathizing with the Tainos. Students took notes and wrote personal responses to the information in their learning logs. Victoria, quoted earlier, wrote the following on the day she realized the kind of man Columbus really was: "Columbus and his crew treated the Tainos as if they were less than human. Columbus made the Tainos into anything he wanted. He killed them if they didn't bring enough gold, made them slaves, and made them become Christian. Christopher Columbus was a very greedy and cruel person."

Students continued to write and perform informal skits and role plays, acting out various parts of the story. They still talked a lot about the need to set other kids straight on the Columbus record and wanted to create a play. After doing a few skits we realized how challenging it would be to impart the story in the form of a play.

There were some problems: the Spaniards couldn't speak to the Tainos because of the language barrier and we couldn't figure out how to portray the interactions between the two groups using only hand signals. I didn't feel comfortable having my students act as Tainos because they really didn't know enough about them to assume their characters. These activities, however, were invaluable in helping my students to view the events through the eyes of the Tainos and to imagine their thoughts and feelings. In the end, we decided to create a documentary type of presentation to share with other students.

During the last four weeks of school, my class continued studying the alternative historical materials and wrote a critical documentary about the conquest, which they later performed for parents and other students in our school.

Writing and then presenting the documentary put my students in the position of being social activists. They took action rather than bemoan not having learned about this historical injustice. They were able to use their new understanding of Columbus in an attempt to tell others the truth.

Before launching this project, I was uncertain about how much they would really understand and afraid that I was teaching material that was developmentally inappropriate. To give the reader some sense of what fourth grade children were able to make of the information we studied, I am including excerpts from the narrative my students wrote for our documentary. In each case, I footnote the particular sources I used to generate the understandings reflected in that narrative. I also include anecdotes of class discussions and activities which occurred. In retrospect, I realize that I underestimated their ability to understand history and historical biases.

Lindsey and Kacey wrote the following statement describing the nature of Taino society to introduce our documentary: "The Tainos respected all things on the earth—people, plants, animals and the rest of the natural world. They took very good care of the earth and also each other. They were caring and compassionate, kind and generous. The Tainos made sure that all people were taken care of, that all had food, shelter and were healthy. There wasn't any homelessness and hunger like we have today. Most things were shared and they only owned things that they needed. The Tainos also didn't believe that any individual could own the land. They had their own religion and their own God. The Tainos were peaceful and friendly people who didn't have wars or slaves."[8]

I think their writing reflects a fairly sophisticated grasp of Taino culture and belief. Their understanding of Tainos was built upon work we had done earlier in the year, when we studied a number of Native American nations from the continental U.S. I had emphasized the vast differences between Native American societies and our own. We read the words of Sitting Bull, Chief Seattle, Black Elk, and others which capture the heart of Native American beliefs about the land and the good life. I explained that Native Americans value community and cooperation much more so than our society, which values the individual and competition. I also explained that Native Americans believe that the land is sacred, life-giving, and deserving of our reverence; that we are intricately bound up with the earth and all living things; and that a good life for humans depends on a healthy and whole mother earth. Throughout our study of Tainos, I contrasted the communitarian and peaceful nature of Taino culture with the exploitative, violent, and materialistic nature of European culture. We explored the beliefs and values driving Columbus's treatment of the Tainos.

I asked my students to consider what it meant for Columbus to speak of the Tainos as we read in his journal.[9] Did he view them as equal human beings deserving of respect and freedom? Did he believe that they had the same rights that he had? This sparked a lively discussion about human rights in general with several students referring to our "class bill of rights" which the class had written in September. One student remarked that if Columbus had been asked to write a "bill of rights" for the Tainos it would have been blank. For our documentary Lauren wrote: "Columbus and his men forced us into slavery. They took some of us back to Spain to be sold as slaves and made many of us work as slaves on our own land. This was horrible for us. Columbus treated us like we had no right to be on earth. He never stopped to think about how he would have felt if he were in our place. Even though we had our own religion he forced us to become Christian. At least he tried to."

During one of our discussions, T.J. invented the following scenario to explain the horror and grief the kidnapped Tainos must have felt when being brought back to Spain. He later wrote it up to be included in our presentation: "Now put yourself in the position of the Tainos but make it in a modern, science-fiction type setting. It would be like this: An alien spaceship lands on earth and kidnaps you and some other people. You realize that the aliens are taking you back to their strange planet to be sold as slaves. You will never see your family, friends or homeland again. How would you feel?"

The class discussed whether we could share all the bloody deeds of Columbus with our intended audience. Frankly, I wasn't too concerned, knowing that most kids are exposed to far more extreme violence in the movies and on television. However, my students were concerned that the younger kids might have nightmares from our presentation if we told all. Carolyn wrote the following compromise: "Columbus and his men did something terrible to my people who didn't bring in enough gold each month. He actually cut their hands off and left them to die. He did other cruel and horrible things that you can read about if you find the right books. We couldn't understand how anyone could make us suffer so much just for gold."

I wanted my students to understand that the Tainos didn't just passively accept these atrocities. I explained that there were many instances when they bravely resisted Columbus's brutal and cruel treatment.[10] In an attempt to convince our audience that the Tainos were active subjects who struggled valiantly to defend themselves, Erin wrote: "We tried many times to defend ourselves and our land. We did not just sit back and allow these terrible things to happen to us. But Columbus and his men had more powerful weapons than we did. We were a peaceful people and we were not prepared for such a powerful enemy."

Toward the end of our preparations for the documentary Rob raised the obvious question: "Why don't any of these books [pointing to the traditional books we had been evaluating] tell about the horrible things that Columbus did to the Tainos?" It was time to explore "the contemporary abuses of historical ignorance,"[11] a challenge for teaching critically with fourth graders. The Columbus myth serves to forestall any critical questioning of U.S. imperialistic foreign policy today. Widespread belief in the myth makes it easy for U.S. officials to get away with invading Vietnam, Grenada, Panama, and so on. Those books teach children that any nation with sufficient military power has the right to invade other lands. In particular, they reinforce blind patriotism and the belief that the United States has a moral imperative to control the "New World Order." But how on earth does one talk to fourth graders about imperialism?

To help my students to understand how certain versions of the Columbus story justify contemporary imperialism, I created and told the following story:

> Pretend that every year at Hawes [our school] you're taught that Columbus was great hero and there are school-wide celebrations in his honor. Each year the principal addresses the school and speaks of Columbus as a man to honor and learn from, a man to respect and emulate. Imagine that this principal is also conducting raids on neighboring schools using the strongest and toughest of Hawes students as her "army." Each time the Hawes army invades another school it takes over the building, confiscates all valuable materials such as computers and books, and brings them back to Hawes. This army also rounds up a number of students from these neighboring schools and brings them back to be the principal's servants.

I asked them to explain the connection between the principal's spirited promotion of the Columbus myth and the invasions of neighboring schools. T.J., the first to understand the analogy, explained to the class: "The principal tried to get everyone to love Columbus because she was doing almost the same thing that he did. If she got the kids to think Columbus was great then they would think she was too." To convey this line of thinking to our audience, Rob—the student who had first asked "Why the lies?"—wrote: "With what many teachers are telling kids and with what most books say about Columbus it makes it seem like it's okay to invade someone else's land and take over. But it's not okay and people should know that. It's time that people learn the truth."

While preparing the documentary, my students critiqued a number of conventional biographies on Columbus found in our school library. Using an evaluation guide by Bill Bigelow,[12] they analyzed these books for bias, omissions, and outright lies. In the documentary, several children shared the most glaring problems with these books and warned their audience to question all that they read and to "do their own research."

Throughout the several weeks of preparing the documentary, my students' energy level was high because they believed they earlier had chosen the important task of telling the other side of the Columbus story. My students were convinced that Columbus was wrong and what he did to the Tainos was unfair. It was now extremely important for my students to have the opportunity to produce social change. During the year, they had learned about numerous social protest movements and now it was their turn to make history, to take a stand and resist.

Initially, my students wanted to tell the other side to their younger schoolmates. Instead, since they created a rather sophisticated documentary, my students performed for the other fourth graders and for the fifth graders and parents. They presented the documentary just three days before the last day of

school, precluding substantial critical follow-up work with the audience. However, the documentary did have a strong impact on the audience. One student
viewer said: "I feel very sad about what happened to the Tainos and really mad
that I never learned this before. I wonder what else we haven't learned the truth
about." Another student later wrote in his journal: "Columbus didn't explore
the new world. He invaded it. He cut off people's hands because he was very
greedy for gold. I think he is a very bad man. A lot of people I've met think that
Columbus is very good. Once I tell them what he really did they tell more
people so everyone who thought he was nice and did good things knows what
he really did. I don't know why he set a flag down and claimed the land for
Spain when he could plainly see that people already lived there."

The fifth grade teachers, as a result of the documentary, have revised
their unit on "The Age of Exploration," making it much more critical. Fortu-
nately, they were moved rather than alienated by the presentation. The teachers
launched this year's exploration unit with a discussion of last year's Columbus
documentary. We made a video of the documentary and, this year, I used it to
initiate my classes' study of Columbus.

When viewed in the larger context of an ongoing struggle for social justice, the impact of my students' activist project is modest. But when I consider
the effect it had on individual students, the power of the project is heartening.
My students felt empowered, however briefly, as social activists and believed
they had a mandate and the ability to make a difference.

Notes

1. Linda Christensen, "Unlearning the Myths that Bind Us," *Rethinking Schools*
(May/June 1991): 15.

2. Bill Bigelow, "Talking Back to Columbus," *Rethinking Columbus* (Milwaukee: Rethinking Schools, 1991) 43. Also see Bill Bigelow, "Discovering Columbus:
Rereading the Past" and "Once Upon a Genocide," *Rethinking Columbus* 6–9, 23–30.

3. See Bigelow, "Once Upon a Genocide" for a critical analysis of elementary
level biographies on Columbus.

4. See page 101 for Bigelow's description of this exercise.

5. Tina Thomas, "The Untold Story," *Rethinking Columbus* 32.

6. Hans Konig, *Columbus: His Enterprise* (New York: Monthly Review Press,
1991); Kirkpatrick Sale, *The Conquest of Paradise: Christopher Columbus and the
Colombian Legacy* (New York: NAL/Dutton, 1991).

7. Francine Jacobs, *The Tainos: The People Who Welcomed Columbus* (New
York: G.P. Putnam's Sons, 1992); Milton Meltzer, *Columbus and the World Around Him*
(New York: Franklin Watts, 1990). Also see Michael Dorris, *Morning Girl* (New York:
Hyperion, 1992).

8. My students read most of chapter 9 in Meltzer's book and chapter 2 in Jacobs's
for background on the Tainos. I gave them a good deal of instructional support for these
texts (e.g., vocabulary, explanations, and discussion) as the materials are written on a

middle school level. I also wrote a summarized and simplified version for them of Jose Barreiro, "A Note on the Tainos," *Confronting Columbus,* ed. John Yewell, Chris Dodge, and Jan DeSirey (North Carolina: McFarland, 1992).

9. See Meltzer 93 and Konig 53–54.

10. Several acts of resistance are described in Jacobs 12 and Bigelow 40.

11. Bigelow 9.

12. See Bigelow 8.

13. Interested teachers who wish to see the quotations used as springboards for class discussions should contact me at: 335 Fifth Avenue, Saddle Brook, NJ 07662. I would like to thank Bill Bigelow, Linda Christensen, and David Sehr for their thoughtful comments on earlier drafts of this article.

Appendix A:
Pupils' Script on Workers Is Ruled Out

Evelyn Nieves

On the last day of school, with a party scheduled, Maria Sweeney's fourth-grade class at the Hawes School was still brooding over the demise of their final project.

"This was our first really serious play," Jessica Greco said.

"We thought we could make a difference," said David Mishler.

And so it went as nineteen students sitting in a circle in the bright, new-looking suburban classroom tried to figure out why their play on Nike and Disney sweatshops had been canceled.

They had planned to perform the piece about conditions at Nike and Disney factories (with one skit about the McDonald's Happyland toy factories in Vietnam) for the whole school. But just before their final dress rehearsal, the principal scrapped the performance. The students could not possibly grasp the issue, she said. The play was not "age appropriate."

Censorship! the students cried. They fired off letters to district officials. But the decision stood: They could perform their play for their parents, in their classroom, and that was it. "Performing for our parents is not like teaching anybody anything," said Larry Fitzmaurice.

Even in Ridgewood, consistently described as having one of the best school districts in the country, it could be argued that ten-year-olds still learning long division can't understand the complexities of corporate exploitation of labor. But Ms. Sweeney's class, which chose the issue after reading an article on Nike in Time for Kids, delved into the subject for a full month.

"They chose this subject even though we hadn't studied it in depth," said Ms. Sweeney, who each year asks her students to choose a current or historic social-justice topic for an end-of-year play.

Under her guidance, the students watched reports on sweatshops on *48 Hours* and *Dateline*. They read articles on the Internet and in daily newspapers and newsweeklies. They wrote to Michael Eisner at Disney (and to Michael Jordan about Nike). They gathered information from the corporations and from workers' advocacy groups. They wrote letters from the point of view of corporate presidents to better understand them.

Ms. Marino, the school principal, remains convinced that the sweatshop issue is beyond the students' level. "They were just going around saying don't wear these clothes, don't go to Disney," she said. The play, she added, didn't strike a balance, didn't show "all the good things these corporations do."

The play became controversial when a parent of a student in another fourth-grade class raised objections in a letter to the district superintendent. Ms. Marino said she heard from other parents and some staff members and students. "Maria is a fabulous, fabulous teacher," Ms. Marino said. "She goes way beyond what's required." But, she added, this play did not work for fourth graders, let alone children in lower grades, who would also see it. With all the anti-Nike talk, she said, Maria Sweeney's class was "hurting students' feelings."

Ms. Sweeney's students said they had gotten heat from other students who could not fathom criticizing Nike, lord of all labels.

Some students said their parents were a little wary about the idea of the play being performed. But two mothers visiting the class said that most parents were upset that it was cancelled. "The school could have limited the play to third, fourth, and fifth graders," said Andrea Mishler, David's mother. "Or parents could have signed a form if they didn't want their children to watch."

Jeanne Russo, whose daughter Josie is in the class, helped gather props and edit the script. "There is not a child in here who does not know what they're talking about," she said. "For Josie, this has taught her how to be a thinker and not take something for granted."

Students agreed. "I know what's happening out there now," said Han Park.

Han was so upset by the play's cancellation that he poured his heart out in his letter to the district: "We were learning about this for a month, learning it inside out. Three days until the actual play . . . then you stopped everything. Every single person in the class is even sadder than sad. Tears ran down my face. The world seemed to have ended. It's like I live in a world with no heart."

What upset him so much? "These workers are not being treated as humans," Han said quietly. "They're like dolls being bitten by dogs who are the bosses."

Appendix B:
Banned in Jersey, Welcomed on Broadway

Stan Karp

The show closed after one night on Broadway, but it was a smash success nonetheless. On October 27, Maria Sweeney's fourth-grade class finally got to present "Justice, Do It!," an original play they wrote last spring about sweatshop labor conditions in Nike and Disney manufacturing plants. Less than a week before the play was to be performed at Hawes Elementary School in Ridgewood, NJ, it was canceled by school officials who deemed it inappropriate for young children.

It was an act of censorship familiar in many schools, where efforts to bring thorny social issues into the classroom often run up against sanitized curricula and nervous administrators fearful of controversy. Issues of social justice are frequently deemed "too political" for the classroom, while the equally political implications of more traditional, mainstream viewpoints—for example those that celebrate patriotic or historical myths—are regularly overlooked.

What was uncommon in this case, however, was the high-profile publicity that followed the play's cancellation, and eventually led to a triumphant performance at the Roundabout Theater in the heart of New York City's theatre district.

Sweeney's students had chosen the sweatshop theme for their year-end play and social studies unit. During her five years as a teacher in Ridgewood, an upscale community known for its excellent schools, Sweeney made it a practice to let children end the year by picking a subject to explore in more depth and to dramatize for the school. Previous classes had chosen Columbus' voyages, South African elections, a famous textile strike out of the labor history of the nearby city of Paterson, and the Montgomery bus boycott. Last year some current events discussions had raised the issue of poorly paid, poorly treated workers, including young children, who made products abroad for two companies very familiar to Hawes' students: Nike and Disney. The class enthusiastically selected the topic and began their research.

Sweeney drew materials from a variety of mainstream news sources. She showed videos from CBS' *48 Hours* on "Nike in Vietnam" and NBC's *Dateline* about child labor in China and Indonesia. She took articles from the *New York Times, U.S. News and World Report,* and *Time for Kids.* These were supplemented with materials from Global Exchange and the National Labor Committee, watchdog groups that promote awareness of exploitative labor practices by U.S.-owned corporations.

Students also wrote for and received materials from the companies themselves, which denied or minimized the charges of worker abuse. They found other resources on the Internet, made charts, and scoured their homes for Nike and Disney products. As a guest speaker, Sweeney invited Jeff Ballinger, a former grant administrator for the Agency for International Development. Ballinger formed a media/information group called Press for Change after spending many years in Asia researching and writing about labor conditions.

Sweeney helped students sift the materials they found for information and for signs of bias. "Throughout this process," she says, "the children were encouraged to consider the information and form their own opinions." Finally, they began to dramatize the information they had compiled into a play.

The play begins with students on the Hawes playground discussing what they'd learned about the people and practices behind the Nike sneakers and Disney toys kids like so much. The scene shifts to a McDonald's where kids are eating a "happy meal" and enjoying the Disney toys that come with it. A Vietnamese student tells his friends about his sister and other Vietnamese teenagers who worked for $2 a day and suffered chemical poisoning on the job while making such products.

Next, the audience is taken to a hut in Haiti where the family's income from making *101 Dalmations* pajamas for Disney doesn't provide enough to eat or allow the mother to stay home with a sick child. Another scene, set in a Haitian factory, shows workers abused for talking about organizing to improve conditions.

Other scenes depict Disney CEO Michael Eisner in his office counting his profits ("one million . . . two million"), as Mickey and Minnie Mouse enter and threaten to turn in their ears unless Disney cleans up its act: "Lots of people out there in this country, many of them kids, are very angry about how the workers in your factories are treated," Mickey and Minnie tell Eisner. "Their lives are nothing like ours, but they're people just like us. . . . They want to be able to feed their kids and send them to school." Eisner is unmoved ("six million, seven million . . ." he resumes as they leave). Another scene shows Vietnamese workers making Nike sneakers for 20 cents an hour who are not permitted to stop long enough to get a drink or go to the bathroom. Like much of the play, the episode dramatizes information drawn from the monitoring reports of human rights groups.

Other scenes show Michael Jordan in an imaginary confrontation with one of his children who says she'd be "happy with a lot less" and just wants "people to be treated right"; and a stockholder being dragged away by security after trying to challenge Nike president Phil Knight at a meeting.

The play ends back at the Hawes playground with students talking about where all this "really depressing" information came from and what they can do about it.

Boycotts, letter writing, protests at home, and labor organizing abroad by Third World workers are the suggestions they come up with. "If we can just get tons and tons of people to join in this movement, I think we can make a difference," one says. "Let's get started!"

Sweeney's students were pumped up about the prospects of bringing their concerns to their schoolmates. As student Josie Russo said later, "We wanted to do this play. We wrote the whole script. We learned our lines. We brought in every single prop. . . . We were doing this play not just to do this play, but to change the minds of the children out there. . . . Not one single kid in the audience we hoped to perform for knew where their sneakers and toys came from. We wanted to change that."

But on a Friday afternoon last June, as Monday's scheduled performance neared, Sweeney was informed by her principal, Cathy Marino, that the show would be canceled. A parent of a Hawes' student, though not one in Sweeney's class, had seen a copy of the script and had written to Superintendent Fred Stokely complaining that Sweeney was "politicizing" the classroom and imposing her own views on the children. Sweeney had been made aware of the complaint, and in fact had responded with a detailed letter to Stokely explaining how the topic was chosen, what resources she had used, including the information from Nike and Disney, and offering to meet with the superintendent and the parent to discuss things further.

But Stokely left the fate of the play up to principal Marino, who along with assistant superintendent Deborah Pearce, decided to cancel the show for the school and allow only a performance for parents in Sweeney's classroom. Though the administration later claimed it was concerned primarily about the play's suitability for younger children at the K–5 school, it apparently never considered allowing a performance for grades 3, 4, or 5. Marino also indicated strongly that she thought both the sweatshop unit and the play were inappropriate for Sweeney's fourth graders.

Sweeney recalls being stunned by the news. Her experience in the district had given her no reason to expect such censorship. In the past, occasional complaints from parents had always been handled by discussing specific concerns and explaining the overall curriculum context of particular activities. But now Sweeney had to tell her students the play was off. It wasn't easy.

One student, Jessica Greco, remembered, "After lunch we came back to the classroom all happy and laughing. We were excited about the play, saying that we couldn't wait until Monday. But when our teacher told us the decision, we all stopped laughing and just froze. It was so quiet you could hear a pin drop, but not for long. Soon there was disbelief, arguing and some yelling. Two people got very upset and cried."

Since neither the principal nor the superintendent ever spoke to the children directly, Sweeney did her best to explain the administration's reasons as they were given to her. School authorities maintained that the issues were complicated and young children could not understand them clearly. Later Marino would say the play wasn't balanced and didn't show "all the good things these corporations do." Stokely told reporters, "The heads of the companies, Nike and Disney, were characterized in an extreme manner, as really being evil."

Sweeney's students seemed to agree that a "terrible thing" had been done, but in their minds it was the school administration that had done it. They wrote eloquent letters of protest.

Ordinarily things might have ended there, with the disappointed students limited to a classroom performance for parents and Sweeney wondering what the implications of the incident might be for her teaching, and perhaps her job. However, when Jeff Ballinger of Press for Change returned to Hawes to catch the play, he was surprised to find the venue had been changed from the large multipurpose room to Room 108. After hearing the story, he contacted a labor reporter at the *New York Times,* who in turn gave the information to one of the Times' New Jersey reporters.

On June 26, Evelyn Nieves devoted her "Our Town" column to the story of the fourth grade play that was banned in Ridgewood. She recounted the events, reporting all sides, sympathetically quoting parents and students as well as district officials.

As everyone soon learned, a lot of people read the *New York Times.*

One was Scott Ellis, who saw the story while riding the subway to work at the Roundabout Theater where he is resident director. Ellis was impressed by the fact that the students were using drama to express their ideas and appalled by the censorship. "How can you say to fourth graders, one, that you don't know what you're talking about, and two, that you can't say it anyway?" he asked. Ellis began to look into the possibility of making his own theatre available.

Disney's Michael Eisner also reads the *New York Times.* According to a story that filtered through the halls at Hawes, Eisner saw the article the morning it appeared while in a meeting with some people who happened to be familiar with Ridgewood and the school. When Eisner read about the principal who thought the children's play deserved cancellation because it didn't show "all the good things these corporations do," Eisner wanted to call to say thank you, and, reportedly, he did.

The *Times* article triggered a flood of other reactions, letters, and media coverage. Sweeney received calls from civil liberties columnist Nat Hentoff and the populist radio commentator Jim Hightower. Ridgewood school officials received letters of protest from parents, labor advocates, and opponents of censorship.

Michael Robbins, the editor of *Audubon* magazine, saw the article and wrote to Sweeney: "Of course what your principal did was censorship; that's the plain, unvarnished truth. And of course ten-year-olds can understand injustice. . . . It also appears to me that they have learned some unexpected lessons from this episode: they have learned about the incendiary power of facts, good reporting, and the exposure of injustice. They have learned how some adults— allegedly leaders and role models—can chicken out when faced with a real-life controversy. They have learned how some grownups fear the power of big,

famous corporations. And they have learned that sometimes it takes real courage to seek out the truth and then say it right out loud."

Along with letters of support and protest came Scott Ellis' offer to help
bring the play to Broadway. A cautious Sweeney hesitantly checked to see if
the superintendent would object. Stokely gave his approval, as long as the
school itself had no official connection to the event.

As the new school year rolled around, the play's authors, now fifth graders
and no longer in Sweeney's class, devoted many after-school hours to working
with Ellis and other theatre personnel to prepare their production for Broadway.
Sweeney and parents put in many hours as well.

As opening night approached, there was another wave of publicity. Sweeney
and some of the students appeared on local all-news radio stations and other
programs, including one of NBC's weekend network morning shows. There
was front-page coverage in the major New Jersey papers as well as reports in
Education Week, the *National News Reporter,* and the New York dailies.

Though she appreciated the publicity and the support it generated, Sweeney
also recalls how superficial much of the coverage was. Most media outlets were
more interested in playing up the "kids' play gets to Broadway" angle than in
dealing with the substantive labor or economic issues involved. Reporters often tended to reduce the issue of sweatshop labor practices and multinational
corporate exploitation of Third World countries to one of "child labor," even
though the use of underage employees was but one aspect of the problems
being raised.

Ridgewood school officials, at least some of whom were clearly uncomfortable with the content of the play and of Sweeney's curriculum, increasingly
confined their public reservations to the matter of the play's "inappropriate-
ness" for the youngest children in Hawes school. As the October premiere approached and the media spotlight grew, district officials spoke equally of the
"wonderful opportunity children were getting to work with theatre professionals," and Superintendent Stokely attended the performance and praised it to
Board of Education members afterwards.

Finally, those connected to the Roundabout Theater (which is coinciden-
tally located next to one of Disney's busy retail outlets) stressed on a number
of occasions that the theatre was supporting the right of the students to express
themselves through drama, not endorsing the political message of the play, although many of the staff volunteers were clearly sympathetic.

Taken together, these responses suggested that being young was hardly the
only, or even the main, obstacle to grappling with the central issues involved,
namely the right of children to take a public stand on issues of social justice and
the merits of the stand these particular children took.

October 27 was an off-night for the Roundabout Theater's regular run of
the musical *1776* (which Ellis pointedly noted is about the country's founding
struggle to establish a democracy). Instead, Kids for Fairness presented *Justice,
Do It!* The 500-seat theatre was filled to near capacity with a celebratory crowd
of parents, supporters, students, and human rights' activists.

The lobby was decorated with artwork about the labor issues, done by other school children in solidarity with the Hawes' students. There were large photos of the student actors and a professional playbill complete with "Who's Who in the Cast" bios, such as the one for "Han Park (Boss/Narrator/Worker) [who] is 10 years old and was born in Korea. His favorite subject is math and he enjoys building rockets. He has guppies, goldfish, and hamsters."

Theatergoers also were handed a folder with background information on the topic, a resource list, and a petition to circulate. The combination of education, research, and activism that first led Sweeney's students to create their play at Hawes was not left behind when they brought it to the "big time."

In the aftermath of what was alternately an alarming, intense, and exhilarating experience, Sweeney knew that her students had been through something they'd never forget. Some may mostly remember the bright lights and attention. But for others the lasting memories will be about the risks and rewards of taking a stand for something you believe in.

As Sweeney says, "I believe that I am preparing children to participate as critical and caring participants in a public democracy. . . . I am giving them experience in taking a stand on important issues and trying to effect social change. I feel this kind of teaching is essential."

To charges that she is "politicizing the classroom," Sweeney would respond that nearly all teaching is value-laden and, in a sense, "political." The solution is not to avoid controversial topics or to pretend that complete "neutrality" is possible or even desirable. Rather it's to present complicated issues fairly and with sensitivity to issues of intimidation and the rights of dissent. Even more important is to help students develop tools of critical social analysis so they can identify and evaluate for themselves the various interests that can influence the "free exchange of ideas."

The best defense against inappropriate political manipulation in the classroom is for students to learn how to critically examine different perspectives, whether they come from their teachers, their textbooks, or other "authoritative sources." They also need to learn that ideas and actions have real consequences and often involve moral choices. To pretend that such issues don't lay hidden behind many classroom lessons is itself a kind of censorship.

Finally, Sweeney reminds her critics that Disney, Nike, and other corporations have multimillion-dollar advertising budgets to get their views across to the public and to kids. Further, she underscores, the companies' views were prominently included in the materials given to her students. "The students had the opportunity to represent Nike or Disney's point of view in the play if they chose to," she said. "If the play is one-sided, it's because this is the side that the children took."

"Banned in Jersey, Welcomed on Broadway" by Stan Karp originally appeared in Rethinking Schools *12.2 (Winter 1997–98): 14–15. Reprinted with permission.*

7

Beyond Thanksgiving

Teaching About Native Americans of New England

Rosemary Agoglia

Editors' Notes: Rosemary Agoglia, of Amherst, Massachusetts'
Common School, effectively argues for the need to teach the story of
Native Americans to elementary students. Her students begin by examining the stereotypical portrayal of Native Americans in schools,
books, and popular culture. Then Agoglia represents Native Americans from their point of view. She does this with "in-depth studies"
of Native American culture over a period of four months. Agoglia's
methods offer students a critical awareness of how discrimination
develops. She shows how to employ a multicultural critical pedagogy within the restraints of a board-dictated curriculum.

Having made the decision to teach my class of twenty-four six-, seven-, and
eight-year-olds about the Native people of New England,[1] I began where most
curriculum development begins, with self education. Dissatisfied with the traditional approach to Native history as an adjunct to Colonial history, I began to
look for resources which would present the Native point of view. It was at this
point that I started to ask myself some important questions: Whose history is
this? Who is writing it? Does it tell the whole story?

I soon realized that these questions were not for me alone. They were as
important, if not more important, than the specific content contained in the many
books which lay before me. I had to include a way to involve my students in
pondering them. Thus we began our study of the Native people of New England.

The class was quite surprised when I introduced our study by asking them
if they had ever had any problems while playing with other people. Lots of
hands went up. After discussing the many ways these situations got resolved, I

asked those who had chosen to get help from an objective third party whether or not their stories ever sounded exactly the same as the stories of their opponents. Very few hands appeared. I asked them why they thought this was so: "Well he/she didn't know what I meant"; "That's just the way it felt to me"; "I didn't understand what he/she was trying to do."

The reasons went on and on. It became clear that we were on our way towards exploring the ideas of historical bias and the importance of hearing all the voices involved in any event in a way that elementary age children could understand. I then explained that for many hundreds of years Native people have been silenced, unable to tell their side of the story to others because for a very long time their history remained unwritten. Although it was passed on from generation to generation, it was never written down for others to read. Europeans, on the other hand, wrote much about themselves and the natives they encountered. Therefore, many of the books we have used to learn about New England history have had only one side of the story. At this point we all agreed that in order to get the whole story we needed to uncover the Native American history as well as the history of Colonial America.

The first step was to look at who *we* are, individually and as a society, and discover how that might affect how we think about Native people. I gathered together a variety of books about Indians.[2] Some of them, such as Bennett Cerf's riddle books and Maurice Sendak's *Alligators All Around,* contained offensive illustrations and stereotyping. (For a more complete list of questionable books, see *Books Without Bias* by Seale and Slapin, listed in the "Teacher Resources.") Others, including most of those cited in the bibliography, were accurate in their content. I asked my class to examine these books, keeping in mind how Native people were portrayed. They were to decide whether the material they identified might be insulting or hurtful to a Native person or whether it showed respect toward Native people. They became the researchers. They examined the materials looking for a voice without feeling responsible for what they heard. Their goal was to look, listen, and understand. Although their understanding could not change what had happened, it certainly could affect the future.

They discovered pictures of Native people threatening non-Native people, pictures of animals used to represent Native people, pictures of Native people living and dressing as they did long ago, pictures which made Native people look silly. There were also books which contained photographs of Native people in modern dress, working at various jobs, attending powwows, working at traditional arts, and telling their history. The discussion which followed helped us all to see how people might develop mistaken ideas about how Indians behave, think, and live. While one picture or story might not be enough to create a negative image, the many pictures and stories we examined, if they were all we saw, certainly could. This exercise was one which we returned to many times during our study of the Natives of New England. Children questioned the pictures they saw in books. They objected when they read phrases like "the last of the Pequots" and they wrote letters to the Atlanta Braves during the World Series explaining why they thought they should change their name. Having engaged in some exercises which helped us better understand how we look at others, we were ready to learn about the history and culture of the Natives of New England.

My development of the historical component of this curriculum was shaped by the guidelines developed at my school[3] for what we call in-depth studies. Having decided to study the Algonquian-speaking people of New England, I introduced into the classroom displays and exhibits that invited questions and exploration: materials and tools used to make wampum, pictures of New England Natives both past and present, displays showing Natives' uses of plants and animals. Activities at the beginning of each day introduced the study through cooking (preparing Native foods), artwork (making beaded leather pouches, porcupine quill jewelry, baskets), scientific exploration (methods of food preservation and tracking) and literature (readings of the many myths and legends).

First we set the people in time and space. After meeting with an archaeologist to discuss how we learn about the distant past, the class examined and sorted stone artifacts on their own. They debated questions of function and what that might tell us about these people who lived so very long ago. A time line put in place by the class encircled the room as a constant reminder of what we meant when we said Native people were here long ago. Next we learned about the people. Their spiritual beliefs were conveyed through the many myths and legends we shared (see Bruchac and Caduto). We studied Native American appearance, traditional dress, food, and shelters through the many activities laid out in the various curriculum guides. Preparing Native foods, building a wigwam, creating a miniature Native village scene, and dressing Native dolls were just some of the activities which helped us to understand and appreciate traditional Native life. In each case materials which were authentic as possible were used. Finally, we looked at the ever widening circles of interaction: family life, community life, and contact with people from other cultures. Columbus Day provided us with a very sobering opportunity to examine what could and did happen when two cultures meet. Children interviewed their parents about what they had learned about Columbus Day in school. They carefully examined the many children's books available on the legacy of Columbus. Once again we found ourselves asking: Whose history is this? Who is telling it? Does it tell the whole story? Vicki Liestman's book on Columbus Day did the best job of answering these questions for young children.

A trip to the Institute of American Indian Studies in Washington, Connecticut; excerpts from the Massachusetts Educational Technologies series *People of the First Light;* and visits from Native people were just some of the ways we underscored the continuance of the many people we learned about into the present day. Eager to share what we had learned at the end of our four month study, we planned a feast with another group in our school who had been studying the Native peoples of the plains. We exchanged foods, traditions, and plays and then listened together as Dovie Thomason, an Oglala Lakota, Kiowa Apache storyteller drew us into the powerful world of Native American stories. Surrounded by parents and friends, warm and well fed, we listened to Dovie's words and learned about ourselves while we laughed and learned about the people who had been telling these stories for thousands of years.

It became clear that each of these experiences provided a context for understanding Native people. Without such a context it would be easy for students to think of Native people merely as a group who lived an interesting life in the woods and made neat little things. Such a shallow image of this culture freezes the people in the past. Indian becomes synonymous with someone dressed in deerskin clothing who hunted for food. The knowledge that Native people of today live in houses, have modern day jobs, and wear modern day clothing is an essential part of the context we need to provide in our teaching. As educators we need to be educated about what we teach, to become sensitized to aspects of another person's culture. This cannot be done by looking at things out of context. In doing so we not only shortchange our students but we run the risk of offending those very people about whom we hope to learn.

Whether we are handed a history or social studies curriculum or are free to decide for ourselves what we may teach, it is important for us as teachers to build bridges between historical studies and the study of cultural diversity. While our general goal might be defined as helping students gain a historical perspective about the peoples and places of the past, a second goal should be to support the value of diversity by helping students develop an appreciation and understanding of cultural commonalities and differences.

Although these are equally important goals, the first goal of historical perspective is the one which consumes much of our time and energy. With careful research and organization, one can pass on a great deal of information about a culture and its people. At best, this means of investigation begins to illustrate how a particular group of people lived, and the events and environment that shaped their existence. However, there are pitfalls connected to these cultural surveys. I have seen many attempts at cultural curriculum which resemble little more than "tourist teaching"—looking at that which is exotic and exciting in a culture in an attempt to interest the student, without ever really "seeing" the people or listening to what they have to say.

The second goal, valuing cultural diversity, is less straightforward. How can we help our students learn to listen to the many voices who are both the makers and subjects of history? Success requires introspection as well as careful observation. In attempting to build an understanding and appreciation of others, we as teachers must understand who *we* are and how that might affect what we see and understand. In this endeavor, we find our own educational experience returning to haunt us, usually taking the form of perpetuating a Eurocentric view of history, in which we identify with a particular interpretation. While the facts remain unambiguous—e.g., that Columbus landed in the "New World" in 1492—the meaning we give to them helps to shape their importance. Therefore, it becomes more important for us to stop identifying with one interpretation and start asking ourselves important questions about the histories that we teach, questions such as: Whose history is this? Who is telling it? What is the purpose of the historian? Who is not there? Why might they not be represented? These questions are all ways of trying to see the whole picture, of including all the voices and views that shape our understanding of the past as well as our awareness of the present. Since there was no definitive source through which to examine all of these questions, I found myself drawing from the many resources cited in the bibliography below. The more perspectives I took in, the more I was able to understand what did happen in the past, whether yesterday or five hundred years ago.

Historical bias, prejudice, and racism are not topics to be reserved for older children. We can't continue to simply teach about how the Wampanoags helped the Pilgrim settlers survive their first winter and how they then celebrated the "First Thanksgiving" together. Merely replacing the stereotype of the "savage Indian," who lived a primitive and somewhat disdainful existence, with that of the "noble savage," who graciously came to the aid of the Pilgrims only to then fade away, is to trade one stereotype for another.

The Wampanoag, Abanaki, Niantic, and Pequot peoples (to name just a few of the many groups which make up the many Indian nations of the Northeast) have a history which began thousands of years before their encounters with the Europeans. Their cultures, rich in history, traditions, beliefs, and ways of life, deserve to be studied in their own right. Their voices are a part of the history of the past and, if one is listening, can still be heard today.

There is much to be gained for all of us as we learn about the first peoples of New England. Their relationship to the environment and their use of resources provide us with many valuable models. By learning about other people, their past and present, our ideas of culture and diversity are broadened. The richness and variety of peoples' beliefs, tastes, and traditions are appreciated rather than frowned upon. We also come to understand better who we are in relation to the world in which we live. We learn how people adapt and change over time. We begin to see how and why the realities of discrimination and conflict develop. The fabric of New England's history becomes stronger as a result of our weaving in all of these threads. It is important that our children not feel responsible for the actions of those who have gone before them. But, by allowing our students to hear the voices that have been silenced, by encouraging them to examine books and other media more critically, we help them become more thoughtful and independent thinkers. In this examination of the past lies our hope for the future.

Notes

1. I use this term as a shorthand throughout this article. However when talking to my students I referred to the specific tribe upon which we focused at any given time. These included the Wampanoag, Pequots, Nipmuk, Narragansett, and Abanaki.

2. I use the terms Native people, Native American and Indian interchangeably throughout this article since to the best of my knowledge none of these terms is more preferred by the people to whom these labels refer.

3. The Common School, an independent elementary school in Amherst, Massachusetts.

Classroom Resources

Aliki. *Corn is Maize, The Gift of the Indians.* New York: Thomas Y. Crowell, 1976.

Batherman, Muriel. *Before Columbus.* Boston, MA: Houghton Mifflin, 1981.

Bradford, William et al. *Homes In The Wilderness: A Pilgrim's Journal of Plymouth Plantation in 1620* (ed. M. W. Brown). Hamden, CT: Linnet Books, 1988.

Bruchac, Joseph. *Return of the Sun: Native American Tales From the Northeast Woodlands.* Watsonville, CA: Crossing Press, 1989.

———. *The Faithful Hunter: Abanaki Stories.* Greenfield Center, New York: Bowman Books, 1988.

———. *The Wind Eagle and Other Abanaki Stories.* Greenfield Center, NY: Bowman Books, 1985.

Cass, James. *Ekahotan—Indians of the Eastern Woodland Series.* Canada: D.C. Heath, 1983.

Cohlene, Terri. *Little Firefly, An Algonquian Legend.* New Jersey: Watermill Press, 1990.

Crompton, Anne Elliot. *The Winter Wife.* Boston, MA: Little Brown, 1975.

Day, Michael, and Whitmore, Carol. *Berry Ripe Moon.* Maine: Tide Grass Press, 1977.

Jones, Hettie, ed. *The Trees Stand Shining.* New York: Walker, 1971.

Lavine, Sigmund A. *Indian Corn and Other Gifts.* New York: Dodd, Mead, 1974.

Liestman, Vicki. *Columbus Day.* Minneapolis, MN: Carolrhoda Books, 1991.

Ortiz, Simon. *The People Shall Continue.* San Francisco, CA: Children's Book Press, 1988.

Peters, Russell. *The Wampanoag of Mashpee.* Massachusetts: Nimrod Press, 1987.

Sewall, Marcia. *The People of the Breaking Day.* New York: Atheneum, 1990.

Shemi, Bonnie. *Houses of Bark.* Chicago, IL: Children's Press, 1983.

Whitehead, Ruth Holmes, and McGee, Harold. *The Micmac: How Their Ancestors Lived 500 Years Ago.* Canada: Nimbus Publishing Limited, 1983

Wilbur, Keith. *The New England Indians.* Chester, CT: Globe Pequot Press, 1978.

———. *Indian Handcrafts.* Chester, CT: Globe Pequot Press, 1990.

Wolfson, Evelyn. *Growing Up Indian.* New York: Walker, 1986.

Yolen, Jane. *Encounter.* New York: Harcourt, Brace, Jovanovich, 1992.

Teacher Resources

American Friends Service Committee. *The Wabanake of Maine and the Maritimes: A Resource Book about Penobscot, Passamaquoddy, Maliseet, Micmac and Abanaki Indians.* Maine: The Maine Indian Program, 1989.

Appleton, Leroy. *American Indian Designs and Decoration.* New York: Dover, 1971.

Bjorklund, Karna L. *The Indians of Northeastern America.* New York: Dodd, 1969.

Brandin, Judith A. *The Native People of the Northeast Woodlands.* New York: The Museum of the American Indian, Heye Foundation, 1990.

Bruchac, Joseph and Caduto, Michael. *Keepers of the Earth.* Colorado: Fulcrum Inc., 1988.

―――. *Keepers of the Animals.* Colorado: Fulcrum Inc., 1991.

Bernstein, Bonnie and Blair, Leigh. *Native American Craft Workshop.* Belmont, CA: David S. Lake, 1982.

Culin, Stewart. *Games of the North American Indian.* New York: Dover, 1975.

Farson, Laurie Weinstein. *The Wampamoag.* New York: Chelsea House, 1989.

Kavasch, Barrie. *Native Harvest.* New York: Random House, 1979.

Molloy, Anne. *Wampum.* New York: Hasting House, 1977.

Robinson, Barbara. *Native American Sourcebook: A Teacher's Resource on New England Native Peoples.* Concord, MA: Concord Museum, 1988.

Seale, Doris and Slapin, Beverly, eds. *Books Without Bias: Through Indian Eyes.* Berkeley, CA: Oyate, 1988.

Wilber, Keith. *Land of the Nonotucks.* Massachusetts: Northampton Historical Society, 1987.

Wolfson, Evelyn. *American Indians: Habitats.* New York: David McKay, 1979.

―――. *American Indian Tools and Ornaments.* New York: David McKay, 1979.

―――. *American Indian Utensils.* New York: David McKay, 1979.

8

On the Road to Cultural Bias

A Critique of The Oregon Trail *CD-ROM*

William Bigelow

Editors' Notes: In this chapter, Bill Bigelow offers a critique of the popular educational CD-ROM, *The Oregon Trail.* In this program, he found a superficial representation of women, African Americans, and Mexicans, and players assuming a white, male perspective. He also reports the exclusion of women's and slaves' actual-lived experience, slavery itself, and the black exclusion laws in Oregon. Further, Bigelow sees the program ignoring the causes of conflict with Native Americans and the destruction of natural resources and Native hunting grounds. Bigelow believes computer-assisted instruction can carry the same cultural biases as books do and warns against the computer as a substitute for teachers. He concludes his piece with ways to develop a critical computer literacy—questions to be asked for an investigation of the cultural biases of CD-ROMs and other educational computer materials.

The critics all agree: *The Oregon Trail* (1993) is one of the greatest educational computer games ever produced. *Prides' Guide to Educational Software* awarded it five stars for being "a wholesome, absorbing historical simulation," and "multi-ethnic," to boot (Pride & Pride, 1992, p. 419). The new version, *The Oregon Trail II* (1994), is the "best history simulation we've seen to date," according to Warren Buckleitner, editor of *Children's Software Review Newsletter* (The Oregon Trail II, 1994). Susan Schilling, a key developer of *The Oregon Trail II* and recently hired by *Star Wars* film maker George Lucas to head Lucas Learning Ltd., promises new interactive CD-ROMs targeted at children 6 to 15 years old and concentrated in math and language arts (Armstrong, 1996).

Because interactive CD-ROMs like *The Oregon Trail* are encyclopedic in the amount of information they offer, and because they allow students a seemingly endless number of choices, the new software may appear educationally progressive. CD-ROMs seem tailor-made for the classrooms of tomorrow. They are hands-on and "student-centered." They are generally interdisciplinary— for example, *The Oregon Trail II* blends reading, writing, history, geography, math, science, and health. And they are useful in multi-age classrooms because they allow students of various knowledge levels to "play" and learn. But like the walls of a maze, the choices built into interactive CD-ROMs also channel participants in very finite directions. The CD-ROMs are programmed by people—people with particular cultural biases—and children who play the new computer games encounter the biases of the programmers (Bowers, 1988). Just as we would not invite a stranger into our classrooms and then leave the room, we as teachers need to become aware of the political perspectives of CD-ROMs and to equip our students to "read" them critically.

At one level, this article is a critical review of *The Oregon Trail* CD-ROMs. I ask what knowledge is highlighted, what is hidden, and what values are imparted as students play the games. But I also reflect on the nature of the new electronic curricula, and suggest some questions teachers can ask before choosing to use these materials with their students. Finally, I offer some classroom activities that might begin to develop students' critical computer literacy.

Playing the Game

In both *The Oregon Trail* and *The Oregon Trail II*, students become members of families and wagon trains crossing the Plains in the 1840s or 1850s on the way to the Oregon Territory. A player's objective, according to the game guidebook, is to safely reach the Oregon Territory with one's family, thereby "increasing one's options for economic success" (The Oregon Trail II, 1994).

The enormous number of choices offered in any one session—what to buy for the journey; the kind of wagon to take; whether to use horses, oxen, or mules; the size of the wagon train with which to travel; whom to "talk" to along the way; when and where to hunt; when to rest; and how fast to travel— is a kind of gentle seduction to students. It invites them to "try on this world view and see how it fits." In an interactive CD-ROM, students don't merely identify with a particular character, they actually adopt his or her frame of reference and act as if they were that character (Provenzo, 1991). In *The Oregon Trail*, a player quickly bonds with the "pioneer" maneuvering through the "wilderness."

In preparation for this article, I played *The Oregon Trail II* until my eyes became blurry. I can see its attraction to teachers. One can't play the game without learning a lot about the geography between Missouri and Oregon. (However, I hope I never have to ford another virtual river again.) Reading the trail guide as one plays teaches much about the ailments confronted on the Oregon Trail and some of the treatments. Students can learn a tremendous amount about the details of life for the trekkers to Oregon, including the kinds of wagons required, the supplies needed, the vegetation encountered along the route, and so forth. And the game has a certain multicultural and gender-fair veneer that, however limited, contrasts favorably with the white male-dominated texts of yesteryear. But as much as the game teaches, it *mis*-teaches more. In fundamental respects, *The Oregon Trail* is sexist, racist, culturally insensitive, and contemptuous of the earth. It imparts bad values and wrong history.

They Look Like Women, But . . .

To its credit, *The Oregon Trail II* includes large numbers of women. Although I didn't count, women appear to make up roughly half the people students encounter as they play. But this surface equity is misleading. Women may be present, but gender is not acknowledged as an issue in *The Oregon Trail*. For example, in the opening sequences, the game requires students to select a profession, any special skills they will possess, the kind of wagon to take, and the city from which to depart. Class is recognized as an issue—bankers begin with more money than saddle makers, for example—but not gender or race. A player cannot choose to be a female or African American.

Without acknowledging it, *The Oregon Trail* maneuvers students into thinking and acting as if they were all males. The game highlights a male lifestyle and poses problems that historically fell within the male domain, such as whether and where to hunt, which route to take, whether and what to trade, and whether to caulk a wagon or ford a river. However, as I began to read feminist scholarship on the Oregon Trail (e.g., Faragher & Stansell, 1992; Kesselman, 1976; Schlissel, 1992), I realized that women and men experienced the Trail differently. It's clear from reading women's diaries of the period that women played little or no role in deciding whether to embark on the trip, where to camp, which routes to take, and the like. In real life, women's decisions revolved around how to maintain a semblance of community under great stress, how "to preserve the home in transit" (Faragher & Stansell, 1992, p. 190). Women decided where to look for firewood or buffalo chips, how and what to cook using hot rocks, how to care for the children, and how to resolve conflicts between travelers, especially between the men.

These were real-life decisions, but, with the exception of treating illness, they're missing from *The Oregon Trail*. Students are rarely required to think about the intricacies of preserving "the home in transit" for 2000 miles. An *Oregon Trail II* information box on the screen informs a player when "morale" is high or low, but other than making better male-oriented decisions, what's a player to do? *The Oregon Trail* offers no opportunities to encounter the choices of the Trail as women of the time would have encountered them and to make decisions that might enhance community and thus "morale." As Lillian Schlissel (1992) concludes in her study, *Women's Diaries of the Westward Journey:*

> If ever there was a time when men and women turned their psychic energies toward opposite visions, the overland journey was that time. Sitting side by side on a wagon seat, a man and a woman felt different needs as they stared at the endless road that led into the New Country. (p. 15)

Similarly, *The Oregon Trail* fails to represent the *texture* of community life on the Trail. Students confront a seemingly endless stream of problems posed by *The Oregon Trail* programmers, but rarely encounter the details of life, especially that of women's lives. By contrast, in an article in the book, *America's Working Women,* Amy Kesselman (1976) includes this passage from the diary of one female trekker, Catherine Haun, in 1849:

> We women folk visited from wagon to wagon or congenial friends spent an hour walking ever westward, and talking over our home life "back in the states" telling of the loved ones left behind; voicing our hopes for the future in the far west and even whispering, a little friendly gossip of pioneer life. High teas were not popular but tatting, knitting, crocheting, exchanging receipts for cooking beans or dried apples or swopping food for the sake of variety kept us in practice of feminine occupations and diversions. (p. 71)

The male orientation of *The Oregon Trail* is brought into sharp relief in the game's handling of Independence Day commemoration. Students-as-pioneers are asked if they wish to "Celebrate the Fourth!" If so, they click on this option and hear loud "Yahoos" and guns firing. Compare this image to the communal preparations described in Enoch Conyers' 1852 diary:

> A little further on is a group of young ladies seated on the grass talking over the problem of manufacturing "Old Glory" to wave over our festivities. The question arose as to where we are to obtain the material for the flag. One lady brought forth a sheet. This gave the ladies an idea. Quick as thought another brought a skirt for the red stripes. . . . Another lady ran to her tent and brought forth a blue jacket, saying: "Here, take this; it will do for the field." Needles and thread were soon secured and the ladies went at their task with a will, one lady remarking that "Necessity is the mother of invention," and the answer came back, "Yes, and the ladies of our company are equal to the task." (Hill, 1989, p. 58)

The contrast of the "Yahoos" and gunfire of *The Oregon Trail* to the collective female exhilaration described in the diary excerpt is striking. This contrast alerted me to something so obvious that it took me a while to recognize. In *The Oregon Trail,* people don't talk to *each other,* they all talk to you, the player. Everyone in *The Oregon Trail*-constructed world directs her or his conversation to you, underscoring the simulation's individualistic ideology that all the world exists for *you,* the controller of the mouse. An *Oregon Trail* more alert to feminist insights and women's experiences would highlight relationships between people, would focus on how the experience affects our feelings for each other, and would feature how women worked with one another to create and maintain a community, as women's diary entries clearly reveal.

As I indicated, large numbers of women appear throughout *The Oregon Trail* simulation, and they often give good advice, perhaps better advice than the men we encounter. But *The Oregon Trail*'s abundance of women, and its apparent effort to be gender-fair, masks an essential problem: The choice-structure of the simulation privileges men's experience and virtually erases women's experience.

African Americans as Tokens

From the game's beginning, when a player starts off in Independence or St. Joseph's, Missouri, African Americans dot *The Oregon Trail* landscape. By and large, however, they are no more than black-colored white people. Although Missouri was a slave state throughout the Oregon Trail period, I never encountered the term "slavery" while playing the game. I found race explicitly acknowledged in only one exchange, when I "talked" to an African American woman along the trail. She said: "I'm Isabella. I'm traveling with the Raleighs and their people. My job is to keep after the cows and watch the children. My husband Fred is the ox-driver—best there is." I wondered if they were free or enslaved, and if we are to assume the Raleighs are white. I asked to know more, and Isabella said: "I was born in Delaware. My father used to tell me stories of Africa and promised one day we'd find ourselves going home. But I don't know if I'm getting closer or farther away with all this walking." The end. Like Missouri, Delaware was a slave state in antebellum days, but this is not shared with students. Isabella offers provocative details, but they hide more than they reveal about her identity and culture.

The Oregon Trail's treatment of African Americans reflects a superficial multiculturalism. Black people are present, but their lives aren't. Attending to matters of race requires more than including lots of black faces or having little girls "talk black": "I think it's time we be moving on now." (This little girl reappears from time to time to repeat these same words. A man who looks Mexican, likewise, shows up frequently to say, with a heavy accent: "Time is a-wasting. Let's head out!")

Although one's life prospects and world view in the 1840s and 1850s—as today—were dramatically shaped by one's race, this factor is invisible in *The Oregon Trail*. *The Oregon Trail* players know their occupations but not their racial identities, even though these identities were vital to the decisions the Oregon Trail travelers made before leaving on their journeys and along the way.

For example, many of the constitutions of societies that sponsored wagon trains specifically excluded blacks from making the trip west. Nonetheless, as Elizabeth McLagan (1980) points out in her history of blacks in Oregon, *A Peculiar Paradise*, blacks did travel the Oregon Trail, some as slaves, some as servants, and even some, like George Bush, as well-to-do pioneers. Race may not have seemed important to *The Oregon Trail* programmers but race mattered a great deal to Bush: Along the Trail, he confided to another emigrant that if he experienced too much prejudice in Oregon, he would travel south to California or New Mexico, and seek the protection of the Mexican government (McLagan, 1980).

And Bush had reason to be apprehensive: African Americans arriving in Oregon Territory during the 1840s and 1850s were greeted by laws barring them from residency. Two black exclusion laws were passed in the Oregon Territory in the 1840s, and a clause in the Oregon state constitution barring black residency was ratified in 1857 by a margin of eight to one—a clause, incidentally, not repealed until 1926.

Upon completion of one of my simulated Oregon Trail journeys, I clicked to see how my life turned out: "In 1855, Bill built a home on 463 acres of land in the Rogue River Valley of Oregon," experienced only "moderate success" and later moved to Medford, "establishing a small business that proved more stable and satisfying." Although *The Oregon Trail* simulation never acknowledges it, "Bill" must have been white because in 1850 the U.S. Congress passed the Oregon Donation Land Act granting 640 acres to free white males and their wives. It is unlikely that a black man, and much less a black woman, would have been granted land in 1855 or have been allowed to start a business in Medford some years later.

Why were whites so insistent that blacks not live in Oregon? The preamble of one black exclusion bill explained that "situated as the people of Oregon are, in the midst of an Indian population, it would be highly dangerous to allow free negroes and mulattoes to reside in the territory or to intermix with the Indians, instilling in their minds feelings of hostility against the white race . . ." (McLagan, 1980, p. 26). And Samuel Thurston, a delegate to Congress from the Oregon Territory, explained in 1850 why blacks should not be entitled to homestead in Oregon:

> The negroes associate with the Indians and intermarry, and, if their free ingress is encouraged or allowed, there would a relationship spring up between them and the different tribes, and a mixed race would ensue inimical to the whites, and the Indians being led on by the negro who is better acquainted with the customs, language, and manners of the whites, than the Indian, these savages would become much more formidable than they otherwise would, and long and bloody wars would be the fruits of the commingling of the races. It is the principle of self preservation that justifies the action of the Oregon legislature. (McLagan, 1980, pp. 30–31)

Thurston's argument carried the day. But *The Oregon Trail* programmers have framed the issues so that race seems irrelevant. Thus, once students-as-pioneers arrive in Oregon, most of them will live happily ever after—never considering the impact that race would have on living conditions.

Just Passing Through?

The Oregon Trail programmers are careful not to portray Indians as the "enemy" of westward trekkers. However, the simulation's superficial sympathy for Native groups masks a profound insensitivity to Indian cultures and to the earth that sustained these cultures. The simulation guidebook lists numerous Indian nations by name—and respectfully *calls* them "nations." The *The Oregon Trail* guidebook explains that emigrants' fear of Indians is "greatly exaggerated."

> Some travelers have been known to cross the entire breadth of the continent from the Missouri River to the Sierra Nevadas without ever laying eye on an Indian, except perhaps for occasional brief sightings from a distance. This is all well and good, for it is probably best for all parties concerned for emigrants and Indians to avoid contact with each other. Such meetings are often the source of misunderstandings, sometimes with regrettable consequences.

Emigrants often spread disease, according to the guidebook, which made the Indians "distrust and dislike" them. The guidebook further warns *The Oregon Trail* players not to over-hunt game in any one place as "few things will incur the wrath of the Indian peoples more than an overstayed welcome accompanied by the egregious waste of the natural resources upon which they depend."

The ideology embedded in *The Oregon Trail* and *The Oregon Trail II* is selfish and goal-driven: Emigrants should care about indigenous people only insofar as they need to avoid "misunderstanding" and incurring the wrath of potentially hostile natives. *The Oregon Trail* promotes an anthropocentric earth-as-natural resource outlook. Nature is a *thing* to be consumed or overcome as people traverse the country in search for success in a faraway land. The simulation's structure coerces children into identifying with white settlers and dismissing non-white others. It also contributes to the broader curricular racialization of identity that students absorb—learning who constitutes the normalized "we" and who is excluded.

The Oregon Trail players need not take into account the lives of others unless it's necessary to do so in order to accomplish their personal objectives. Thus, the cultures of Plains Indians are backgrounded. The game marginalizes their view of the earth. Contrast, for example, the Indians' term "mother earth" with *The Oregon Trail* term "natural resource." The metaphor of earth as mother suggests humans in a reciprocal relationship with a natural world that is alive, that nourishes us, and that sustains us. On the other hand, a resource is a thing to be used. It exists *for* us, outside of us, and we have no obligations in return.

The consequences of the Oregon Trail for the Plains Indians, the Indians of the Northwest, and for the earth were devastating. In fairness to *The Oregon*

Trail, students may hear some of the details of this upheaval as they play. For example, on one trip I encountered a "Pawnee Village." Had I paid attention to the warning in the guidebook to "avoid contact" I would have ignored it and continued on my trip. But I entered and "talked" to the people I encountered there. A Pawnee woman said: "Why do you bother me? I don't want to trade. The things that we get from the white travelers don't make up for all that we lose." I clicked to hear more. "We didn't know the whooping cough, measles, or the smallpox until your people brought them to us. Our medicine cannot cure these strange diseases, and our children are dying." I clicked on "Do you have any advice?" Angrily, she said, "No. I just want you to leave us alone." The implication is that if I just "leave [them] alone" and continue on the trail I can pursue my dream without hurting the Indians.

However, this interpretation hides the fact that the Oregon Trail itself, not just contact with the so-called pioneers, devastated Indian cultures and the ecology of which those cultures were an integral part. Johansen and Maestas' (1979) description of the Lakota language for talking about these pioneers helps us see how they were regarded by the Indians:

> [The Lakota] used a metaphor to describe the newcomers. It was *Wasi'chu,* which means "takes the fat," or "greedy person." Within the modern Indian movement, *Wasi'chu* has come to mean those corporations and individuals, with their governmental accomplices, which continue to covet Indian lives, land, and resources for private profit. *Wasi'chu* does not describe a race; it describes a state of mind. (p. 6)

The *Wasi'chu* cut down all the cottonwood trees found along the rich bottom lands of plains rivers—trees which "offered crucial protection during winter blizzards as well as concealing a village's smoke from its enemies. In lean seasons, horses fed on its bark, which was surprisingly nourishing" (Davidson & Lytle, 1992, p. 114).

The Oregon Trail created serious wood shortages, which even the *Wasi'chu* acknowledged. "By the Mormon guide we here expected to find the last timber," wrote overlander A. W. Harlan in describing the Platte River, "but all had been used up by others ahead of us so we must go about 200 miles without any provisions cooked up." A few weeks later, in sight of the Black Hills, Harlan wrote: "[W]e have passed many cottonwood stumps but no timber . . ." (Davidson & Lytle, 1992, p. 115).

Wasi'chu rifles also killed tremendous numbers of buffalo that Plains Indians depended upon for survival. One traveler in the 1850s wrote that, "The valley of the Platte for 200 miles presents the aspect of the vicinity of a slaughter yard, dotted all over with skeletons of buffaloes" (Davidson & Lytle, 1992, p. 117). Very soon after the beginning of the Oregon Trail the buffalo learned to avoid the Trail, their herds migrating both south and north. Edward Lazarus (1991) points out in *Black Hills/ White Justice: The Sioux Nation Versus the United States—1775 to the Present* that "the Oregon Trail did more than move the buffalo; it destroyed the hunting pattern of the Sioux, forcing them to follow the herds to the fringes of their domain and to expose themselves to the raids of their enemies" (p. 14).

However, wrapped in their cocoons of self-interest, *The Oregon Trail* players push on, oblivious to the mayhem and misery they cause in their westward drive. This is surely an unintended, and yet intrinsic, part of the game's message: Pursue your goal as an autonomous individual, ignore the social and ecological consequences: "look out for number one."

No Violence Here

The Oregon Trail never suggests to its simulated pioneers that they should seek permission of Indian nations to travel through their territory. And from this key omission flow other omissions. The simulation doesn't inform players that, because of the disruptions wrought by the daily intrusions of the westward migration, Plains Indians regularly demanded tribute from the trekkers. As John Unruh, Jr. (1993), writes in *The Plains Across:*

> The natives explicitly emphasized that the throngs of overlanders were killing and scaring away buffalo and other wild game, overgrazing prairie grasses, exhausting the small quantity of available timber, and depleting water resources. The tribute payments . . . were demanded mainly by the Sac and Fox, Kickapoo, Pawnee, and Sioux Indians—the tribes closest to the Missouri River frontier and therefore those feeling most keenly the pressures of white men increasingly impinging upon their domains. (p. 169)

Wasi'chu travelers resented this Indian-imposed taxation and their resentment frequently turned to hostility and violence, especially in the later years of the Trail. The Pawnee were "hateful wretches," wrote Dr. Thomas Wolfe in 1852, for demanding a 25 cent toll at a bridge across Shell Creek near the North Platte River (Unruh, 1993, p. 171). Shell Creek and other crossings became flashpoints that escalated into violent skirmishes resulting in the deaths of settlers and Indians.

Despite the increasing violence along the Oregon Trail, one choice *The Oregon Trail* programmers don't offer students-as-trekkers is the choice to harm Indians. Doubtlessly MECC, the publisher of *The Oregon Trail,* is not anxious to promote racism toward Native peoples. However, because simulation players can't hurt or even speak ill of Indians, the game fails to alert students that white hostility was one feature of the westward migration. The omission is significant because the sanitized non-violent *The Oregon Trail* fails to equip students to reflect on the origins of conflicts between whites and Indians. Nor does it offer students any insights into the racial antagonism that fueled this violence. In all my play of *The Oregon Trail,* I can't recall any blatant racism directed at Indians. But as Unruh (1993) points out, "The callous attitude of cultural and racial superiority so many overlanders exemplified was of considerable significance in producing the volatile milieu in which more and more tragedies occurred" (p. 186).

The End of the Trail

Soon there will come from the rising sun a different kind of man
from any you have yet seen, who will bring with them a book and
will teach you everything, after that the world will fall to pieces.

—Spokan Prophet, 1790
(Limerick, 1987, p. 39)

A person can spend two or three hours—or more—playing one game of *The
Oregon Trail* before finally reaching Oregon Territory. Upon arrival, a player
is awarded points and told how his or her life in Oregon turned out. Yet the
game fails to raise vital questions about one's right to be there in the first place
and what happened to the people who were there first.

In its section on the "Destination," the guidebook offers students its wisdom on how they should view life in a new land. It's a passage that underscores
the messages students absorb while engaged in the simulation. These comfort-
ing words of advice and social vision are worth quoting at length:

> Once you reach the end of your journey, you should go to the nearest large
> town to establish your land claim. If there are no large towns in the area,
> simply find an unclaimed tract of land and settle down. . . . As they say, pos-
> session is nine-tenths of the law, and if you have settled and worked land that
> hasn't yet been claimed by anyone else, you should have little or no trouble
> legally establishing your claim at a later time. As more and more Americans
> move into the region, more cities and towns will spring up, further increasing
> one's options for economic success. Rest assured in the facts that men and
> women who are willing to work hard will find their labors richly rewarded,
> and that you, by going west, are helping to spread American civilization from
> ocean to ocean across this great continent, building a glorious future for gen-
> erations to come! (The Oregon Trail II, 1994)

The Lakota scholar and activist Vine Deloria, Jr. (1977), in his book,
Indians of the Pacific Northwest, offers a less sanguine perspective than that included in the CD-ROM guidebook. People coming in on the Oregon Trail
"simply arrived on the scene and started building. If there were Indians or previous settlers on the spot they were promptly run off under one pretext or another. Lawlessness and thievery dominated the area" (p. 53). From 1850 on, using provisions of the Oregon Donation Act, thousands of "settlers" invaded
"with impunity."

As Deloria points out, there were some in Congress who were aware that
they were encouraging settlers to steal Indian land, and so Congress passed the
Indian Treaty Act requiring the United States to get formal agreements from
Indian tribes. Anson Dart, appointed to secure land concessions, pursued this
objective in a despicable fashion. For example, he refused to have the treaties
translated into the Indians' languages, instead favoring "Chinook jargon," a
non-language of fewer than 300 words good for trading, giving orders, and little

else. Dart's mandate was to move all the Indians east of the Cascades, but he decided some tribes, like the Tillamooks and Chinooks, should keep small amounts of land as cheap labor reserves:

> Almost without exception, I have found [the Indians] anxious to work at employment at common labor and willing too, to work at prices much below that demanded by the whites. The Indians make all the rails used in fencing, and at this time do the boating upon the rivers: In consideration, therefore, of the usefulness as labourers in the settlements, it was believed to be far better for the Country that they should not be removed from the settled portion [sic] of Oregon if it were possible to do so. (Deloria, 1977, p. 51)

Meanwhile, in southwestern Oregon white vigilantes didn't wait for treaty niceties to be consummated. Between 1852 and 1856 self-proclaimed Volunteers attacked Indians for alleged misdeeds or simply because they were Indians. In August of 1853, one Martin Angel rode into the Rogue River Valley gold mining town of Jacksonville shouting, "Nits breed lice. We have been killing Indians in the valley all day," and "Exterminate the whole race" (Beckham, 1991, p. 103). Minutes later a mob of about 800 white men hanged a 7-year-old Indian boy. In October 1855, a group of whites massacred 23 Indian men, women, and children. This incident began the Rogue Indian war, which lasted until June 1856 (Beckham, 1991). Recall that this is the same region and the same year in one *Oregon Trail* session where "Bill" built a home and experienced "moderate success," but, thanks to *The Oregon Trail* programmers, he learned nothing of the social conflicts swirling around him.

Nor did Bill learn that, even as a white person, he could protest the outrages committed against the Rogue River Valley Indians, as did one anonymous "Volunteer" in a passionate 1853 letter to the *Oregon Statesman* newspaper:

> A few years since the whole valley was theirs [the Indians'] alone. No white man's foot had ever trod it. They believed it theirs forever. But the gold digger come, with his pan and his pick and shovel, and hundreds followed. And they saw in astonishment their streams muddied, towns built, their valley fenced and taken. And where their squaws dug camus, their winter food, and their children were wont to gambol, they saw dug and plowed, and their own food sown by the hand of nature, rooted out forever, and the ground it occupied appropriated to the rearing of vegetables for the white man. Perhaps no malice yet entered the Indian breast. But when he was weary of hunting in the mountains without success, and was hungry, and approached the white man's tent for bread; where instead of bread he received curses and kicks, ye treaty kicking men—ye Indian exterminators think of these things.—*A Soldier* (Applegate & O'Donnell, 1994, p. 34)

The Oregon Trail hides the nature of the Euro-American invasion in at least two ways. In the first place, it simply fails to inform simulation participants what happened between settlers and Indians. To *The Oregon Trail* player, it doesn't feel like an invasion; it doesn't feel wrong. After one of my arrivals, in 1848, "Life in the new land turned out to be happy and successful for Bill, who always cherished bittersweet but proud memories of the months spent on the Oregon Trail." (This struck me as a rather odd account given that I had lost all 3 of my children on the trip.) The only person that matters is the simulation player. I was never told whether life turned out equally "happy and successful" for the Klamaths, Yakimas, Cayuses, Nez Percés, Wallawallas, and all the others who occupied this land generations before the *Wasi'chu* arrived. The second way the nature of the white invasion is hidden has to do with the structure of the simulation. For a couple hours or more the player endures substantial doses of frustration, tedium, and difficulty. By the time the Willamette or Rogue River Valleys come up on the screen we, the simulated trekkers, feel we *deserve* the land, that our labors in transit should be "richly rewarded" with the best land we can find.

Data Deception and Thoughts on What to Do About It

In the Beatles' song, all you need is love; in *The Oregon Trail,* all you need are data. *The Oregon Trail* offers students gobs of information: snake bite remedies, river locations and depths, wagon specifications, ferry costs, and daily climate reports. Loaded with facts, it feels comprehensive. Loaded with people voicing contrasting opinions, it feels balanced. Loaded with choices, it feels democratic. But the simulation begins from no moral or ethical standpoint beyond individual material success; it contains no vision of social or ecological justice, and, hence, promotes a full litany of sexist, racist, and imperialist perspectives, as well as exploitive perspectives of the earth. And simultaneously, it hides these biases. The combination is insidious, and makes interactive CD-ROMs like this one more difficult to critique than traditional textbooks or films. The forced identification of player with simulation protagonist leaves the student no option but to follow the ideological map laid out by the programmers.

Nonetheless, my critique is not a call to boycott the new "edutainment" resources. But we need to remember that these CD-ROMs are not teacher substitutes. The teacher's role in analyzing and presenting these devices in a broader ethical context is absolutely vital. Thus, teachers across the country must begin a dialogue toward developing a critical computer literacy. We need to figure out ways to equip students with the ability to recognize and evaluate the deep moral and political messages imparted by these CD-ROMs as they maneuver among the various computer software programs.

Before choosing to use CD-ROMs that involve people and places, like *The Oregon Trail*—or, for example, its newer siblings *The Yukon Trail, The Amazon Trail,* and *Africa Trail*—teachers should consider the following questions.

- **Which social groups are students *not* invited to identify with in the simulation?** For example, Native Americans, African Americans, women, and Latinos are superficially represented in *The Oregon Trail*, but the "stuff" of their lives is missing.

- **How might these social groups frame problems differently than the simulation?** As we saw in the foregoing critique of *The Oregon Trail*, women tended to focus more on maintaining community than on hunting. Native Americans had a profoundly different relationship to the earth than did the Euro-American "tamers of the wilderness."

- **What decisions do simulation participants make that may have consequences for social groups not highlighted in the simulation? And what are these consequences?** Although the very existence of the Oregon Trail contributed to the decimation of Plains and Northwest Indians, simulation participants are never asked to consider the broader effects of their decision-making. What may be an ethical individual choice may be unethical when multiplied several hundred thousand times. In this respect, CD-ROM choice-making both reflects and reinforces conventional notions of freedom that justify disastrous social and ecological practices.

- **What decisions do simulation participants make that may have consequences for the earth and non-human life?** Similarly, a simulation participant's choice to cut down trees for firewood may be rational for that individual, but may also have deleterious effects on the ecological balance of a particular bio-region.

- **If the simulation is time-specific, as in the case of *The Oregon Trail*, what were the social and environmental consequences for the time period following the time represented in the simulation?** The wars between Indians and the U.S. Cavalry in the latter decades of the nineteenth century are inexplicable without the Oregon Trail as prologue.

- **Can we name the ideological orientation of a particular CD-ROM?** The question is included here simply to remind us that all computer materials—indeed, all curricula—*have* an ideology. Our first step is to become aware of that ideology.

These questions are hardly exhaustive, but may suggest a useful direction to begin thinking about CD-ROMs as they become increasingly available and begin to cover more and more subjects.

Finally, let me use the example of *The Oregon Trail* to introduce some ways teachers can begin to foster a critical computer literacy. Once we have identified some of the social groups that are substantially missing in a CD-ROM activity like *The Oregon Trail*, we can try to locate excerpts from diaries, speeches, or other communications of members of these groups. We can then engage students in role play where, as a class, students face a number of Oregon Trail problems. For example, class members could portray women on the Oregon Trail and decide how they would attempt to maintain a community in transit. Or they might role play a possible discussion of Oglala people as they confront the increasingly disruptive presence of *Wasi'chu* crossing their lands.

Students might be asked to list all the ways African Americans would experience the Oregon Trail differently than Euro-Americans—from the planning of the trip to the trip itself. (It's unlikely, for example, that every white person on the streets of Independence, Missouri, said a friendly "Howdy," to the blacks he encountered, as each of them does to the implied but unacknowledged white male *Oregon Trail* simulation player.) Students also could assume a particular racial, cultural, or gender identity, and note whether the choices or experiences described in the simulation make sense from the standpoint of a member of their group. For example, would a typical African American in Missouri in 1850 be allowed to choose from which city to begin the trek west?

As we share with students the social and ecological costs of the Oregon Trail, we could ask them to write critical letters to each of the "pioneers" they portrayed in the simulation. Some could represent Rogue River Valley Indians, Shoshoni people, or even Mother Earth. For instance, how does Mother Earth respond to the casual felling of every Cottonwood tree along the Platte River? A Native American elder or activist could be invited into the classroom to speak about the concerns important to his or her people and about the history of white-Indian relations.

We could encourage students to think about the politics of naming in the simulation. They could suggest alternative names for the Oregon Trail itself. For example, the historian of the American West, Frederick Merk (1978), aptly calls the Oregon Trail a "path of empire." Writer Dan Georgakas (1973) names it a "march of death." Other names might be "invasion of the West," or "The 20-year trespass." Just as with Columbus's "discovery" of America, naming shapes understanding, and we need classroom activities to uncover this process.

Students could write and illustrate children's books describing the Oregon Trail from the standpoint of women, African Americans, Native Americans, or the earth.

After doing activities like these, students could "play" *The Oregon Trail* again. What do they see this time that they didn't see before? Whose world view is highlighted and whose is hidden? If they choose, they might present their findings to other classes or to teachers who may be considering the use of CD-ROMs.

The Oregon Trail is no more morally obnoxious than other CD-ROMs or curricular materials with similar ideological biases. My aim here is broader than merely shaking a scolding finger at MECC, publisher of *The Oregon Trail* series. I've tried to demonstrate why teachers and students must develop a critical computer literacy. Some of the new CD-ROMs seem more socially aware than the blatantly culturally insensitive materials that still fill school libraries and book rooms. And the flashy new computer packages also invoke terms long sacred to educators: student empowerment, individual choice, creativity, and high interest. It's vital that we remember that coincident with the arrival of these new educational toys is a deepening social and ecological crisis. Global and national inequality between haves and have-nots is increasing. Violence of all kinds is endemic. And the earth is being consumed at a ferocious pace. Computer programs are not politically neutral in the big moral contests of our time. Inevitably, they take sides. Thus, a critical computer literacy, one with a social and ecological conscience, is more than just a good idea—it's a basic skill.

References

Applegate, S., & O'Donnell, T. (1994). *Talking on paper: An anthology of Oregon letters and diaries.* Corvallis, OR: Oregon State University Press.

Armstrong, D. (1996, February 23). Lucas getting into education via CD-ROM. *The San Francisco Examiner,* pp. E-I–E-2.

Beckham, S. D. (1991). Federal-Indian relations. *The First Oregonians.* Portland, OR: Oregon Council for the Humanities.

Bowers, C. A. (1988). *The cultural dimensions of educational computing: Understanding the non-neutrality of technology.* New York: Teachers College Press.

Davidson, J. W., & Lytle, M. H. (1992). *After the fact: The art of historical detection.* New York: McGraw-Hill.

Deloria, Jr., V. (1977). *Indians of the Pacific Northwest.* Garden City, NY: Doubleday.

Faragher, J., & Stansell, C. (1992). Women and their families on the overland trail to California and Oregon, 1842–1867. In F. Binder & D. Reimer (Eds.), *The way we lived: Essays and documents in American social history, Vol. I* (pp. 188–195). Lexington, MA: Heath.

Georgakas, D. (1973). *Red shadows: The history of Native Americans from 1600 to 1900, from the desert to the Pacific Coast.* Garden City, NY: Zenith.

Hill, W. E. (1989). *The Oregon Trail: Yesterday and today.* Caldwell, ID: Caxton Printers.

Johansen, B. & Maestas, R. (1979). *Wasi'chu: The continuing Indian wars.* New York: Monthly Review.

Kesselman, A. (1976). Diaries and reminiscences of women on the Oregon Trail: A study in consciousness. In R. Baxandall, L. Gordon, & S. Reverby (Eds.), *America's working women: A documentary history—1600 to the present* (pp. 69–72). New York: Vintage.

Lazarus, E. (1991). *Black Hills/White justice: The Sioux Nation versus the United States—1775 to the present.* New York: HarperCollins.

Limerick, P. N. (1987). *The legacy of conquest: The unbroken part of the American west.* New York: W. W. Norton.

McLagan, E. (1980). *A peculiar paradise: A history of Blacks in Oregon. 1788–1940.* Portland, OR: The Georgian Press.

Merk, F. (1978). *History of the westward movement.* New York: Knopf.

The Oregon Trail [Computer software]. (1993). Minneapolis, MN: Minnesota Educational Computer Company.

The Oregon Trail II [Computer software]. (1994). Minneapolis, MN: Minnesota Educational Computer Company.

Pride, B,, & Pride, M. (1992). *Prides' guide to educational software.* Wheaton, IL: Crossway Books.

Provenzo, Jr., E. F. (1991). *Video kids: Making sense of Nintendo.* Cambridge, MA: Harvard University Press.

Schlissel, L. (1992). *Women's diaries of the westward journey.* New York: Schocken.

Unruh, Jr., J. D. (1993). *The plains across: The overland emigrants and the trans-Mississippi west, 1840–1860.* Urbana, IL: University of Illinois Press.

"On the Road to Cultural Bias: A Critique of The Oregon Trail *CD-ROM" by William Bigelow originally appeared in* Rethinking Schools *10.1 (Fall 1995): 14–18. Reprinted with permission.*

9

What Happened to the Golden Door?

Linda Christensen

Editors' Notes: In this essay, Linda Christensen details her experiment negotiating her Literature in History curriculum with her Portland, Oregon, high school students. She asked her students to complete "real" research that would help tell the stories of immigrants not found in textbooks. They worked together in groups, researching original letters, files, and rare documents of immigrants to present lessons in class. Christensen candidly describes the problems the students encountered, which raises important questions about the kinds of sources used. Christensen's report includes lively descriptions of her students' projects and the lessons they taught. She reminds us of the difficulties and rewards of turning our courses over to our students.

At Eureka High School, immigration equaled Ellis Island. We watched old black-and-white film strips of Northern Europeans filing through dimly lit buildings. My textbooks were laced with pictures of the Statue of Liberty opening her arms to poor immigrants who had been granted an opportunity to "pull themselves up by their bootstraps" when they passed through America's door:

> Give me your tired, your poor,
> Your huddled masses yearning to breathe free,
> The wretched refuse of your teeming shores.
> Send these, the homeless, tempest-tost, to me,
> I lift my lamp beside the golden door.

I felt pride at being part of a country that helped the unfortunate, including my own family.

Years later when I visited Angel Island in San Francisco Bay, I learned about another immigration that hadn't been mentioned in my high-school or college texts. I walked through the deserted barracks where painted walls covered the poems of immigrant Chinese who viewed the "Golden Mountain" through a barbed wire fence. I felt angry that yet another portion of U.S. history had been hidden from me. Between 1910 and 1940, the "tired, poor, wretched refuse" from Asian shores were imprisoned on Angel Island before being accepted as "resident aliens" or rejected at the "golden door." As historian Ronald Takaki notes, "Their quarters were crowded and unsanitary, resembling a slum. 'When we arrived,' said one of them, 'they locked us up like criminals in compartments like the cages in the zoo'" (1989, 237). Turning their anger and frustration into words, the Chinese carved poems on the building's wooden walls. Their poems stood in stark contradiction to the Statue of Liberty's promise:

America has power, but not justice.
In prison, we were victimized as if we were guilty.
Given no opportunity to explain, it was really brutal.
I bow my head in reflection but there is nothing I can do. (Lai et al. 1986, 58)

All Europeans were eligible for citizenship once they passed through Ellis Island, a right denied to Asians until the mid-1940s.

In 1995 when California voters passed Proposition 187, which, if implemented, will deprive so-called illegal immigrants of health care and schooling, I decided to teach about immigration, not just the traditional version, but the more dangerous and unspoken immigration that denies access to large numbers of potential immigrants based on color or politics.

Beyond these political reasons, I had personal and educational reasons to teach this unit. It was the last quarter of the year in Literature in U.S. History, a combined junior level untracked history and English class that met 90 minutes a day for the entire year. The days had warmed up and the students smelled summer. If I said the word "essay," "interior monologue," or "role play," I could hear a collective moan rise from the circle and settle like stinky fog around my head.

For three quarters, my planning book had been filled with lessons attempting to teach students how to become critical readers of history and literature. They'd written essays, critiques, short stories, personal narratives, poems, and interior monologues analyzing their own lives as well as the history and contemporary issues that continue to deprive Native Americans of land and economic opportunities. They'd also reflected critically on the enslavement of Africans, starting with life in Africa before slavery as well as forced immigration and resistance. We examined the literature and history of the Harlem Renaissance, the Civil Rights Movement, and contemporary issues. They read and critiqued presidential speeches, historical and contemporary novels and poems written by people from a variety of backgrounds. They were ready to do their own investigation and teaching—putting into practice their analytical skills.

Fourth quarter I wanted them to conduct "real" research—not the scurry-to-the-library-and-find-the-closest-encyclopedia-and-copy-it-word-for-word kind of research, but research that made them ask questions about immigration policies, quotas, and personal stories that couldn't be lifted from a single text. I wanted them to learn to use the library, search for books, look up alternative sources, find the Ethnic NewsWatch, search the Oregon Historical Society's clipping files, photo files, and rare documents room. I wanted them to interview people, read novels and poetry that told the immigrant's story in a more personal way. Through this kind of thorough research, I hoped they would develop an ear for what is unsaid in political speeches and newspaper articles, that they would learn to ask questions when their neighbors or people on the bus began an anti-immigrant rap.

Setting the Stage

I started fourth quarter by outlining my goals and expectations. I do this each term, so students know what kinds of pieces must be in their portfolio, for example, a literary essay comparing two novels, an essay exploring a historical issue, a poem that includes details from history, etc. As part of the opening of the quarter ceremonies, I passed out an outline of their upcoming project. I wanted a lengthy deadline so students would have the opportunity to work the entire quarter on the project.

Before students started their research, I modeled how I wanted the lessons taught by presenting Chinese and Japanese immigration. While students who come through the Jefferson network of elementary, middle, and high schools get at least surface background knowledge of Native Americans and African Americans, they appear to know less about Asian or Latino literature or history. In fact, students are often surprised that the Japanese and Chinese faced any prejudice.[1]

During the lessons on Japanese Americans, students examined Executive Order 9066 signed by President Roosevelt, which gave the military the right to force Japanese Americans from their homes and businesses into camps surrounded by barbed wire and guard towers. Because these "resident aliens" and U.S. citizens were allowed to take only what they could carry to the "camps," they were forced to sell most of their possessions in a short period of time. Students read "Echoes of Pearl Harbor," a chapter from *Nisei Daughter* by Monica Sone, where she describes her family burning their Japanese poetry, kimonos, breaking their Japanese records, destroying anything that could make them look like they cherished their Japanese heritage. Students wrote moving poetry and interior monologues imagining they were forced to leave their homes,

businesses, and treasured possessions. "Becoming American" was written by
Khalilah Joseph: [2]

> I looked into the eyes of my Japanese doll
> and knew I could not surrender her
> to the fury of the fire.
> My mother threw out the poetry
> she loved;
> my brother gave the fire his sword.
> We worked hours
> to vanish any traces of the Asian world
> from our home.
> Who could ask us
> to destroy
> gifts from a world that molded
> and shaped us?
> If I ate hamburgers
> and apple pies,
> if I wore jeans,
> then would I be American?

Recently, I came across *Beyond Words: Images from America's Concentration Camps,* a fascinating book of personal testimony and artwork produced in the camps: black-and-white drawings, watercolors, oil paintings and pieces of interviews that gave me a window into the lives of the imprisoned Japanese. While I showed slides of the artwork, students I prompted ahead of time read "Legends from Camp" by Lawson Inada, "The Question of Loyalty," by Mitsuye Yamada, and segments of the internees' interviews that matched pictures on screen. With images and words of the prisoners in their minds, students wrote their own poems. Thu Throung's poem is called "Japanese Prisoners":

> Guards watch us.
> They wrap us around
> in barbed wire fences
> like an orange's meat
> that never grows outside its skin.
> If the orange's skin breaks,
> the juice drains out.
> Just like the Japanese behind the wire fence.

We watched and critiqued the somewhat flawed film, *Come See the Paradise,* and talked about the laws that forbade Japanese nationals from becoming citizens or owning land.[3] Students read loyalty oaths imprisoned Japanese American citizens were forced to sign. After learning about the "No No Boys," men who refused to sign the oath, and their subsequent imprisonment in federal penitentiaries, students argued about whether or not they would have signed the loyalty oath if they'd been interned (Houston and Houston 1973, 58).

Students also looked at the number of immigrant Chinese allowed in the country compared to European immigrants. For example, in 1943 when Congress repealed the Chinese Exclusion Act because of China's alliance with the United States against the Japanese, 105 Chinese were allowed to enter Angel Island while 66,000 English immigrants passed through Ellis Island (Lowe 1988).

The Research Begins

Students started on their own projects during the same time period I presented the Chinese and Japanese immigration. They had two 30-minute sessions the first week to discuss what they knew, itemize what they needed to find, and list the resources they had (people to interview, books at home, potential videos to use, outside resources like Vietnamese, Russian, or Latino teachers or district-wide coordinators.) During the following weeks, while I continued my presentations, they were given varied amounts of time to conduct research: 45 minutes to prepare for the library, a full day at the library, additional 90-minute periods as we got closer to deadline, and so on.

At the end of each period of "research/preparation" time, students turned their information in to me so I could see if they made headway, ran into a block, needed a push or help. During this research period, I moved between groups, listening in, asking questions, making lists of questions they raised but didn't answer, questioning literary choices when a piece was by a writer from the immigration group but didn't deal with any of the issues we were studying.

During this time, it was not unusual to see some of my students gathered around a television in the hallway outside my door or in the library as they watched and critiqued videos, looking for potential sections to show to the class. Travis, Roman, and Sophia, who were individual researchers, could be seen translating notes or cassette tapes for their stories. Sometimes they met to talk over stories or ideas for their presentation.

The Mexican group had the most members—too many, really. They watched videos together and then split the rest of the work: Danica and Komar collected and read books to find a story; Shannon researched Cesar Chavez and wrote a profile to hand out to the class; Heather gathered information for a debate on Proposition 187; Stephanie and Stacey coordinated the group, collecting information from each subgroup, fitting research into a coherent lesson plan, and creating a writing lesson that would pull information together for the class; Rosa, the only group member fluent in Spanish, talked with recent immigrants in ESL classes and the Latino coordinator to find speakers, videos, and stories to feed to her group.

Before I end up sounding like a movie script starring Michelle Pfeiffer, let me quickly insert into this idyllic classroom a word or two of other things you might see: kids whining and competing for my attention, *RIGHT NOW;*

students gossiping about a fight, a guess-who's-going-out-with . . . , an upcoming game, or a movie they saw last night; a sly student attempting to take advantage of the chaos to catch up on math or Spanish; the slippery students who said they were going to the library or to see an ESL coordinator, but who actually sneaked into the teachers' cafeteria for coffee or outside for a smoke. There were also two students who attended regularly and might have learned something through other people's work, but who produced no work themselves, and a few others who rode the backs of their group's work, contributing a little in spurts, but not making the sustained efforts of most students. The ESL coordinators, librarians, and I developed an easy communication system regarding passes. I called students and parents at home to talk about their lack of work. While the calls pushed the back-riding students who made some effort, I failed to bring the "slackers" into the research fold.

Besides the usual chaos a teacher might expect when turning over the curriculum to students, I simultaneously hit another problem. I'd set up immigrant groups that I knew would have some interesting and contradictory stories because I was familiar with their history and literature. While students did accept some of the groups I'd proposed: Mexican, Haitian, Cambodian, Irish, and Vietnamese, others argued vehemently that they be allowed to choose the immigrant group they would study. Our previous lessons on resistance and solidarity had certainly taken root within each of the class members, and I was the object of their solidarity. A few wanted to research their own family's immigration stories: Greek, Jewish, Macedonian, and Russian. Several African American students wanted to study immigrants from Africa or from the African Diaspora. Most were happy to study Haiti, one of my original groups; one student chose to study Eritrea, since Portland has a larger population of Eritreans than Haitians. I agreed; in fact, he made an excellent choice. We ended our first rounds with the following research groups: Cambodians, Eritreans,[4] Greeks, Haitians, Irish, Jewish, Macedonians, Mexicans, Russians, and Vietnamese. This first dialogue marked the end of my control over the history and literature presented in class. And I was nervous because I knew almost nothing about Greek and Macedonian immigration and not much more about the Russians.

Ultimately, the contrast between groups made for great discussion. In my class of 31 students, three had immigrated from Vietnam, one from Russia, one from Cambodia; several students were second generation Americans from Greece, Ireland, Nicaragua, and Mexico; half of the class' ancestors had been enslaved Africans, and one girl's grandmother was the only surviving member of her family after the Holocaust. But I can imagine a more homogenous classroom where this might not be the case. In my high school English class over twenty years ago, 29 students were white and one was Black. Around Portland today, I can cite similar profiles. These ratios would have made me demand more diversity in the research if all students wanted to study their own heritage. I do think it is important to negotiate the curriculum with students, and I'm sure some students would be more interested in researching their own past than researching the past of others, but sometimes, in order to surface issues of race and class inequality, it is necessary to move beyond our personal histories.

Research Problems

Prior to the beginning of the unit, I spent time in the public library and the Oregon Historical Society (OHS) library, finding sources, articles, books, practicing computer research programs, before bringing my students across town. OHS officials were friendly and helpful, but told me that I couldn't bring the entire class to their library: I'd have to bring one or two at a time after school or on Saturdays. And they closed at 5 P.M.

In addition to limited library time, I discovered that the easily accessible research materials did not have a critical page in their spines; they just restated the textbook version. I wanted students to learn the "whole truth," not just a watered-down version that left out facts that might complicate the issues. I figured that part of research is getting lots of material and then deciding what is important to present so that others hear a fuller truth. But when I discovered that much of what students were reading only told one side of the immigration story—the same side I learned in high school—I made an effort to put other facts in students' hands as well. We searched computer files of Ethnic News-Watch and alternative news and magazine sources. Although many students dutifully read the computer-generated articles, most of these pieces were too academic or required extensive background knowledge to understand. If we had relied solely on these sources of information—either textbook or alternative—many students would have come away with material that they might have been able to cite and copy into a readable paper, but they wouldn't have understood much about the underlying political situations their immigrant group faced.

After the library research, I linked students with people or information that might provide facts and stories not available in the library. The Haitian group, for example, read articles but hadn't comprehended what was going on: Who was Papa Doc? How was the United States involved? What was happening with Aristide? I distributed copies of the Network of Educators on the Americas' (NECA) booklet *Teaching About Haiti,* which gave them historical and political analysis they needed in order to make sense of the newspaper and magazine articles. The novel *Krik? Krak!* by Edwidge Danticat developed their personal connection; she gave faces and voices to the people on the boats, to those who lived in fear. The names in the newspaper became real: Aristide, Tontons Macoutes, boat people, refugees. (The group's enthusiasm for the novel caught ón. I'd purchased five copies, and there were arguments over who got to read *Krik? Krak!* after group members finished.)

Students became wonderfully devious researchers, using their own connections to gain information. They learned to find back doors when the front doors closed and windows when all of the doors were locked. But sometimes these back door, through-the-window type researches posed another problem:

What if personal history omitted vital historical facts and perspectives? While I could help students who studied immigrant groups that I knew something about, I had little time to read and research the Macedonians, Greeks, and Russians. Travis was thoroughly confused when his research revealed a snarled web of history involving Greece, Bulgaria, and a historic trade route through the mountains. His research took him back to 146 B.C., when Rome conquered the Kingdom of Macedonia, and forward to today. He wanted to know why his grandfather immigrated. Instead of untangling the web of Macedonian history, he spent time with his grandfather, talking, asking questions, going through photo albums, relying on his personal relationships to decode the past. He arranged for a day at the Macedonian lodge, where he interviewed men his grandfather's age about their immigration experiences. Because of my own limited knowledge of events in Macedonia, I let him. This was history via personal story—how much or how little of the history was included, I wasn't sure.

Likewise, when Meghan and I met one Saturday at the Oregon Historical Society, we discovered the letters James Mullany, an Irish immigrant, wrote to his sister in Ireland in the mid 1800s. In one letter, he pleaded with his sister not to mention that he was Catholic: "their [sic] is a strong prejudice against them here on account of the people here thinking it was the Priests that caused the Indian war three or four years ago."[5] Interesting. But in another letter he wrote of the Snake Indians who attacked a train of 45 whites, "only 15 survived but some of them died of starvation . . . [A] company of soldiers . . . found them living of [sic] the bodyes [sic] of them that were killed by the [I]ndians."[6] Could we count these letters as historic evidence? Whose voices weren't included? What stories might the Snake Indians have told?

Students using voices of immigrants or novels to tell the history created a dilemma for me: What happens when personal narratives exclude the stories of large groups of other people or neglect important historical facts? When and how do I intervene? If students tell only their own stories or draw on personal testimonies, is that "inaccurate" history? As an English teacher who weaves literature and history together, who values personal stories as eyewitness accounts of events and who encourages students to "tell their stories," I began to question my own assumptions.

The Vietnamese group, occupying Tri's corner between the windows and closet, underscored my "history versus personal story" dilemma. Their student-told account emphasized a pro-American stance around the Vietnam War but said nothing, for example, of U.S. support for French colonialism, its creation of "South Vietnam," or its devastating bombardment of the Vietnamese countryside. How could I challenge the story these students grew up hearing from parents and elders in their community?

With Meghan's research, we'd studied historical accounts of Native Americans in the Northwest, so we knew that Mullany's letters lacked facts about land takeovers and Indian massacres. But I didn't have time to teach the unit on Vietnam that Bill Bigelow and I developed when we taught the class together, so I also worried that the rest of the class would come away without an understanding of the key role the United States played in the Vietnam War; and without that understanding, how would they be able to critique other U.S. interventions?

I talked with Cang, Tri, and Thu and gave them resources: a timeline that reviewed deepening U.S. involvement in Vietnam and numerous readings from a critical standpoint. I also introduced them to the film, *Hearts and Minds,* which features testimony from numerous critics of the war, as well as prominent U.S. antiwar activists like Daniel Ellsberg. Without a sustained dialogue, this insertion seemed weak and invasive. More so than my talks with Travis and Meghan, because their research was at a greater distance from their lives. But I learned a lesson: Personal story does not always equal history. This lingers as a vexing teaching dilemma.

The Presentation

Once presentation deadlines hit, students argued over dates and order—who got to go first, last, etc. Our biggest struggle came around the issue of time. Students lobbied for longer time slots. The Mexican group was especially ardent. They'd found great movies as well as short stories, informational videos, and a guest speaker from PCUN, the local farm workers union, about working conditions and the boycott of Garden Burgers, a national veggie burger sold in stores and restaurants across the country.[7] They figured they needed at least a week, possibly two. We had five weeks left: four for presentations and a last sacred week to finish portfolios and evaluations. Rosa said, "Look how many days you used when you taught us about the Japanese and Chinese. Two weeks on each! Aren't the Latinos as important as the Asians?" They bargained with single person groups, like the Russians and Greeks, for part of their time.

A week or so prior to presentations, groups submitted detailed lesson plans. I met formally with each group to make sure all requirements were covered, but also questioned choices. During previous weeks, I'd read every proposed story and novel selection, watched each video, went over writing assignments: I didn't want any surprises on their teaching day.

The power of my students' teaching was not in just the individual presentations, where students provided historical information in a variety of mostly interesting and unique lesson plans, but also in the juxtaposition of these histories and stories. Students created a jazz improvisation, overlaying voices of pain and struggle and triumph with heroic attempts to escape war, poverty, or traditions that pinched women too narrowly into scripted roles. Their historical research and variety of voices taught about a more varied history of immigration than I'd ever attempted to do in the past.

But the presentations were also like improvisation in that they were not as tightly connected and controlled as a rehearsed piece I would have conducted. There were off notes and unfinished strands that seemed promising but didn't deliver an analysis that could have strengthened student understanding of immigration. Few students found research on quotas, few had time left in their presentation to engage in a discussion that linked or compared their group to another. The Haitian group, for example, tied our past studies of Columbus and the Tainos to present Haiti, but didn't develop the history of Duvalier or Aristide or the involvement of the United States.

Although presentations varied in length and depth, most gave us at least a look at a culture many students weren't familiar with, and at best, a strong sense that not only did racial and political background determine who gets in to this country, but also how they live once they arrive.

The Cambodian group arranged for Sokpha's mother to come to class, as well as a viewing of the film, *The Killing Fields*. Sokpha's mother told of her life in Cambodia, of hiding in the deep tunnels her father built to keep them safe from U.S. bombs, of her fear of snakes at the bottom of the tunnel that scared her almost as much as the bombs. She talked about the Khmer Rouge, the Vietnamese, and the United States. On her father's deathbed, he said, "Go to America. Leave Cambodia." She did. Shoeless, nine months pregnant with Sokpha, and carrying a three-year-old on her back, she walked for three days and three nights from Cambodia into Thailand, dodging land mines that killed some of her fellow travelers. She also spoke of difficulties here—how her lack of language skills have kept her from finding a good job, her reliance on Sokpha, the breakdown of their culture, the Americanization of her children.

The Haitians presented background history tying the modern struggle in Haiti with previous history lessons; their strengths were chilling descriptions of the refugees, their choice of story, their research into Haitian culture, and their writing assignment. Read aloud by a male and a female student, the two-voice story "Children of the Sea" portrayed a political young man who dared to speak out against the Haitian government, writing to his lover as he rides a sinking boat in search of refuge in the United States. His lover writes of the increased military violence of the Tontons Macoutes, who make parents have sex with their children, rape and torture suspected supporters of Aristide (Danticat).

Cang, from the Vietnamese group, recounted Vietnam's history through a time line. Thu's stories of escape and life in the refugee camps created nightmare scenes for her fellow students of drownings, rapes, and the difficulties of families who got separated. Tri pointed out the geographical settlements of immigrant Vietnamese and their induction into the United States. He talked about the struggle of the Vietnamese shrimp fisherman in the Gulf, the attempts of the KKK to drive the fishermen out of the region,[8] and the creation of Little Saigon in California, a space where the Vietnamese have forged a community inside the United States, not unlike many immigrants who came before them.

The student writing assignments generated excellent poems and personal narratives. After Sophia spoke about her mother's experiences, she said her inheritance from her mother was the strength to pursue her goals even when she faces opposition. Her assignment for the class: "Write about something you treasure from your family. It might be an heirloom, like a ring, but it can also be a story, a memory, a tradition, a personal trait. Write it as a poem, a personal narrative, or a story." Komar Harvey wrote an essay about his family's love of music:

> You can hear music on the porch before you enter our house. Tunes climb through those old vinyl windows and mailbox and drift into everybody's ears in the neighborhood. If you came during the holiday season you could hear the Christmas bells chiming through the static of that old crackling phonograph needle. You hear the rumbling voice of Charles Brown as if he were digging a hole up in the living room, "Bells will be ringing". . . Nobody graces our door during those Christmas months without a little Charles ringing his bells in their ears.

After talking about the efforts of his grandfather's struggles to get to the United States, Travis asked students to write a personal narrative about an obstacle they overcame in their life. Cang wrote about his difficulty learning English in the face of classmates' ridicule. His narrative had a profound effect on students. I have not changed or corrected his language because it is part of the story:

> [After he left Vietnam, he was in the Philippines.] In 1989 we came to America. That's when I started to go to school. I went to all of the classes I had, but I felt the blonde and white-skinned people not respected me. They make joke over the way I talk . . . I'll never give up, I say to myself . . . One day I'm going to be just like them on talking and writing, but I never get to that part of my life until now. Even if I can understand the word, but still I can't pronounce it, if I do pronounce it, it won't end up right. Truly, I speak Vietnamese at home all the time, that's why I get used to the Vietnamese words more than English, but I'll never give up what I have learned. I will succeed with my second language.

The Mexican group took several days for their presentation. They taught about the theft of Mexican land by the United States, immigration border patrols, the effect of toxic sprays on migrant workers, the migrants' living conditions in Oregon. During this time, we also debated Proposition 187: Should the United States deny services to illegal immigrants? Then the presenters asked the class to write a persuasive essay taking a point of view on the question.

One day we watched the movie *Mi Familia,* about a "Mexican" family whose original homeland was in California. As we watched, we ate tamales and sweet tacos that Rosa and her mother-in-law lugged up three flights of stairs. Then we wrote food poems that tied us to our culture. Sarah LePage's "Matzah Balls" is a tribute to her grandmother:

> Grandma's hands,
> wise, soft, and old,
> mold the Matzah meal
> between the curves of each palm.
> She transforms our heritage

into perfect little spheres.
Like a magician
she shapes our culture
as our people do.
This is her triumph.
She lays the bowl aside
revealing her tired hands,
each wrinkle a time
she sacrificed something for our family.

Evaluation

On our last day, students overwhelmingly voted that immigration was the unit they both learned the most from and cared the most about. Komar, the first to speak, said, "I never realized that Cambodians were different from Vietnamese. Sokpha's family went through a lot to get here, so did Tri's, Thu's, and Cang's." Stacey, a member of the Haitian group added, "I learned that the United States isn't just black and white. I learned that my people are not the only ones who have suffered in this country." Khalilah noted that she hadn't realized what research really meant until she struggled to find information about the Haitians. While others added similar points about various groups or presentations they learned from, Travis summed up the conversation by saying, "I didn't know anything about Proposition 187 or the discrimination immigrants have faced because that wasn't part of my family's history. I didn't know that there was discrimination about who got in and who was kept out of the United States, and now I do."

I felt that students learned from each other about immigrants' uneven and unfair treatment. The Statue of Liberty's flame and rhetoric had met with a history, told by students, that dimmed her light. But they had also learned lessons that would alter their interactions with the "Chinese"—actually Korean—storekeeper at the intersection of Martin Luther King Jr. and Fremont. At Jefferson, one of the most offensive scenes I have witnessed in the hallways or classrooms is the silencing of immigrant Asian, Russian, and Mexican students as they speak their own languages or struggle to speak English. Throughout the year, Cang, Thu, and Tri's personal testimony during discussions or read-arounds about the pain of that silencing as well as their stories about fighting with their parents or setting off firecrackers in their school in Vietnam created much more awareness in our classroom than any lecture could have. I credit our study of history, for example, the Mexican American War, as part of that change, but through this student-led unit on immigration, I watched students crack through stereotypes they had nurtured about others. Students who sat by their lockers on C-floor were no longer lumped together under the title "Chinese"; they became Vietnamese, Cambodian, Laotian. Students no longer mimicked the sound of their speech as a put-down. Latino students who spoke Spanish near the door on the west side of the building were no longer seen as outsiders who moved into the neighborhood with loud cars and lots of children, but as political exiles in a land that had once belonged to their ancestors. The Russian students who moved together like a small boat through the halls of Jefferson were no longer odd, but seekers of religious freedom.

Throughout fourth quarter, I tossed and turned at night questioning my judgment about asking students to teach such an important part of history—and the consequence that much history would not be taught. But after hearing their enthusiasm and their changed perceptions about their classmates, the world, and research, I put my critique temporarily on hold. Turning over the classroom circle to my students allowed them to become the "experts" and me to become their student. While I lost control and power over the curriculum and was forced to question some key assumptions of my teaching, I gained an incredible amount of knowledge—and so did they.

Notes

1. I have to thank my former student Mira Shimabukuro, who pointed out my own lack of attention to these groups, and Lawson Inada, professor at Southern Oregon State College, who served as my mentor in these studies.

2. Many of the student poems used in this article are printed in our literary magazine, *Rites of Passage*. The magazine may be purchased through the NECA catalogue or by contacting me at Jefferson High School, 5210 N. Kerby St., Portland, OR 97217.

3. For example, like many films about an oppressed people, *Come See the Paradise* features a white man in the lead role.

4. The student studying Eritreans left school, so I will not report on his project.

5. Letters from James Mullany to his sister Mary Mullany, August 5, 1860. Oregon Historical Society Mss 2417, p. 10.

6. Mullany, November 5, 1860, p. 14.

7. For more information on the boycott, write PCUN, 300 Young Street, Woodburn, OR 97071, or call them at (503) 982-0243.

8. See the film *Alamo Bay,* which despite its white hero main character flaw does tell some of the story of Vietnamese immigrant fishermen.

References

Asian Women United of California. 1989. *Making Waves: An Anthology of Writings by and About Asian American Women*. Boston: Beacon Press.

Chin, Frank, Jeffery Paul Chan, Lawson Fusao Inada, Shawn Wong. 1991. *Aiiieeeee! An Anthology of Chinese American and Japanese American Literature*. New York: Penguin Books.

Danticat, Edwidge. 1991. *Krik? Krak!* New York: Vintage Books.

Gesensway, Deborah, and Mindy Roseman. 1987. *Beyond Words: Images from America's Concentration Camps*. Ithaca: Cornell University Press.

Harvey, Komar, Khalilah Joseph, Sarah LePage. 1996. "We Treasure Music." *Rites of Passage*. Portland, OR: Jefferson High School.

Houston, Jeanne Wakatsuki, and James D. Houston. 1973. *Farewell to Manzanar*. Boston: San Francisco Book Company/Houghton Mifflin.

Inada, Lawson Fusao. 1993. *Legends from Camp*. Minneapolis: Coffee House Press.

Kim, Elaine H. 1982. *Asian American Literature*. Philadelphia: Temple University Press.

Lai, Him Mark, Genny Lim, Judy Yung. 1986. *Island: Poetry and History of Chinese Immigrants on Angel Island 1910–1940*. San Francisco: San Francisco Study Center. (P.O. Box 5646, San Francisco, CA 94101)

Lowe, Felicia. 1988. *Carved in Silence*. San Francisco: National Asian American Telecommunications Association. (415-552-9550)

Okada, John. 1957. *No-No Boy*. Boston: Charles E. Tuttle Co.

Sone, Monica. [1953] 1979. *Nisei Daughter*. Seattle: University of Washington Press. (Originally printed by Little, Brown and Company.)

Sunshine, Catherine A., and Deborah Menkhart. 1994. *Teaching About Haiti*. 3d ed. Washington, DC: Network of Educators on the Americas. (202-806-7277)

Takaki, Ronald. 1989. *Strangers from a Different Shore: A History of Asian Americans*. New York: Viking Penguin.

Yamada, Mitsuye. 1976. *Camp Notes*. San Lorenzo, CA: Shameless Hussy Press.

"What Happened to the Golden Door?" by Linda Christensen originally appeared in Rethinking Schools *11.1 (Fall 1996): 1, 4–5, 20, 21. Reprinted with permission.*

10

The Human Lives Behind the Labels

*The Global Sweatshop, Nike,
and the Race to the Bottom*

William Bigelow

Editors' Notes: Bill Bigelow shares some unique strategies for teaching about the global sweatshop in high school global studies and history courses. By asking a soccer ball questions about how it was made, by playing the "Transnational Capital Auction" game where they entice "Capital" to set up production in their country, by global clothes hunting, his students learn the causes behind the exploitation of child labor in Third World countries by American companies such as Nike and Disney. Asked to go beyond anger to action, Bigelow's students come up with some impressively creative written work. (To read more about activist approaches toward the study of sweatshops, see the appendices to Chapter 6.)

I began the lesson with a beat-up soccer ball. The ball sat balanced in a plastic container on a stool in the middle of the circle of student desks. "I'd like you to write a description of this soccer ball," I told my high school Global Studies class. "Feel free to get up and look at it. There is no right or wrong. Just describe the ball however you'd like."

Looks of puzzlement and annoyance greeted me. "It's just a soccer ball," someone said.

Students must have wondered what this had to do with Global Studies. "I'm not asking for an essay," I said, "just a paragraph or two."

At their request, some of the students' names used in this article have been changed.

As I'd anticipated, their accounts were straightforward—accurate if uninspired. Few students accepted the offer to examine the ball up close. A soccer ball is a soccer ball. They sat and wrote. Afterwards, a few students read their descriptions aloud. Brian's is typical:

> The ball is a sphere which has white hexagons and black pentagons. The black pentagons contain red stars, sloppily outlined in silver . . . One of the hexagons contains a green rabbit wearing a soccer uniform with "Euro 88" written parallel to the rabbit's body. This hexagon seems to be cracking. Another hexagon has the number 32 in green standing for the number of patches that the ball contains.

But something was missing. There was a deeper social reality associated with this ball—a reality that advertising and the consumption-oriented rhythms of U.S. daily life discouraged students from considering. "Made in Pakistan" was stenciled in small print on the ball, but very few students thought that significant enough to include in their descriptions. However, these three tiny words offered the most important clue to the human lives hidden in "just a soccer ball"—a clue to the invisible Pakistanis whose hands crafted the ball sitting in the middle of the classroom.

I distributed and read aloud Bertolt Brecht's poem "A Worker Reads History" as a tool to pry behind the soccer-ball-as-thing:

> Who built the seven gates of Thebes?
> The books are filled with names of kings.
> Was it kings who hauled the craggy blocks of stone?
> In the evening when the Chinese wall was finished
> Where did the masons go? Imperial Rome
> Is full of arcs of triumph. Who reared them up? . . .
>
> Young Alexander conquered India.
> He alone?
> Caesar beat the Gauls.
> Was there not even a cook in his army? . . .
>
> Each page a victory.
> At whose expense the victory ball?
> Every ten years a great man,
> Who paid the piper?

"Keeping Brecht's questions in mind," I said, after reading the poem, "I want you to *resee* this soccer ball. If you like, you can write from the point of view of the ball, you can ask the ball questions, but I want you to look at it deeply. What did we miss the first time around? It's not 'just a soccer ball.'" With not much more than these words for guidance—although students had some familiarity with working conditions in poor countries—they drew a line beneath their original descriptions and began again.

Versions one and two were night and day. With Brecht's prompting, Pakistan as the country of origin became more important. Tim wrote in part:

"Who built this soccer ball? The ball answers with Pakistan. There are no real names, just labels. Where did the real people go after it was made?" Nicole also posed questions: "If this ball could talk, what kinds of things would it be able to tell you? It would tell you about the lives of the people who made it in Pakistan . . . But if it could talk, would you listen?" Maisha played with its colors and the "32" stamped on the ball: "Who painted the entrapped black, the brilliant bloody red, and the shimmering silver? Was it made for the existence of a family of 32?" And Sarah imagined herself as the soccer ball worker: "I sew together these shapes of leather. I stab my finger with my needle. I feel a small pain, but nothing much, because my fingers are so calloused. Everyday I sew these soccer balls together for 5 cents, but I've never once had a chance to play soccer with my friends. I sew and sew all day long to have these balls shipped to another place where they represent fun. Here, they represent the hard work of everyday life." When students began to consider the human lives behind the ball-as-object, their writing also came alive.

Geoffrey, an aspiring actor, singer, and writer, wrote his as a conversation between himself and the ball:

> "So who was he?" I asked.
>
> "A young boy, Wacim, I think," it seemed to reply.
>
> I got up to take a closer look. Even though the soccer ball looked old and its hexagons and other geometric patterns were cracked, the sturdy and intricate stitching still held together.
>
> "What that child must've gone through," I said.
>
> "His father was killed and his mother was working. Wacim died so young. . . . It's just too hard. I can't contain these memories any longer." The soccer ball let out a cry and leaked his air out and lay there, crumpled on the stool. Like his master, lying on the floor, uncared for, and somehow overlooked and forgotten.

Students had begun to imagine the humanity inside the ball; their pieces were vivid and curious. The importance of making visible the invisible, of looking behind the masks presented by everyday consumer goods, became a central theme in my first-time effort to teach about the "global sweatshop" and child labor in poor countries. (I did an abbreviated version of this unit with my U.S. history classes. Some of the student writing here is theirs.)

Teaching About the Global Sweatshop

The paired soccer ball writing assignment was a spur-of-the-moment classroom introduction to Sydney Schanberg's June 1996 *Life* magazine article, "Six Cents an Hour." Schanberg, best known for his *New York Times* investigations of Cambodia's "killing fields," had traveled to Pakistan and posed as a soccer ball exporter. There, he was offered children for $150 to $180 who would labor for him as virtual slaves. As Schanberg reports, in Pakistan children as young as six are "sold and resold like furniture, branded, beaten, blinded as punishment for wanting to go home, rendered speechless by the trauma of their enslavement." For pennies an hour, these children work in dank sheds stitching soccer balls with the familiar Nike swoosh and logos of other transnational athletic equipment companies.

Nike spokesperson, Donna Gibbs, defended her company's failure to eliminate child labor in the manufacture of soccer balls: "It's an ages-old practice," she was quoted as saying in Schanberg's article, "and the process of change is going to take time." But as Max White, an activist with the "Justice. Do It NIKE!" coalition, said when he visited my global studies class last month, "Nike knew exactly what it was doing when it went to Pakistan. That's why they located there. They went because they *knew* child labor was an 'ages-old practice.'"

My initial impulse had been to teach a unit on child labor. I thought that my students would empathize with young people around the globe, whose play and education had been forcibly replaced with the drudgery of repetitive work—and that the unit would engage them in thinking about inequities in the global division of labor. Perhaps it might provoke them to take action on behalf of child workers in poor countries.

But I was also concerned that we shouldn't reduce the growing inequalities between rich and poor countries to the issue of child labor. Child labor could be entirely eliminated and that wouldn't affect the miserably low wages paid to adult workers, the repression of trade unions and democratic movements, the increasing environmental degradation, and the resulting Third World squalor sanitized by terms like "globalization" and "free trade." Child labor is one spoke on the wheel of global capitalism, and I wanted to present students with a broader framework to reflect on its here-and-now dynamics. What I share here is a sketch of my unit's first draft—an invitation to reflect on how best to engage students in these issues.

The Transnational Capital Auction

It seemed to me that the central metaphor for economic globalization was the auction: governments beckoning transnational corporations to come hither—in competition with one another—by establishing attractive investment climates (e.g., by maintaining low-wage/weak union havens and not pressing environmental concerns). So I wrote what I called "The Transnational Capital Auction: A Game of Survival." I divided students into seven different "countries," each of which would compete with all the others to accumulate "friendly to Capital points"—the more points earned, the more likely Capital would locate in that country. In five silent auction rounds, each group would submit bids for minimum wage, child labor laws, environmental regulations, conditions for worker organizing, and corporate tax rates. For example, a corporate tax rate of 75 percent won no points for the round, but a zero tax rate won 100 points.

(There were penalty points for "racing to the bottom" too quickly, risking popular rebellion, and thus "instability" in the corporate lexicon.)

I played "Capital" and egged them on: "Come on group three, you think I'm going to locate in your country with a ridiculous minimum wage like $5 an hour? I might as well locate in the United States. Next round, let's not see any more sorry bids like that one." A bit crass, but so is the real-world downward spiral simulated in the activity.

At the game's conclusion, every country's bids hovered near the bottom: no corporate taxes, no child labor laws, no environmental regulations, pennies an hour minimum wage rates, union organizers jailed, and the military used to crush strikes. As I'd anticipated, students had breathed life into the expressions "downward leveling" and "race to the bottom." In the frenzied competition of the auction, they'd created some pretty nasty conditions, because the game rewarded those who lost sight of the human and environmental consequences of their actions. I asked them to step back from the activity and to write on the kind of place their country would become should transnational Capital decide to accept their bids and locate there. I also wanted them to reflect on the glib premise that underlies so much contemporary economic discussion that foreign investment in poor countries is automatically a good thing. And finally I hoped that they would consider the impact that the race to the bottom has on their lives, especially their future work prospects. (That week's *Oregonian* carried articles about the Pendleton Co.'s decision to pull much of its production from Oregon and relocate to Mexico.) I gave them several quotes to reflect on as they responded:

- "It is not that foreigners are stealing our jobs, it is that we are all facing one another's competition." *William Baumol, Princeton University economist*

- "Downward leveling is like a cancer that is destroying its host organism— the earth and its people." *Jeremy Brecher and Tim Costello, authors* Global Village or Global Pillage

- "Globalization has depressed the wage growth of low-wage workers [in the United States]. It's been a reason for the increasing wage gap between high-wage and low-wage workers." *Laura Tyson, Chair, U.S. Council of Economic Advisers*

Many global issues courses are structured as "area studies," with units focusing on South America, sub-Saharan Africa, or the Middle East. There are obvious advantages to this region-by-region progression, but I worried that if I organized my global studies curriculum this way, students might miss how countries oceans apart, such as Indonesia and Haiti, are affected by the same economic processes. I wanted students to see globalization as, well, global— that there were myriad and far-flung runners in the race to the bottom.

This auction among poor countries to attract Capital was the essential context my students needed in order to recognize patterns in such seemingly diverse phenomena as child labor and increased immigration to the world's so-called developed nations. However, I worried that the simulation might be too convincing, corporate power depicted as too overwhelming. The auction metaphor was accurate but inexorable: Students could conclude that if transnational Capital is as effective an "auctioneer" as I was in the simulation, the situation for poor countries must be hopeless. In the follow-up writing assignment, I asked what if anything people in these countries could do to stop the race to the bottom, the "downward leveling." By and large, students' responses weren't as bleak as I feared. Kara wrote: "Maybe if all the countries come together and raise the standard of living or become 'capital unfriendly' then capital would have no choice but to take what they receive. Although it wouldn't be easy, it would be dramatically better." Adrian suggested that "people could go on an area-wide strike against downward leveling and stand firm to let capital know that they won't go for it." And Matt wrote simply, "revolt, strike." Tessa proposed that people here could "boycott products made in countries or by companies that exploit workers."

But others were less hopeful. Lisa wrote, "I can't see where there is much the people in poor countries can do to stop this 'race to the bottom.' If the people refuse to work under those conditions the companies will go elsewhere. The people have so little and could starve if they didn't accept the conditions they have to work under." Sara wrote, "I don't think a country can get themselves out of this because companies aren't generous enough to help them because they wouldn't get anything out of it."

What I should have done is obvious to me now. After discussing their thoughts on the auction, I should have regrouped students and started the auction all over again. Having considered various alternative responses to the downward spiral of economic and environmental conditions, students could have practiced organizing *with* each other instead of competing *against* each other, could have tested the potential for solidarity across borders. At the least, replaying the auction would have suggested that people in Third World countries aren't purely victims; there are possible routes for action, albeit enormously difficult ones.

T-Shirts, Barbie Dolls, and Baseballs

We followed the auction with a "global clothes hunt." I asked students to: "Find *at least* ten items of clothing or toys at home. These can be anything: T-shirts, pants, skirts, dress shirts, shoes, Barbie dolls, baseballs, soccer balls, etc.," and to list each item and country of manufacture. In addition, I wanted them to attach geographic location to the place names, some of which many students had never heard of (for example, Sri Lanka, Macau, El Salvador, and Bangladesh). So in class they made collages of drawings or magazine clippings of the objects they'd found, and with the assistance of an atlas, drew lines on a world map connecting these images with the countries where the items were produced.

We posted their collage/maps around the classroom, and I asked students to wander around looking at these to search for patterns for which kinds of goods were produced in which kind of countries. Some students noticed that electronic toys tended to be produced in Taiwan and Korea; that more expensive shoes, like Doc Martens, were manufactured in Great Britain or Italy; athletic shoes were made mostly in Indonesia or China. On their "finding patterns" write-up, just about everyone commented that China was the country that appeared most frequently on people's lists. A few kids noted that most of the people in the manufacturing countries were not white. As Sandee wrote, "The more expensive products seem to be manufactured in countries with a higher number of white people. Cheaper products are often from places with other races than white." People in countries with concentrations of people of color "tend to be poorer so they work for less." We'd spent the early part of the year studying European colonialism, and some students noticed that many of the manufacturing countries were former colonies. I wanted students to see that every time they put on clothes or kick a soccer ball they are making a connection, if hidden, with people around the world—especially in Third World countries—and that these connections are rooted in historic patterns of global inequality.

From here on, I saturated students with articles and videos that explored the working conditions and life choices confronting workers in poor countries. Some of the resources I found most helpful included: *Mickey Mouse Goes to Haiti*, a video critiquing the Walt Disney Co.'s exploitation of workers in Haiti's garment industry (workers there, mostly women, make 28 cents an hour; Disney claims it can't afford the 58 cents an hour workers say they could live on); a CBS *48 Hours* exposé of conditions for women workers in Nike factories in Vietnam, reported by Roberta Baskin; several Bob Herbert "In America" *New York Times* columns; a November 3, 1996, *Washington Post* article, "Boot Camp at the Shoe Factory Where Taiwanese Bosses Drill Chinese Workers to Make Sneakers for American Joggers," by Anita Chan; *Tomorrow We Will Finish*, a UNICEF-produced video about the anguish and solidarity of girls forced into the rug-weaving industry in Nepal and India; and an invaluable collection of articles called a "Production Primer," collected by "Justice. Do It NIKE!," a coalition of Oregon labor, peace, and justice groups.

I indicated above that the advantage of this curricular globe-trotting was that students could see that issues of transnational corporate investment, child labor, worker exploitation, poverty, and so on were not isolated in one particular geographic region. The disadvantage was that students didn't get much appreciation for the peculiar conditions in each country we touched on. And I'm afraid that, after awhile, people in different societies began to appear as generic global victims. This was not entirely the fault of my decision to bounce from country to country, but was also a reflection of the narrow victim orientation of many of the materials available.

I was somewhat unaware of the limits of these resources until I previewed a 25-minute video produced by Global Exchange, *Indonesia: Islands on Fire*. One segment features Sadisah, an Indonesian ex-Nike worker, who, with dignity and defiance, describes conditions for workers there and what she wants done about them. I found her presence, however brief, a stark contrast to most of the videos I'd shown in class that feature white commentators with Third World workers presented as objects of sympathy. Although students generated excellent writing during the unit, much of it tended to miss the humor and determination suggested in the *Islands on Fire* segment and concentrated on workers' victimization.

Critique Without Caricature

Two concerns flirted uncomfortably throughout the unit. On the one hand, I had no desire to feign neutrality—to hide my conviction that people here need to care about and to act in solidarity with workers around the world in their struggles for better lives. To pretend that I was a mere dispenser of information would be dishonest, but worse, it would imply that being a spectator is an ethical response to injustice. It would model a stance of moral apathy. I wanted students to know these issues were important to me, that I cared enough to do something about them.

On the other hand, I never want my social concerns to suffocate student inquiry or to prevent students from thoughtfully considering opposing views. I wanted to present the positions of transnational corporations critically, but without caricature.

Here, too, it might have been useful to focus on one country in order for students to evaluate corporate claims—e.g., "Nike's production can help build thriving economies in developing nations." I'd considered writing a role play about foreign investment in Indonesia with roles for Nike management as well as Korean and Taiwanese subcontractors. (Nike itself owns none of its own production facilities in poor countries.) This would have provoked a classroom debate on corporate statements, where students could have assessed how terms like "thriving economies" may have different meanings for different social groups.

Instead, I tried in vain to get a spokesperson from Nike, in nearby Beaverton, to address the class; I hoped that at least the company might send me a video allowing students to glean the corporate perspective. No luck. They sent me a PR packet of Phil Knight speeches and their "Code of Conduct," but stopped returning my phone calls requesting a speaker. I copied the Nike materials for students, and they read with special care the Nike Code of Conduct and did a "loophole search"—discovering, among other things, that Nike promises to abide by local minimum wage laws, but never promises to pay a *living* wage; they promise to obey "local environmental regulations" without acknowledging how inadequate these often are. Having raced themselves to the bottom in the transnational capital auction, students were especially alert to the frequent appearance of the term "local government regulations" in the Nike materials. Each mention might as well have carried a sticker reading WEASEL WORDS.

I reminded students of our soccer ball exercise, how we'd missed the humanity in the object until we read Bertolt Brecht's poem. I asked them to write a "work poem" that captured some aspect of the human lives connected to the products we use everyday. They could draw on any situation, product, individual, or relationship we'd encountered in the unit. As prompts, I gave them other work poems that my students had produced over the years. Students brainstormed ways they might complete the assignment: from the point of view of one of the objects produced, or that of one of the workers; a dialogue poem from the point of view of worker and owner, or worker and consumer; a letter to one of the products, or to one of the owners (like Oregon-based Phil Knight, CEO of Nike). Cameron Robinson's poem, below, expressed the essence of what I was driving at with the assignment.

Masks

Michael Jordan soars through the air,
on shoes of un-paid labor.
A boy kicks a soccer ball,
the bloody hands are forgotten.
An excited girl combs the hair of her Barbie,
an over-worked girl makes it.
A child receives a teddy bear,
Made in China has no meaning.
The words "hand made" are printed,
whose hands were used to make them?
A six year old in America starts his first day of school,
A six year old in Pakistan starts his first day of work.
They want us to see the ball,
not to see the millions of ball stitchers.
The world is full of many masks,
the hard part is seeing beneath them.

As we read our pieces aloud (I wrote one, too), I asked students to record lines or images that they found particularly striking and to note themes that recurred. They also gave positive feedback to one another after each person read. Sandee wrote: "I liked the line in Maisha's paper that said, 'My life left me the day I stitched the first stitch. . . .' I like Antoinette's paper because of the voice. It showed more than just pain, it also reflected a dream"—an ironic dream of a sweatshop worker who wants to flee her country for the "freedom" of the United States. Dirk had written a harshly worded piece from the point of view of a worker for a transnational company; it drew comments from just about everyone. Elizabeth appreciated it because "he used real language to express the feelings of the workers. As he put it, I doubt that the only thing going through their minds is 'I hate this job.'" As a whole the writings were a lot angrier than they were hopeful; if I'd missed it in their pieces, this came across loud and clear in students' "common themes" remarks. As Jessica wrote, "One of the things I noticed was that none of the [papers] had a solution to the situation they were writing about." Maisha agreed: "Each paper only showed animosity . . ."

I expected the unit to generate anger, but I hoped to push beyond it. From the very beginning, I told students that it was not my intention merely to expose the world's abuse and exploitation. A broader aim was to make a positive difference. For their final project, I wanted students to *do* something with their knowledge—I wanted to give them the opportunity to act on behalf of the invisible others whose lives are intertwined in so many ways with their own. I wasn't trying to push a particular organization, or even a particular form of "action." I wanted them simply to feel some social efficacy, to sense that no matter how overwhelming a global injustice, there's always something to be done.

The assignment sheet required students to take their learning "outside the walls of the classroom and into the real world." They could write letters to Phil Knight, Michael Jordan, or President Clinton. They could write news articles or design presentations to other classes. I didn't want them to urge a particular position if they didn't feel comfortable with that kind of advocacy; so in a letter they might simply ask questions of an individual.

They responded with an explosion of creativity: three groups of students designed presentations for elementary school kids or for other classes at Franklin; one student wrote an article on child labor to submit to the *Franklin Post,* the school newspaper; four students wrote Phil Knight, two wrote Michael Jordan, and one each wrote the Disney Co., President Clinton, and local activist, Max White.

Jonathan Parker borrowed an idea from an editorial cartoon included in the "Justice. Do It NIKE!" reader. He found an old Nike shoe and painstakingly constructed a wooden house snuggled inside, complete with painted shingles and stairway. He accompanied it with a poem that reads in part:

> There is a young girl
> who lives in a shoe.
> Phil Knight makes six million
> she makes just two.
> When Nike says "just do it"
> she springs to her feet,
> stringing her needle
> and stitching their sneaks.
> With Nike on the tongue,
> The swoosh on the side,
> the sole to the bottom,
> she's done for the night . . .
> When will it stop?
> When will it end?
> Must I, she says,
> toil for Nike again?

The "sculpture" and poem have been displayed in my classroom and have sparked curiosity and discussion in other classes, but Jonathan hopes also to have it featured in the display case outside the school library.

Cameron, a multi-sport athlete, was inspired by a *Los Angeles Times* article by Lucille Renwick, "Teens' Efforts Give Soccer Balls the Boot," about

Monroe High School students in L.A. who became incensed that all of their school's soccer balls came from Pakistan, a child labor haven. The Monroe kids got the L.A. school board there to agree to a policy to purchase soccer balls only from countries that enforce a prohibition on child labor.

Cameron decided to do a little detective work of his own, and discovered that at the five Portland schools he checked, 60 percent of the soccer balls were made in Pakistan. He wrote a letter to the school district's athletic director alerting him to his findings, describing conditions under which the balls are made, and asking him what he intended to do about it. Cameron enclosed copies of Sydney Schanberg's "Six Cents an Hour" article, as well as the one describing the students' organizing in Los Angeles—hinting further action if school officials didn't rethink their purchasing policies.

One student, Daneeka, bristled at the assignment, and felt that regardless of what the project sheet said, I was actually forcing them to take a position. She boycotted the assignment and enlisted her mother to come in during parent conferences to support her complaint. Her mother talked with me, read the assignment sheet, and—to her daughter's chagrin—told her to do the project. Daneeka and I held further negotiations and agreed that she could take her learning "outside the walls of the classroom" by "visiting" on-line chat rooms where she could discuss global sweatshop issues and describe these conversations in a paper. But after letting the assignment steep a bit longer, she found a more personal connection to the issues. Daneeka decided to write Nike about their use of child labor in Pakistan as described in the Schanberg article. "When I was first confronted with this assignment," she wrote in her letter, "it really didn't disturb me. But as I have thought about it for several weeks, child labor is a form of slavery. As a young black person, slavery is a disturbing issue, and to know that Nike could participate in slavery is even more disturbing." Later in her letter, Daneeka acknowledges that she is a "kid" and wants to stay in fashion. "Even I will continue to wear your shoes, but will you gain a conscience?"

"Just Go with the Flow"

At the end of the global sweatshop unit, I added a brief curricular parenthesis on the role of advertising in U.S. society. Throughout the unit, I returned again and again to Cameron Robinson's "masks" metaphor:

> The world is full of many masks,
> the hard part is seeing beneath them.

I'd received a wonderful video earlier in the year, *The Ad and the Ego,* that, among other things, examines the "masking" role of advertising—how ads hide the reality of where a product comes from and the environmental consequences of mass consumption. The video's narrative is dense, but because of its subject matter, humor, and MTV-like format, students were able to follow its argument so long as I frequently stopped the VCR. At the end of part one, I asked students to comment on any of the quotes from the video and to write other thoughts they felt were relevant. One young woman I'll call Marie, wrote in part: "I am actually tired of analyzing everything that goes on around me. I am tired of looking at things at a deeper level. I want to just go with the flow and relax."

I'd like to think that Marie's frustration grew from intellectual exhaustion, from my continually exhorting students to "think deep," to look beneath the surface—in other words, from my academic rigor. But from speaking with her outside of class, my sense is that the truer cause of her weariness came from constantly seeing people around the world as victims, from Haiti to Pakistan to Nepal to China. By and large, the materials I was able to locate (and chose to use) too frequently presented people as stick figures, mere symbols of a relationship of domination and subordination between rich and poor countries. I couldn't locate resources—letters, diary entries, short stories—that presented people's work lives in the context of their families and societies. And I wasn't able to show adequately how people in those societies struggle in big and little ways for better lives. The overall impression my students may have been left with was of the unit as an invitation to pity and help unfortunate others, rather than as an invitation to join with diverse groups and individuals in a global movement for social justice—a movement already under way.

Another wish-I'd-done-better, that may also be linked to Marie's comment, is the tendency for a unit like this to drift toward good guys and bad guys. In my view, Nike *is* a "bad guy" insofar as it reaps enormous profits as it pays workers wages that it knows full well cannot provide a decent standard of living. They're shameless and they're arrogant. As one top Nike executive in Vietnam told Portland's *Business Journal:* "Sure we're chasing cheap labor, but that's business and that's the way it's going to be"—a comment that lends ominous meaning to the Nike slogan "There is no finish line." My students' writing often angrily targeted billionaire Nike CEO Phil Knight and paired corporate luxury with Third World poverty. But corporations are players in an economic "game" with rules to maximize profits, and rewards and punishments for how well those rules are obeyed. I hoped that students would come to see the "bad guys" less as the individual players in the game than as the structure, profit imperatives, and ideological justifications of the game itself. Opening with the Transnational Capital Auction was a good start, but the unit didn't consistently build on this essential systemic framework.

Finally, there is a current of self-righteousness in U.S. social discourse that insists that "we" have it good and "they" have it bad. A unit like this can settle too comfortably into that wrong-headed dichotomy and even reinforce it. Teaching about injustice and poverty "over there" in Third World countries may implicitly establish U.S. society as the standard of justice and affluence. There is poverty and exploitation of workers here, too. And both "we" and "they" are stratified based especially on race, class, and gender. "We" here benefit very unequally from today's frantic pace of globalization. As well, there are elites in the Third World with lots more wealth and power than most people in this society. Over the year, my global studies curriculum attempted to confront these complexities of inequality. But it's a crucial postscript that I want to emphasize as I edit my "race to the bottom" curriculum for future classes.

Enough doubt and self criticism. By and large, students worked hard, wrote with insight and empathy, and took action for justice—however small. They were poets, artists, essayists, political analysts, and teachers. And next time around, we'll all do better.

"The Human Lives Behind the Labels: The Global Sweatshop, Nike, and the Race to the Bottom" by William Bigelow originally appeared in Rethinking Schools *11.4 (Summer 1997): 1, 12–16. Reprinted with permission.*

11

Tales from an Untracked Class

Linda Christensen

Editors' Notes: Outraged at the race and class bias of tracking,
Linda Christensen describes an experiment "untracking" her English
classes. Ten years of teaching "remedial" English taught Christensen
that notions of great differences in student abilities are false. She
finds that students have different sets of skills because of their education histories, but do not have different intellectual capabilities.
Christensen explodes the myths of tracking, a pervasive school practice not supported by research. She argues that by changing teaching
methods (and attitudes), an untracked class can develop students'
strengths. She also shares her methods for helping students develop
their writing abilities.

It's teacher "work" day—two days before students arrive—and I'm trying to
reconstruct my classroom between faculty, department, and union meetings.
Mallory leans over my desk, her dancer's body rounding in the third month of
pregnancy. "I need to transfer to your fifth period class because the parenting
class is only offered sixth. I hope this class is all mixed up like last year's."

Mallory reads over my temporary student enrollment list, telling me about
the students I don't already know. "Oh, he's bad, Ms. Christensen. He talked all
the time in math last year. I don't think he's passed a class yet. Oh, the Turner
brothers are in here. They are the smartest kids in our class. I swear they've
never gotten less than an A the whole time they've been in school."

The class is starting to sound good. Hopefully, Barbara Ward and Annie
Huginnie, the two senior counselors, have given me "mixed up" classes of students again: failures and successes, neighborhood and magnet students, per-
formers and nonperformers, "advanced," and "remedial."

Unhooking One Class

I untracked my English classes several years ago. I knew tracking was unjust, and I didn't want to perpetuate the myths about academic ability that tracking imparts. I also wanted to demonstrate that it was possible to teach a wide range of students in one class, to present a model for our school. After ten years of teaching remedial English, I also knew I couldn't stand teaching one more low-tracked class. Even if my seniority allowed me the privilege of teaching advanced classes, morally, I couldn't teach them any longer.

Tracking helps create, then legitimates, a social hierarchy within a school based on perceived differences in student ability. Students in higher tracks have access to college preparatory classes: algebra, geometry, calculus, chemistry, physics. But even in the traditional subjects—English and social studies—students participate in different educational experiences. Even the titles of classes are telling: Global Issues for college-bound students, Geography Skills for the vocationally tracked. Students in advanced classes read whole books, write papers, complete library research that prepares them for college, while students in lower track classes typically read light bites of literature and history—short stories or adolescent novels. Their writing, if they write, tends to remain in the narrative, personal storytelling mode rather than moving to the analytical.

Beyond the lack of preparation for academic tasks, the larger problem I witness as a teacher is the embedded beliefs students leave these classrooms with. Students in advanced classes come to believe they earned a privilege that is often given them based on race, class, or gender, while students in remedial classes learn they are incapable of completing more difficult work.

But I wonder what other messages my students learn when they see a majority of white students or magnet students in advanced classes. Do they believe that white students are smarter than students of color? That students who don't live in our neighborhood know more than neighborhood students? When we allow tracking, especially tracking that privileges one race, one class, or one gender over another, we may unwittingly allow students to walk away with these assumptions.

When I decided to untrack, I asked the counselors to place a variety of students in my classes. And they do. I typically teach four classes a day: Literature in American History, a two-period block class that I coteach with Bill Bigelow, and two sections of Contemporary Literature and Society, a senior-level course. (This is not a full load; I work as director of the Portland Writing Project for part of my day.) Each of these classes fulfills the requirement for junior- and senior-level English classes. The English department and the administration approved both courses as variations in the regular curriculum. Depending on the time my classes are offered, they are more or less diverse.

Myths and Misunderstandings

After teaching untracked classes for several years, I've come to believe that the notion of great differences in student ability is false. Many of the students who come from "remedial" classes are quite bright. But the abilities they bring to class often go unrecognized because they aren't the skills traditional education has prized. Anyone who has taught low-skilled classes know this. During my first years of teaching, I couldn't keep up with the verbal sparring in my Title I (now Chapter I) reading classes. Students beat me quite handily in verbal battles about going to the bathroom, eating food, and chewing gum in class.

Because of the difference in students' education histories, they come with different sets of skills, but not necessarily different sets of intellectual capabilities. The students who typically perform well in class have better reading, writing, geographic, and math skills. They have better work habits. They know how to study. They are often voracious readers. They have written more essays and know how to put together a well-organized paper. They are confident of their ability as students. Whereas many "remedial" students still have problems with the basics in punctuation, spelling, sentence structure, and grammar. They don't know where to begin or end a sentence much less a paragraph or an essay. Many have never read a complete book by their junior or senior year in high school. Many never do homework. They are often intimidated when it comes to traditional class work, or they have made a choice to slide by.

But often the most creative students in my mixed ability classes are the students who have not succeeded in school. Previously in my low-skilled English classes, this creative energy funneled into "stinging" each other, hurling insults. Now it finds outlets in poetry, dialogues, oral work. (This is not to say my classroom is perfect; I battle side talk daily.) In my experience, many previously low-tracked students have a great ear for dialogue because their listening and speaking skills are more finely honed. These students tend to be playful, talkative, adept at role plays, debates, and class discussions. They are risk takers.

Steven, for example, literally jumps into the middle of a debate. Once, in a unit on the politics of gender, he strode to the center of our circle and acted out how he believes women have a shopping mall approach to men. Steven pretended he was a woman inspecting each man as if he were a piece of merchandise, then tossing him aside when someone better came along. Although he had difficulty writing an essay on the topic, his spontaneous "presentation" during discussion was well argued and gave students a metaphoric framework for many of their debates on the topic.

Each group of students (as well as each individual student) presents their own problems. While most of the "advanced" students complete their class work and homework on time, too often they write "safe" papers. Chris, a potential valedictorian, summed it up when he asked, "What do I have to do to get an

A?" Not what tools must I be capable of using, not what knowledge will I need to understand about literature, writing, society, history, but what must I get done. My goal is to shake them out of their safety, to create a desire to write, instead of a desire to complete the work, to awaken some passion for learning, to stop them from slurping up education without examining it. I want them to walk around with notepads, ready for their next poem, story, or essay, but I also want them to question themselves and the world: in fact, I want them to question the privilege that placed them into advanced or honors classes. I want the same for my low-skilled students, but additionally, I am challenged to harness their verbal dexterity onto paper and motivate them to work outside of class. But I also want to provoke them to examine the inequalities that landed many of them in low-skilled classes in the first place.

Who Benefits?

Another myth about ending ability grouping is that "low" students automatically benefit while advanced students automatically languish. Some folks think that top students end up playing teacher to their not so bright peers in an untracked class—and unfortunately this is sometimes true. Adam, a senior, writes of his experience in this role:

> I was always the one the teacher looked at when someone else needed help. "Oh, Adam can help you." It's not the usual form of discrimination, but I realize now how much it bothered me when I was in grade school. "Well, so and so isn't a good student, he needs extra help, we'll make him partners with Adam. Adam won't mind spending his extra time explaining things to so and so."

This problem tends to erupt when a class is untracked but the curriculum and methodology remain the same. It's the worst case scenario that proponents of tracking use to scare us into maintaining the status quo. They assume that top students master the material quickly and must either tap their toes or play teacher while remedial students struggle. This situation places students who arrive feeling one down educationally at a further disadvantage, but it also takes time away from advanced students who should be working at the edge of their ability instead of repeating what they already know.

But if we turn the practice of students as teachers around and look at it differently, if we shift perceptions about who teaches in a classroom, then we acknowledge that all students can be teachers. When there is real diversity in the class, students teach each other by sharing their strengths: Steven's improvisation on gender issues, Jessica's dialogue, Tony's metaphoric analysis of the politics of language, Adam's ability to punctuate, Tivon's synthesis of political issues into concrete images, Curtina's images in her poetry, Joe's insight into how social politics reverberate in the 'hood.

Students also teach each other by telling the stories of their lives or debating issues from diverse perspectives. Scott thought that racism had disappeared after the '60s. When Millshane told about her brother's death at the hands of a white man who was never punished for the crime, when she described the cross burning in front of her house, when Suntory wrote about the hour it took for 911 to respond after a round of gun shots were fired into his house, Scott's education about race relations became real.

As Jessica noted in her class evaluation:

> This is the first English class in three years where I have been around different students. All of us have been tracked into separate little migrating groups forever stuck with each other. I think that having so many different thinking minds made it rich. All the experiences we shared were exciting and new. It made us debate things because most often we didn't agree with each other. But we listened and we all think a little bit differently now. Don't you wish the whole world could be like our class?

Of course this notion of students as teachers implies a major shift in the structure, content, and methodology of the class.

Changing the Curriculum

I was moved to untrack my classes because of the injustice I saw in students' education. But I continue to teach untracked courses because they make better classes—for teachers and students.

Now instead of constructing my curriculum around a novel in my English classes, I teach thematic units that emphasize the social/political underpinnings of my students' lives: the politics of language, men and women in society and literature, the politics of cartoons and mass media. The point is not to teach a certain novel or a set of facts about literature, but to engage students in a dialogue, to teach them to find connections between their lives, literature, and society. And most important, to teach them to question what is too often accepted. The same is true in my Literature in American History course. We no longer march through the year chronologically. "Essential" questions provide the focus for each unit.

In the politics of language section of my Contemporary Literature and Society class, I ask "Is language political?" There is no one text that answers the question. A variety of readings—novels, plays, essays, short stories, poems—as well as role plays, discussions, improvisations, writing from our lives, all serve as "texts." Think of it as a symphony or a choir. Each text, each student's life, adds an instrument or voice to the discussion. The texts are interwoven, but the recurring refrain is made up of the students' stories and analysis—their voices, either in discussion or in read-arounds of their own pieces, hold the song together.

For example, instead of teaching students Standard Written Edited English as if it were the only way to speak and write, as if it were the language agreed upon as the best choice, I ask them to question that policy. Because many of the seniors are either preparing for or avoiding the SATs, I begin the unit by giving them a sample test, then exploring how they felt about it. Most felt humiliated. We explore why a test for college admissions should make them feel like that. We ask why there should be tests to keep some people in and some people out of college. Statistics from FairTest that break down SAT scores by race, class, and gender provide students another perspective. They try to analyze what these data mean. Are women less intelligent than men? Are rich people smarter than poor people? If not, how can we explain the difference in scores? What other explanations can we find?

"The Cult of Mental Measurement," a chapter from David Owens' book *None of the Above,* gives historical background to their analysis. Then we look at how language affects different groups. We read George Bernard Shaw's *Pygmalion* and look at the intersection of class and language. Through "The Achievement of Desire," a chapter from Richard Rodriguez's book, *Hunger of Memory,* students examine how people whose first language is not English change when they assimilate. We also read parts of *Talkin' and Testifyin'* by Geneva Smitherman. For many students, African American and European American, this is the first time they've studied the historical roots of the African American language. For some, this is an affirmation of their home language, a winning back of pride in themselves and their families; for others, it is an opportunity to explore misconceptions about language.

The change in content to thematic units with a focus on essential questions shifts the educational domain from memorizing the rules to questioning the rules. This is sometimes uncomfortable. There are no easy-to-answer, machine-scorable tests at the end of the unit. There is no "getting it done." Sometimes, there isn't even agreement. The shift in terrain from consumption of knowledge to the questioning and examining of assumptions moves students of diverse abilities away from the lock-step nature of a skills approach while at the same time challenging them with a rigorous, accessible curriculum.

Our explicit focus on the politics of language and education plays an additional key role in untracking my classes. Because tracking has to one degree or another shaped students' academic self-conception, especially low-tracked students, taking a critical look at this process helps them rethink their potential. As my teaching partner Bill Bigelow writes in an article on untracking the social studies classroom:

> [t]he unequal system of education, of which tracking is an important part, needs a critical classroom examination so that students can expose and expel the voices of self-blame, and can overcome whatever doubts they have about their capacity for academic achievement.

Changing Strategies

It's hard to parse out techniques. They don't easily divide into reading, writing, social studies, English. Is writing interior monologues and poetry about a historical novel a reading strategy, a writing strategy, or a way to deepen students' understanding of history or literature? When students begin writing poetry, drama, essays, fiction, their reading of those genres change. They read with a new kind of awareness—they look at blocking, dialogue, imagery, use of evidence instead of reading for answers. When students begin making a social analysis of a text, where does English end and social studies begin? Just as untracking makes us question the notion of "good" kids and "bad" kids, changing classroom practice blurs borders between content areas and strategies. Nothing is quite so tidy.

Some of the readings discussed above are quite difficult—for all students. And this provides a roadblock or a dilemma for those of us who want to untrack classes. How do we continue to read challenging literature when not all of our students are capable of reading it? Do we "dummy down" the curriculum and deny capable students access to a rigorous curriculum or do we give different assignments to students based on their reading levels? Although I've done both in the past, as well as providing students a choice of novels within a theme, I grew uncomfortable with those options.

Improvisations, dialogue journals, poetry, and interior monologues as well as other strategies teach students in any class to question rather than read for answers. But in an untracked class, these methods equalize access to reading as well as push students to discuss content. Not every student in my class completes the readings by the due date, but they can still be involved in the discussion. Often the class talk entices them to read and provides a meaningful context for them to understand the text.

Improvisations

Now I use a variety of strategies to give students access to the readings. For example, with *Pygmalion* I use improvisations. I divide the students into small groups, give each group a provocative scene and ask them to create an improvisation which will help the class understand what took place in that particular section of the play. As a small group they discuss the scene and make meaning. As I circulate from group to group, I catch snatches of questions: What is going on? Who is Freddie? And then moving to higher level discussions: Why does Eliza throw the slipper at Higgins? Why doesn't she fight back when he calls her a "squashed cabbage leaf?" Doesn't this remind you of . . . ?

The groups provide access to the entire class as they reread, reinterpret, and act out the text. Goldie and Antonia rewrote the script in modern Jefferson language. Steffanie and Licy worked with the original script on the bath scene. Students stay in character on "stage" as the class questions them. Disagreements about the interpretation of a scene lead to engaged dialogue about character motivation, author's intent, and society. Often, we're sent back to the original text to "prove" our point to the class. Although I usually begin by modeling the kinds of questions I want students to ask, they quickly take over. This year in my second period class, Mark's statement, "Henry didn't love Eliza, he considered her a professional equal," kept the class debating for an hour. In sixth period, Licy questioned whether Eliza's life improved with her new knowledge or brought her misery. As Licy's questions suggest, the improvs permit all students access to important issues about the politics of language.

The improvs are not an end; they are means to provoke meaningful discussion about literature or history in a way that enables all students to participate, no matter what their reading level.

Dialogue Journals

Improvisations are neither appropriate nor valuable for all texts. The method I most frequently use to equalize access to articles, essays, stories, and novels is the dialogue journal (otherwise known as double entry journal, talk back journal, note taking/note making). The purpose of the journal is to teach students to read closely, to encourage them to ask questions of the author, but also to find out what confuses them in the piece. I try to get students to question, to make connections with other readings or life experiences, instead of reading to consume.

In the dialogue journal, students become the authors of their own questions about readings. Sometimes at the beginning of class, I ask students to read over their dialogue journals and circle questions or comments they want to discuss. After they've assembled their contributions, I divide students into small groups and ask them to talk with each other using their questions/comments as a starting point. I tell each group to bring one or two questions or statements to the whole class for discussion. Here's a sample from my junior Literature in American History class discussion about the novel *River Song* by Craig Lesley:

Group #1 returns to full class discussion with the following question: Is Craig Lesley racist, sexist, homophobic when he makes the Mexican jokes, etc. or is he just trying to develop Danny's character?

Angela: I think he's just trying to show what Danny is like.

Aaron: Okay, but then why does he have to keep bringing [racist remarks] up? Couldn't he just have him make those jokes during the first few chapters, then leave it alone? When he keeps doing it, it's an overkill. It seems like with the Native American issues there is so much to cover, why spend time making jokes about Mexicans or male nurses?

Janice: Wouldn't he have to keep doing it if it's a characteristic? I mean he couldn't just do it for a few chapters then stop or else his character wouldn't be consistent.

Aaron: Yeah. I hadn't thought of that.

Sarah: I think he's trying to make a point about the Native American culture—that since they are consistently being put down—alcoholism, lazy—that they put other people down, other racial groups.

Aiden: I think he's just trying to make it realistic. That's how people talk; they make fun of others.

Jim: Maybe he's trying to make us think about the racism, that's why he puts in so many—and against so many groups.

Aaron: But couldn't he do that and then have someone make a comment about it—like Pudge? When Danny makes a joke, couldn't she say, "Hey, that's not funny. Think about how people talk about Indians"?

Janice: Yeah. Because people do that in real life too—stop someone when they're telling a racist joke.

The class becomes more democratic. This questioning method puts students in charge of the discussion rather than the teacher. It validates their questions. Sometimes in large group discussions when the teacher talks about symbolism or a well-read student discusses the imagery in a passage, some students are too intimidated to ask the simple questions. Students have an opportunity to try out ideas on this small group before taking the point to a large group.

Again, students learn from each other, by challenging each other's assumptions and listening to someone else's opinion. Claire wrote, "I got ideas I wouldn't have thought of, interpretations I would not have considered. When I really thought about all of it, I acquired some new skills from [my classmates]."

While writing dialogue journals, students stand outside of the text and ask questions or make comments, whereas the writing of interior monologues and poems from the literary or historical character's point of view encourages students to examine why characters act the way they do. These tactics put students inside the literature and history. They breathe life into content that can seem dry, factual and distant from students' lives. For example, in the following poem "To Die Without Weeping: The Atomic Bomb on Japan," Cresta borrows language from the book *Hiroshima* and writes about the bombing of Hiroshima:

Near the center
it was as hot as the sun
and people became nothing.
Windless.
Their heads bowed in expressionless silence,
butterflied patterns of kimonos
scarring shoulders and backs.
Cries for water echo off destroyed lives,

moans of pain haunt the shadows of men,
as if their spirits left
so that we do not forget too quickly
our people buried together.

As black rain falls
plants flourish wildly in the wreckage.
A city of death blanketed in flowers,
morning glories twist around lifeless bodies,
regenerating towards the sky,
ignoring those who have died without weeping.

Her poem puts us inside Japan. We no longer count bodies from a distance. Instead we feel the pain and see the destruction close up. We talk about the personal toll of the bombing. Historic decisions become embedded in real people's lives—lives that students, at least momentarily, have touched.

Interior monologues also help erase the distance between people separated by time, race, nationality, and gender. In this form, students get inside a character's head and write thoughts and feelings about a situation from that person's perspective. Typically, students read pieces of literature or history or view slides, videos, or paintings in class as prompts and then imagine the character's thoughts. Heather wrote from the point of view of an enslaved woman raped by her "master"; George wrote from the mind of a soldier who watched his friend die. Erika's interior monologue came from a Japanese American girl's point of view as she burned all of her Japanese toys and books before the Japanese internment. By getting in touch with their own pain and loss, students learn to empathize with others. This deepens their reading. Instead of reading words, they read lives.

There is no right answer in these exercises. As I tell students, "The only way you can do this wrong is to not do it." I begin by sharing examples from previous years so students will understand what I want. The student pieces advance classroom knowledge and dialogue about content, in these cases history, but also about reading and writing. One of the points I try to make is that neither history nor literature is inevitable. People made choices.

Filtering reading through improvisations, dialogue journals, interior monologues, poetry, and class discussions slows the class down. We don't "cover" as many novels, as much history, as we did before. But students learn more. They discover how to dig beneath the surface, how to make connections between texts and their own lives. Last year in class evaluations students let me know in no uncertain terms that the units they enjoyed and learned the most from were the units we spent months on; the units they enjoyed the least were the ones where I "bombarded [them] with readings" that I didn't give them time to digest.

I remind myself that taking time to carefully teach students how to "talk back" to text pays off throughout the year because these practices teach students to read and respond critically. In her class evaluation Lily wrote, "I look at the world as a question now. When I read the newspaper, I don't know if I can believe what it is saying. I always read more than one history book, and definitely question what CNN is saying. The press has a way of changing stories to make them sound good so that the paper will sell. I think the historians did the same thing."

These techniques also allow students from different literacy backgrounds a way to join in the conversation. There's no one way, no right way to talk about literature and history.

Changing Writing Strategies

Few students, regardless of their ability, see themselves as writers. So my first challenge is to change students' perceptions about writing and their ability. I tell them: Don't worry about grammar, punctuation, or spelling on the first drafts, just write, then revise. I try to get them to kick the editor out of their heads.

The threshold for success should be low enough for all students to cross over. The climate should be welcoming enough for everyone to want to try. Whatever we write, wherever we begin should be cause for celebration. I know this sounds like some kind of fairy tale magic—"just believe enough and your dream will come true." But as corny as it sounds, it's true. Maybe part of it is that if teachers believe in a student's capacity to learn, they will. But I think part of it is rewriting the student mind set, replacing the belief, "I don't know how to write or read or discuss," with the belief that they can.

The read-around is where the fairy dust that converts nonwriters to writers happens. The circle is necessary so everyone is a part of the class. (This also cuts down on discipline problems because all students are visible and accountable.) As students and I read our pieces, classmates take notes and give positive feedback to the writer. I talk about three kinds of feedback: content, style, and "me too." They can respond to the content of the piece—what did they like about the arguments, the ideas of the writing. They can respond to the style of the piece. I ask them to be specific. What line, what phrase did they like? Did they like the imagery, the repetition? Instead of working on a deficit model— what's wrong with this piece—we work on a positive model—what's right with this piece. What can we learn from it? They can also respond, after they've given the writer feedback, with a "me too" story that tells how the writer's experience stimulated a memory. As Pete noted in his class evaluation:

> The way you have us make comments (what did you like about [the piece of writing]) has helped me deal with people. My skin is thick enough to take a lot of abuse just because I've always had a fairly high opinion of some of the things I can do. I didn't realize a lot of other people don't have that advantage. After a while I found out positive criticism helped me more than negative too.

·Students learn from each other. They provide each other with accessible models. I encourage them to listen for what "works" in the writing of their peers, and then steal those techniques and use them in their own pieces. In their portfolio evaluations, they write about what they learn from each other's writing as a way of discussing the changes in their writing.

Erika wrote in her portfolio:

> My classmates played a huge role in improving my writing. Without them I wouldn't be able to write at all. When listening to people's pieces I find things to use in my own work. When I hear Jessica or Courtney read a piece I listen to their "attitude" and try to bring it into my own writing. When I hear Amianne and Rose's description I then try to reach deeper into my own vocabulary. And when I hear Rachel's and Adam's true life stories, I search back in time to find something that happened in my life worth writing about.

In an untracked class, the fear is that advanced students will read and students who have been placed in low-tracked classes will be silenced. But that has not proven true. I begin with low threat assignments: write about your name; write about an event in your life; write from the point of view of a character. At the beginning of the year, I ask students to write a compliment to each of their classmates about their piece. The message is: anyone who reads will receive positive feedback. No one will be thrown to the wolves. We do critique writings later, but always the initial feedback is what works. All students are fearful when they share. They feel exposed and vulnerable. Their hands shake, their voices quaver, clearly, they are nervous. Although Sharon was afraid to read for the first quarter of the year, she eventually read:

> One thing I need to learn is to read my pieces out loud because I might think my piece is scum but it might be just dandy to another. I think it was good that we had read-arounds because you got a chance to hear what people thought about our pieces and that leads to rewrites.

Heather wrote:

> When I listen to other people's writing, I hear things I love or wish I'd written myself. Most of the time that's where I get my inspiration. Sometimes I catch myself saying, "I wish I could write like so-and-so." Then I think, "What was it about his/her piece that I liked?" When I figure that out, I'm that much closer to being a better writer. I use their papers as examples. I steal their kernels of ideas and try to incorporate it into my own writing. For example, I love how Ki uses her personal history in her writing, so I try that out for myself. I like Lisa's use of unusual metaphors, so I try as hard as I can to steer clear of the generic type I've been known to use in the past.

As with the reading, not all students in an untracked class arrive on the due date with a paper in hand. To be sure, some students haven't taken the time to do the work, but others can't find a way to enter the work; they either don't know where to start or feel incapable of beginning. Even my pep talks about "bending the assignment to find your passion" or "just write for thirty minutes; I'll accept whatever you come up with as a first draft" don't entice these students. That's why I'm not a stickler about deadlines. During read-arounds the students who wrote papers will spawn ideas for those who either couldn't write or who haven't learned homework patterns yet. They will teach them how to find a way to enter the assignment. Sometimes students write a weak "just to get it done" paper, then hear a student's piece that sends them back home to write.

Conflict and Consciousness

As we solve problems, we create them. Untracking raised issues I haven't had to deal with before. At Jefferson, ability grouping tends to divide down race and class lines, so there is less tension over these issues in homogeneously grouped classes—usually because one group feels too marginalized to speak out. This is not true in a "mixed up class"—especially when the curriculum I teach explicitly examines and challenges race, class, and gender inequities. Students who have been privilieged feel the weight and sometimes the guilt of that privilege. While other students feel outrage when they understand that "their prison decorated with modern illusion is still a prison," as my student Tivon wrote. Put these two emotions, guilt and outrage, together in fifty-five minute periods and the result is conflict.

Race and class can become tender wounds where students and teacher either learn from one another or create inseparable gulfs. A student I'll call Paul wrote, "This is the first time in my history as a student where I would cry because of a class . . . I cried because I was a white male who had been through the scholars program, oblivious to tracking."

Some turned that shame into anger. European Americans didn't want to feel guilty about the past or the present. In one class after the Rodney King verdict, almost every topic turned into a discussion on race, and the discussion always left someone feeling anxious, at the very least. As one student wrote in her evaluation, "I found myself contributing less to the class than I normally do. I had always thought of this class as a place where I could be free to express my ideas and have those ideas be respected, even if everyone doesn't agree with them, but instead a lot of the time I found it to be a place where I had to watch my tongue for fear of being labeled a racist." Later she added, "I know hearing what a lot of people had to say made me feel uncomfortable, but it changed some of my perceptions about the world, and our class."

Sekou, an African American male, provided an alternative perception to the same class:

> It gets almost scary when we begin to touch on controversial racial issues or uncover other sheets that seemed to be intentionally pulled over our eyes. Everyone feels the seriousness in the room, but for some it turned them away. They became disgruntled with the class. "This always happens," some said. But to me, it is beautiful. It makes me look forward to discussions, and I look

forward to taking part. I think about the issues on my own outside of class. That never happened to me before. Class had always been separate from the real world. Finally, there is a connection.

Unfortunately, there is no quick exercise that makes inequality go away. This conflict and the discomfort have become more pronounced since the uprising in Los Angeles. It's more acute in the senior year when students are competing for scholarships and entry into colleges.

I try to structure my Literature in American History class around movements where people worked together for change. I talk about constructing alternative moral ancestors—people we want in our family/racial history because they worked to end oppression. As Johanna wrote, "I'm glad we studied the abolitionists; they restored my faith in my race. I learned not to feel guilty for what my ancestors did. I am free to choose my own moral ancestors, and I have."

I take Bill Bigelow's idea of looking at the use of pronouns—who is the "we" students identify with? For example, when Leah said, "How did the Nez Perce feel when we took their land?" the class looked at the "we." Did we identify with the settlers or with the people who were trying to keep land for the Nez Perce? Licy, a Mexican American senior, told Joachim, a foreign exchange student from Germany, "You don't have to feel guilty unless you identify with the part of the system that denies people their rights."

Is there an alternative to this conflict? Change is sometimes painful. I don't want my students feeling tongue-tied, but protecting them from reality is not a trade-off I'm willing to make.

Conclusion

We can't just wish tracking away. There are too many barriers and too much resistance on too many levels. The evidence against tracking is mounting. Parents, teachers, administors, and students need to be convinced that we can deliver a rigorous, challenging education for everyone in untracked classes. In addition to making a case against the injustice of tracking, we need to create a vision of education that serves all children. I am hopeful that change is possible. Teachers in my school and around the district are questioning practices that before were taken for granted. Now is the time for the education community to prove that justice and quality education are possible.

"Tales from an Untracked Class" by Linda Christensen originally appeared in Rethinking Schools *7.2 (Winter 1992–93): 1, 19–22. Reprinted with permission.*

12

Teaching Math Across the Curriculum

Bob Peterson

Editors' Notes: In this essay, Bob Peterson describes how students can overcome "number numbness." Instead of presenting abstract number problems or remote number puzzles and stories, Peterson uses interdisciplinary, multicultural, and student-centered approaches. Math comes alive for students when it is connected to their generative themes, their conditions, their experiences, and to popular culture. Peterson shares strategies for using math to help students understand our society's inequalities, especially the impact of race, class, and gender. This essay is not for math teachers alone; it reminds us of the dangers of isolating academic knowledge from experience and offers ways we all can use math in the courses we teach.

I recently read a proposal for an innovative school and it set me thinking about math. It wasn't the proposal's numbers that got my mind going, but rather the approach to structuring math into the curriculum. I disagreed with it.

The plan called for the curriculum to be divided into three areas—math/science, the arts (including fine arts and language arts), and history/philosophy. Blocks of time were set aside for a unified approach in each area. As I mulled over the proposal and thought of my experience in a self-contained fifth-grade classroom, I realized I was uneasy with the proposed curricular divisions, specifically the assumption that science and math belong together as an unified block. It reminded me of how some elementary teachers integrate the curriculum by lumping language arts and social studies together in one strand, and math and science in another.

It also raised several questions for me. Why place math and science together, and not math and social studies? What are the political and pedagogical assumptions behind such an approach? Why shouldn't reformers advocate math in all subject areas? Why not have "math across the curriculum," comparable to "writing across the curriculum?"

One reason reformers have advocated changes in how math is structured is because of the historic problems with math instruction itself: rote calculations, drill and practice ad nauseum, endless reams of worksheets, and a fetish for "the right answer." These have contributed to "number numbness" among students, and ultimately among the general population when students become adults.

But the problem is deeper than a sterile teacher-centered and text-driven approach. "Number numbness" also has its roots in how math is segregated in schools and kept separate from the issues that confront students in their daily lives. Most students don't want to do abstract exercises with numbers or plod through text-based story problems that have them forever making change in some make-believe story. The curriculum rarely encourages students to link math and history, math and politics, math and literature—math and people.

There are unfortunate consequences when math is isolated. First, the not-so-subtle message is that math is basically irrelevant except for success in future math classes, or if you want to be a scientist or mathematician. Second, students learn that math is not connected to social reality in any substantive way. Thus students approach math in the abstract and never are encouraged to seriously consider the social and ethical consequences of how math is sometimes used in this society. Third, if students are not taught how math can be applied in their lives, they are robbed of an important tool to help them fully participate in society. An understanding of math and how numbers and statistics can be interpreted is essential to effectively enter most debates on public issues such as welfare, unemployment, and the federal budget. For example, even though the minimum wage is higher than it has ever been, in constant dollars it is the lowest in forty years. But you need math to understand that.

When I first began teaching fifteen years ago, I was dissatisfied with "number numbness" but wasn't sure what to do about it. My growth as a teacher first came in the area of language arts and reading. I increasingly stressed that students should write for meaningful purposes, and read books and stories that were connected to their lives. Thus I had children read and discuss whole books, conducted writing workshops, and had students read and write in science and social studies. My math, however, remained noticeably segregated from the rest of the curriculum, even though I increasingly emphasized problem solving and the use of manipulatives.

More recently, with the help of my teacher colleague Celín Arce and publications from the National Council of Teachers of Mathematics, I have begun to view math as akin to language. I believe that math, like language, is both a discipline unto itself and a tool to understand and interact with the world and other academic disciplines. Just as written and oral language helps children understand their community, so can written and oral mathematics. Just as teachers stress the need for "writing across the curriculum," I believe it is important to advocate "math across the curriculum." Just as students are expected to write for meaningful purposes, they should do math for meaningful purposes.

Plans to integrate math into science are a step in the right direction. And assuming that the science curriculum is "meaningful," the teaching of mathematics will improve. But I believe linking math with science is only a beginning, and should be followed with integration of math across the curriculum. I have found that my fifth graders, for instance, are particularly interested in social issues. Thus integrating math with social studies is an effective way to bring math alive for the students. (Before I go any further, I want to make two important clarifications. First, I don't mean to imply that distinct math "minilessons" aren't important. They are, just as such lessons are necessary in reading and writing. I also want to make clear that integrating math with social studies does not necessarily make the teaching more student-centered or the content more concerned with issues of social justice. Those important components depend on the teacher's philosophical and pedagogical beliefs.)

In the past few years I have tried in a variety of ways to integrate mathematics—from the simplest understanding of number concepts to more complex problem solving—with social studies. In the interests of clarity (my classroom life is never so neatly ordered), I outline these approaches as: Connecting Math to Students' Lives; Linking Math and Issues of Equality; Using Math to Uncover Stereotypes; Using Math to Understand History.

Connecting to Students

The starting point of many teachers is to build on what students bring into the classroom, and to connect curriculum to the students' lives. Math is a great way to do this. I usually start the year with kids exploring, in small groups, how math is used in their homes and communities. They scour newspapers for numbers, cut them out, put them on poster paper and try to give sense to their meanings, which at times is difficult. They interview family members about how they use math and write up their discoveries. As part of a beginning-of-the-year autobiography, they write an essay "numeric me" tying in all the numbers that connect to their lives, from height and weight, to number of brothers and sisters, to addresses, phone numbers, and so forth. I also ask them to write a history of their experiences in math classes, what they think about math, and why.

This process starts a yearlong conversation on what we mean by mathematics and why it is important in our lives. As the class becomes increasingly sensitive to the use of numbers and math in news articles, literature, and in everyday events, our discussions help them realize that math is more than computation and definitions, but includes a range of concepts and topics—from geometry and measurements to ratios, percentages, and probability.

As part of the autobiography project we also do a timeline. We start by putting the students' birth dates and that of their parents and grandparents on a class timeline that circles the outer perimeter of my classroom (and which is used throughout the year to integrate dates that we come across in all subject areas). The students also make their own timelines—first of a typical day and then of their life. In these activities, students use reasoning skills to figure out relations between numbers, distance, time, fractions, and decimals.

I also use another beginning-of-the-year activity that not only builds math skills but fosters community and friendship. The whole class discusses what a survey or poll is and brainstorms questions that they would like to ask each other. After I model one survey, each student surveys classmates about a different topic. Kids, for example, have surveyed classmates on their national origin, their favorite fast food restaurant, music group, or football team, or what they think of our school's peer mediation program. Each student tabulates his or her survey data, makes a bar graph displaying the results, and reflects on what they have learned in writing. Later in the year they convert the data into fractions and percentages and make circle graphs. I encourage the students to draw conclusions from their data, and hypothesize why the results are the way they are. They then present these conclusions orally and in writing.

This activity is particularly popular with my students, and often they will want to do more extensive surveys with broader groups of people. The activity lays the basis for more in-depth study of polling and statistics around issues such as sampling, randomness, bias, and error. For extensive curricular ideas on the use of polls and statistics in social studies, see *The Power of Numbers* curriculum published by the Educators for Social Responsibility.

Math and Inequality

To help my students understand that mathematics is a powerful and useful tool, I flood my classroom with examples of how math is used in major controversies in their community and in society at large. I also integrate math with social studies lessons to show how math can help one better understand our society's inequalities. Kids are inherently interested in what is "fair," and using math to explore what is and isn't "fair" is a great way to get kids interested in all types of math concepts, from computation, to fractions, percentage, ratios, averages, and graphing.

For example, during October and November, there is often lots of discussion of poverty and hunger in my classroom, related either to the UNICEF activities around Halloween or issues raised by the Thanksgiving holiday. This is a good time to use classroom simulation exercises to help the children understand the disparity of wealth in the United States and around the world. In one lesson, I provide information on the distribution of population and wealth in the six continents, and then have the children represent that information using different sets of color chips. After working with the students so they understand the data, we do a class simulation using a map of the world that is painted onto our playground. Instead of chips to represent data we use the children themselves, and I tell them to divide themselves around the playground map in order to represent the world's population distribution. I then use chocolate chip cookies, instead of chips, to represent the distribution of wealth, and hand out chocolate chip cookies accordingly. As you can imagine, some kids get far more chocolate chip cookies than others, and lively discussions ensue. Afterward, we discuss the simulation and write about the activity.

Not only does such a lesson connect math to human beings and social reality, it does so in a way that goes beyond paper and pencil exercises; it truly brings math alive. I could just tell my students about the world's unequal distribution of wealth. But that wouldn't have the same emotional impact as when they see classmates in the North American and European sections of the map get so many more cookies even though they have so many fewer people.

I also use resources such as news articles on various social issues to help the students analyze inequality. The students, again in small groups, study data such as unemployment or job trends, convert the data into percentages, make comparisons, draw conclusions, and make graphs. This is a great way to help students understand the power of percentages. Because they also use a computerized graph-making program, they realize how the computer can be a powerful tool.

One group, for example, looked at news stories summarizing a university report on the ten thousand new jobs created in downtown Milwaukee due to commercial development. According to the report, African Americans held fewer than 8 percent of the new jobs, even though they live in close proximity to downtown and account for 30 percent of the city's population. In terms of the higher-paying managerial jobs, Latinos and African Americans combined held only 1 percent, while white residents who are overwhelmingly from the suburbs took almost 80 percent of the new managerial jobs. Using this data, my students made bar graphs and pie graphs of the racial breakdown of people in different jobs and in the city population. They compared the graphs and drew conclusions. They then did a role play with some students pretending to be representatives of community organizations trying to convince the mayor and major corporations to change their hiring practices. What began as a math lesson quickly turned into a heated discussion of social policy. At one point, for example, a student argued that the new jobs should be split—⅓ Black, ⅓ Latino, and ⅓ white, because those are the three principal nationality groups in Milwaukee. Others disagreed. Needless to say, this led to an extensive discussion of what is "fair," of reasons why minorities had so few of the jobs created downtown, and what it would take for things to be different.

Math, Stereotypes, and Voice

It is important for students to be aware of whose voice they are hearing as they read history books or the newspaper, or watch a movie. Who gets to narrate history matters greatly, because it fundamentally shapes the readers' or viewers' perspective. We can analyze these things with kids and help them become more critical readers of the books and other media. In this process math plays an important role.

I usually start with something fairly easy. I have my students analyze children's books on Columbus, tabulating whose views are represented. For instance, how many times do Columbus and his men present their perspective, versus the number of times the views of the Taíno Indians are presented. The students, using fractions and percentages, make large graphs to demonstrate their findings and draw potential conclusions. Large visual displays—bar graphs made with sticky tape, for instance—are good points of reference to discuss and analyze. Math concepts of percentages, proportions, and comparisons can be used to help kids discuss the statistics they've uncovered and the graphs they've made.

A similar tabulation and use of percentages can be used to analyze popular TV shows for the number of "put downs" versus "put ups," who is quoted or pictured in newspapers, stereotypes of females in popular cartoons, who is included in textbooks, and who is represented in the biography section of the school library. (See "Math and Media" in *Rethinking Our Classrooms: Teaching for Equity and Justice* [1994].)

Numbers and History

As we study history in my classroom, we pay particular attention to dates and data. I try to highlight those numbers that relate to social movements for equity and justice. For example, as we look at women's struggle for equality we try to imagine what it was like for Susan B. Anthony to go to work as a teacher and get paid $2.50 a week, exactly half the salary of the previous male teacher. Lots can be done with such a statistic—from figuring out and graphing the difference on an annual or lifetime basis, to looking for wage differentials in other occupations and time periods, including the present. I have found children particularly interested in looking at the wages paid to child workers—whether it be in coal mines or textile mills. We compare such wages to the price of commodities at the time, to the wages of adult workers, and to the wealth that was accumulated by the owners of industry. Such historical connections can be easily linked to present-day concerns over U.S. child labor and minimum wage laws or to international concerns over multinational corporations exploiting child labor in Asia to make consumer goods for their worldwide markets.

One math/history connection that can range in sophistication depending on the level of the students is to look at who is represented in different occupations and areas of power in our society, and how that has changed over time. For example, students can figure out what percentage of the signers of the Constitution were slave holders, common working people, women, wealthy businessmen who held bonds, and so forth. A similar exercise would be to analyze U.S. presidents, or the people our country has chosen to honor by putting their faces on currency and coins. Such historical number-crunching can take a contemporary turn if you have students analyze the gender and racial breakdown of the U.S. House and Senate, the editors of major newspapers, or the CEOs of Fortune 500 companies.

It's important for students to understand that such numbers are not permanent fixtures of our social structure, but have changed as result of social movements such as the Civil Rights or women's movements. To demonstrate this, a teacher might have students tally the current percentage of African Americans or women in selected professional occupations and compare it to the 1960s, before the rise of affirmative action.

Another area is to teach the history of math, pointing out the contributions of various non-European cultures and civilizations to mathematical thought. Greek mathematicians, for instance, were heavily influenced by their predecessors and counterparts in Africa and Asia. Arab mathematicians inspired European Renaissance scholars. The Mayans were one of the first peoples to develop the concept of zero and make sophisticated mathematical calculations. I have used a unit on the Mayan counting system of a base 20 with my fifth graders to demonstrate such sophistication and to help students expand their understanding of place value.

Conclusion

The level of sophistication and complexity of the math we use in our classrooms naturally depends on the developmental level of our students. Teachers, however, too often underestimate what students are capable of doing. To the degree that I am able to provide quality instruction, clear modeling, and activities that are purposeful, I am usually pleased with the enthusiasm with which my kids take on such math-based projects and the success they have in doing them.

I have found that as a result of trying to implement "math across the curriculum"—and in particular, integrating math and social studies—my students' interest and skill in math have increased, in terms both of their understanding of basic concepts and of their ability to solve problems. Furthermore, they can better clarify social issues, understand the structures of society, and offer options for better social policies.

Kids need every tool they can get to make this world—their world—a better place. Mathematics is one such important tool.

References

Bigelow, Bill, et al., eds. 1995. *Rethinking Our Classrooms: Teaching for Equity and Justice.* Milwaukee: Rethinking Schools, Ltd.

Folbre, Nancy, and the Center for Popular Economics. 1995. *The New Field Guide to the U.S. Economy.* New York: New Press.

Frankenstein, Marilyn. 1989. *Relearning Mathematics: A Different Third R—Radical Maths.* London: Free Association Books.

Gross, Fred, et al. 1993. *The Power of Numbers, A Teacher's Guide to Mathematics in a Social Studies Context.* Cambridge: Educators for Social Responsibility. Available from ESR, 23 Garden St., Cambridge, MA 02138. 800-370-2515.

National Council of Teachers of Mathematics. 1989. *Curriculum and Evaluation Standards for School Mathematics.* Reston, VA: NCTM.

———. 1991. *Curriculum and Evaluation Standards for School Mathematics Addenda Series, Grade K–6,* edited by Miriam A. Leiva. Reston, VA: NCTM.

Nelson, David, Joseph Gheverghese, and Julian Williams. 1993. *Multicultural Mathematics: Teaching Mathematics from a Global Perspective.* New York: Oxford University Press.

Rose, Stephen J. 1992. Social Stratification in the United States poster. New York: New Press.

U.S. Department of Labor. 1994. *By the Sweat and Toil of Children: The Use of Child Labor in American Imports.* Washington, DC: U.S. Department of Labor.

Zaslavsky, J. 1993. *Multicultural Mathematics.* Portland, ME: Weston Walch.

"Teaching Math Across the Curriculum" by Bob Peterson originally appeared as "Number Numbness: Teaching Math Across the Curriculum" in Rethinking Schools *10.1 (Fall 1995): 1, 4–5. Reprinted with permission.*

13

Negotiating Mathematics

Susan Hyde

Editors' Notes: In this chapter from the extraordinary book *Negotiating the Curriculum* edited by Garth Boomer and Nancy Lester, Susan Hyde describes her experiment negotiating the curriculum with her Year 8 mathematics class in Banksia Park High School, South Australia. Hyde transformed the traditional classroom into one in which students helped design the course, worked collaboratively, and rewrote parts of the assigned textbook. She offers many teaching strategies and shows how this long-term process can help develop students' self-confidence and self-direction. Hyde's inclusion of student voices reveals both enthusiasm for and resistance to her teaching methods; she is not afraid to share some of the problems that go along with such an experiment. Her examples of how students rewrote math texts are good instances of critical literacy invented from the bottom up.

When I decided to negotiate the curriculum with my Year 8 mathematics class, I had already had experience with the model in teaching science. I had also experimented with certain teaching strategies appropriate to the model in the mathematics classroom. Before I discuss these I want to consider what negotiating the curriculum implies in the light of teacher and student experiences of learning and teaching.

Effects of Curriculum Negotiation

Negotiating the curriculum is not an alternative teaching strategy or a way of breaking the monotony of second term. It involves the development of the teacher's understanding of the learning process and of how to provide conditions in which learning can best occur. It is a curriculum design that is developed by students and teachers in the classroom.

One of the basic attitudes in this design is teachers' confidence in their students' ability to learn and make informed decisions about their learning. We know that people know *how* to learn, because people learn to speak a language from ages zero to five, not to mention walking, eating, dressing themselves, drawing etc. They may have help, of course, but not in the form of formal instruction or prescription. However, by the time most people enter secondary school they have had seven years' experience of being told how to learn. In my experience this has a variety of effects, which manifest themselves when I offer a negotiable curriculum to my students.

Student Reactions to Offers of Negotiation

Firstly, there are those students who are *thankful and amazed* when they realize that at last they will be able to learn in the way they know they can learn. They are pleased because I am treating their self-confidence with respect. They react responsibly to helping to make decisions about class activities, and they help others to stick to the decisions. These are usually students who are interested in learning what is offered at school—who have put up with teacher direction because they have been very, or reasonably, successful at passing tests and achieving standards (and because they feel that they are powerless to change teachers' attitudes, or even to suggest it).

Other students view the offer with *suspicion,* because they don't really think that I will go through with it. They don't trust me. They approve of my attitude, but their experience of teachers allowing them to make decisions about what they will do is not vast. They think that I am "conning" them. These students involve themselves reservedly at first, but once they see that I am serious their involvement becomes more enthusiastic. They need encouragement and react well to praise. They are quick to react when I do tell them to do something and, justifiably, demand reasons for my direction. They react well to my inquiries about how they are going about their learning, but I have to be careful how I word any suggestions about how they might do it better, because they often interpret this as a direction and follow it out of habit. These students usually have been "turned off" to the degree of accepting that what happens in the classroom is likely to be boring. They have mostly experienced inconsistent success with tests and grades, depending on how bored they have been with the topic. They are usually cynical and either quietly go through the motions expected by the teacher, with their "brains in neutral," or become disruptive, determined to thwart the teacher's plan of action.

There are also those students who are *dismayed* at the whole idea, because they can't understand how they will learn anything if I or someone else doesn't tell them what to do. If left to themselves they will flounder in confusion and never get anything done. Some refuse even to start. These students need a lot of attention, and certainly more guidance, until they become more confident in their abilities. Above all, they need help in starting to learn a new "topic," because they can't trust their own judgements about what they already know about the subject. I try to help them by involving them in discussions about what interests them and what they have experienced. This helps them to realize what they know, so they can choose a starting point. I try to help by offering a limited set of alternatives to make their choice easier. Once they have chosen a starting point they need attention and encouragement right through the learning process. These students usually have experienced a lot of failure and have little self-confidence. They have either become very dependent on prescription or learnt how to avoid schoolwork as much as possible.

Finally, there are those students who react with *contempt*. In their opinion I am shirking my responsibilities by not giving the class a prescription for learning (the teacher is the expert) and allowing students to help each other (after all, that is cheating). They resent my attitude of encouragement to the disruptive persons in the class, and criticise and complain about the 'discipline' in the classroom. They want me to be more judgmental and to compare students with each other. They are continually asking "How much is this worth?" or "What grade will I get for this?" They refuse to help, or resent helping, other students. Understandably, these students are not usually popular with the rest of the class, and therefore their influence is not very great amongst their peers. However, they can influence me because their attitude can plunge me into paranoia about doing something different. Their expectations of me are those which I am trying to avoid and indeed unlearn, so I oscillate between outright confrontation or reasonable persuasion when dealing with these students. Interestingly enough, they may be bright, competitive students, super-confident from being so successful, or they may be those who have been so turned off by failure and humiliation that they criticize my attitudes and actions simply because I belong to that hated class of people—teachers. They are very often boys, and their attitude is often partly sexist (women are not to be taken seriously). They often approve of the competitive and prescriptive atmosphere in which they usually learn at school and have learned to succeed at the expense of others.

The Need for Confidence

I have written at length about this because I want to emphasize that negotiating the curriculum implies that the teacher has confidence in his/her students' ability to learn and make decisions about their learning. It is important to realise that the majority of students have not had this experience. In fact they have been learning quite the opposite for most of their school life. This conditioning can cause a lot of problems and barriers for a teacher who is attempting to make his/her classroom open and collaborative and means that students will be at different starting points.

Another reason I mention this is because students have to be confident of their own ability to learn. In some cases this takes quite a while to develop, depending on what experience the student has had. This is why I insist that a negotiable curriculum results from an attitude that has to be shared and developed by teacher and student. It is not a teaching strategy or method, and it is not just an interesting way to approach weather or graphs. It is a long-term, continuously developing and improving relationship between teacher, students and learning.

Planning the Course Together

During 1979 I was one of a group of teachers at Banksia Park High School involved in what we called the *classroom-based curriculum study*. Essentially, we decided to get our classes involved . . . in planning their year's courses in mathematics, science and humanities.

During the first few weeks of the term, we involved our classes in discussions about the learning process, the nature of the subject and learning that subject in the classroom. We did this because we believed that these discussions would focus their attention on the learning process, as well as giving them a more informed basis on which to make decisions about the content and skills to be learnt in the particular subject areas.

At first I was rather apprehensive at the thought of students planning a mathematics course. However, they coped with planning this subject very easily—in fact, often more easily than with planning the other subjects. I was amazed at how much they knew about mathematics and how easily they could justify learning about the topics they chose. Really, this is not so surprising, because they had already experienced seven years of learning mathematics (which was certainly more than they had experienced of learning science).

Once we had planned the course we then used the book with which they were provided to find appropriate exercises (Franklin and Preece, 1973). In reality the basic content of the course was not really negotiable, because they were limited to a certain extent by the graded exercises and concepts covered by the book. However, it was understood that the content of the book could be (and was) added to, rearranged, rewritten and left out according to the needs of the course that we had planned.

Planning the Topic Work

At first I planned the exercises for the class. I gave them a set of exercises and discussion topics to be finished with the time we had planned for the topic. I did this because I wanted to show them how the book worked, and to give them a model for a plan. The work that I set was negotiable in that they could change the plan for their own needs. For instance, they could negotiate to leave out certain exercises if they already knew how to do the problems well. They could also ask for extra ones if they were finding them hard to understand. They responded very well to this. Both fast and slow learners took advantage of it. (The class was a mixed ability group.) Each student had to negotiate with me before making the change. In almost every case the student's judgment of his/her understanding of the exercise and whether he/she needed to omit it or needed more practice was right. It certainly made me realize that there must be quite a few students who either sit in mathematics classes being bored by doing many exercises in which they don't need practice, or rarely have the satisfaction of knowing that they understand how to do a type of problem, simply because teachers refuse to trust students' judgments about their learning.

After a couple of topics, I asked those students who had finished their work before the time limit whether they would like to help set the next topic work instead of doing extension work. They did this and produced an excellent topic for the class. Gradually, more students became involved in this, some working as a group to plan for others. Others planned their own topic work, and sometimes a group of friends would work on a common plan.

It was very interesting to see how the students actually planned their own work. The number of students who did this varied with each topic, depending on how confident they felt with the subject matter. By the end of the year, most students were planning their work for each topic, and if they didn't plan their own work they had several versions from which to choose: mine, their friends' etc.

The way in which they sequenced the work was varied also. I think that we take it for granted that mathematics must be learnt in a certain sequence, and in some cases it is necessary to know about one concept before another can be understood. Most students accepted the sequence that the book offered. However, it is most significant that some students varied the sequence according to what they knew or didn't know. Others varied it according to interest. For instance, during a topic called Decimals, Fractions and Percentages, some students sequenced the exercises so that they learnt about decimals in relation to percentages, decimals in relation to fractions, fractions in relation to percentages etc. In other words, they chose a bit out of one chapter, then a bit out of the next, then dropped back to the other chapter for a few exercises and so on.

This all sounds very rosy and easy, but for some students the experience was traumatic at times. Primarily, they were faced with the realization that they had to take the responsibility for the amount and quality of their learning. In a conventional mathematics classroom students depend on the teacher for set work, and thus can complain if the work is too hard or too easy. Some students set their work too hard, confident that they could complete it with understanding, and faced disillusionment when they could not cope with it—especially if I had advised them that this would happen. In most cases they needed a lot of encouragement to continue to direct themselves. Some other students set work that was too easy for them. They then had to face the realization that they were underestimating their ability, and this also affected their confidence to direct themselves. "I can't do it," they would say. However, some students persisted in playing the game of "bludging," mainly because they were afraid to fail again. They then had to face confrontation with me about responsibility and taking advantage of the power that they had agreed to use properly.

You see, a negotiable curriculum is not just a wishy-washy attempt by a teacher to let students do what they feel like. It is a process by which the teacher can help to develop students' confidence and self-direction, often against all experience and conditions of both teacher and student. This process is ongoing and is based on the developing relationship between teacher and student. This relationship must be based on honesty about confidence, ability and personality, and is therefore filled as often with confrontation and disillusionment as it is with warm feelings of cooperation and friendship. Students find this traumatic at times, because usually they are not used to being granted responsibility for decisions that affect the quality and quantity of learning. The teacher has to be sensitive to all of this and to know when to relieve a student from the responsibility until his/her confidence is regained, and when to insist that the student does not try to opt out of making decisions.

It helps, and in fact is essential, for the students to be aware of this developing process. This is why I consider it very important to involve students in discussions about the learning process, and about what self-directed learning implies for them. These discussions should continue throughout the process, and should help the students to rationalize some of the strong emotions they are feeling.

Collaborative Learning Atmosphere

The relationships between the students in a classroom are also very important if the classroom is to be open and collaborative. The basic idea is that learners collaborate and share ideas and information to help each other to learn. In mathematics it is as important as in any other subject that students have plenty of practice in explaining verbally what they know, what they mean or how to do something. Teachers, especially, are familiar with the experience of increasing their understanding of a particular concept or method through having had to explain it many times.

In the classroom the teacher has to allow this to happen. Students, of course, always help their friends to do mathematics when sitting next to each other—that is, if they are allowed to talk in class. But the traditional mathematics classroom is very quiet and orderly, so it is not surprising that the value of students talking about mathematics and helping each other is very underrated by most mathematics teachers.

The competitive atmosphere in the traditional classroom also does not encourage students to help each other. Why should they? They may be helping other students to get better marks. I was very surprised when I realized that often the seemingly brightest students in a mathematics class have a very poor ability to explain what they know.

In my classroom students could help each other, as well as get out of their seat to find someone else to help them if their neighbour could not. At other times, when everyone was working and lots of hands were going up for help, I would organize a student or two to aid me in giving help to those who needed it. Several students in the classroom spent one lesson per week helping another student.

The discussion that follows (from a tape transcript) is part of an interview conducted by a colleague with some members of this class:

Interviewer: Someone said the kids help. Is that very common?

Mandy: Yeah.

Bridget: Oh, sort of, like my friend didn't know how to do fractions, so I had to sit down and help her.

Stephen: Yeah, she sometimes picks people that know what they're doing to help the others that don't.

Michelle: And if they've finished it and they know what to do and they've got it all right and that.

Interviewer: Have any of you people helped someone else?

All Students: Yeah . . . I have . . .

Interviewer: All right. Well, what do you get out of helping someone else? Doesn't that interfere with . . . ?

Students: (interrupting) Helps us too.

Interviewer: How does it help you?

Michelle: Well, by saying it to them we're learning the same too, like we're learning more.

Stephen: No, we're not. We're learning the same, but we're just sort of revising it over ourselves with other people and they know what to do.

Interviewer: What do the other kids think of having a kid help them?

Bridget: Oh, they don't mind. The kid talks to them in sort of their own language or whatever you like to call it.

Mandy: Yeah, with the teachers, they might go too fast and they might not understand it.

Bridget: They might say, oh, "these denominators," and that, and some kids don't understand what they are or something.

Scott: If the kids don't understand, when a teacher says it, they sort of . . . They say it, they explain it to you, then you say, well, you don't know how to do it and they go mad at you. But when a kid does it, they explain it through a couple of times.

Interviewer: You reckon kids are better at that?

Students: Yeah.

Mandy: That's if they know what they're doing.

Bridget: Oh, teachers can do it too, but you know, other kids . . .

Interviewer: Don't you think that's the teacher's job?

Students: Yeah.

Scott: But kids can do it better.

Bridget: But kids can understand . . . like kids that have got problems understand kids better than they can understand the adults.

Interviewer: Why's that, do you reckon?

Bridget: I dunno, they sort of talk the same . . . I dunno, the teachers talk bigger and longer words that the kids don't understand.

Stephen: Yeah, and probably they don't understand, and so when other people [kids] help, and that, they understand what they are saying.

Interviewer: Mmmmmmm, all right.

Some teachers became rather worried when I mentioned that my students helped each other, because they were afraid that the students would not teach each other properly. This fear is well founded in classrooms where students are not allowed to help each other. One of the most crucial discussions that students should have before they do this on an organised scale is how to help someone best. They also need to be aware, as were the students involved in the above discussion, of how it helps the person doing the explaining as well.

Teaching Strategies

There are certain teaching strategies that I found appropriate to the negotiation model in the mathematics classroom. They were adapted from those that I use when teaching science. They included brainstorming, class discussion, group discussion and offering a range of audiences for writing and information presented by students for other class members to learn. They were not distinct entities, because a combination could be used in any one lesson. They were based on the principle that learning should be an active process, involving the learner's prior knowledge and language as he/she comes to grips with the language and concepts involved in the new information. Two factors were basic to the success of these strategies:

1. There must be an *emphasis on meaning* in the mathematics classroom. Students must know that mathematics is about *understanding* as well as getting the right answer. It is possible, and I've seen it many times, that students know how to get the right answer but not be sure about why they get it. All they do is to memorize the steps to get that answer. However,

memorization of method is much easier when it is rooted in meaning—then the student understands what the steps are about. I think that we owe more to our students than a promise that when they get to Year 11 they will understand the steps they are doing in Year 8.

2. The teacher must give the class (both students and teacher) *time to develop class and group discussion skills.* The students have to learn to share their ideas, ask each other questions and, above all, feel confident that what they say is seen as a valuable contribution. The teacher has to learn to help these discussions to continue without interfering with the students' flow of thought. In particular, the teacher has to learn new responses to students' explanations that are partially incorrect, in order to encourage the students to be more explicit, instead of telling them that they are wrong. This latter response encourages the "guess the answer in the teacher's head" game, which is prevalent in many classroom discussions in schools.

A lot more could be said about how these skills are developed in the classroom. However, the main point that I want to emphasize is that it takes time for both teacher and students to adjust to the different roles involved. The payoff in the quality and involvement of the students' learning is well worth the time.

Writing Mathematics

Writing rules, definitions and explanations of methods is excellent for giving students the opportunity to make meaning in mathematics. Every now and then my mathematics class had what we called a *writing lesson.* They chose a rule, concept or method that they had been working with, and tried to generate the definition, rule or method for themselves. We usually *brainstormed* the idea first and then took the ideas to *group discussion,* where they worked out what they should write. After that the *groups reported back,* and we discussed the writing.

The following definitions were generated by group discussion about factors:

Factor definitions (First attempt)

Factor is a number that will go in another number.

Factors are whole numbers that can divide equally into another number.

Factors are a set of numbers that divide evenly into one another.

Factors are whole numbers which can divide evenly into any whole number like: 15—the factors are 1, 5, 3, and 15. The factors of a number are whole numbers that go into another number.

Factors are numbers that can be divided into a certain number, like 4.

When the Year 8 students saw what the other groups had written they began to discuss the adequacy of the various definitions. They continued this in group discussion with the aim of improving their own definitions. During these discussions I spent my time going around, asking sticky questions to encourage them to be more explicit. When the groups reported back their definitions were more explicit, and some of them quite adequate:

Factor definitions (Second attempt)

The factors of a number are whole numbers which will go into this number equally.

Factors are whole numbers which divide evenly into another number evenly: e.g. factors of 10 are 1, 2, 5, 10; the factors of the number 16 are 1, 2, 4, 8, 16.

Factors are a set of whole numbers that divide evenly into one whole number, e.g. 30; 1, 15, 2, 5, 6.

Factors are numbers that can divide into a certain number.

At the end of this lesson, students were feeling very pleased with themselves, because they had worked out for themselves what factors are, written some mathematics, talked a lot of mathematics and read a lot. Mathematics was making sense.

A similar sort of strategy was a very efficient way to teach mathematical method. At the end of the discussions and writing, the students could explain in their own words why and how to do each step in the method involved. It was certainly a more efficient and rewarding way for most learners to come to grips with both the concepts and methods of mathematics than just listening to me practising my explanations with a piece of chalk in my hand.

A very important aspect of this writing was that the students were writing for themselves. I wanted my students to value this and to know that they *could use writing for learning.* One way to demonstrate this to them was to get a student who was not sure how to explain what he/she was doing actually to write it out. This helped the student to understand what he/she was doing as well as to memorize the method.

The most powerful aspect for me when the students were writing for themselves and for the other students, was that I got to see their writing in the formative stages. (This is not usually possible when students are writing to me as examiner.) I found it an excellent opportunity to introduce new terminology or to help them to understand a particular concept when it was relevant and meaningful to them.

Rewriting the Textbook for Other Students

My students also wrote mathematics for each other, and they enjoyed doing this. The writing involved dividing a particular section of work amongst groups of students. During the group work they examined the text to decide whether it needed revision of the explanations and/or exercises. This approach was particularly suitable for geometry, where the textbook that we used approached geometry in an abstract way that made it particularly indecipherable for students.

It is important for students to be given direct experience with the language of mathematics. The language of mathematics is very accurate and descriptive, and if one is familiar with the concepts and terms involved, it is a very useful and meaningful language. Learning to be able to articulate the meaning of certain concepts involves the development of language that can best describe the concepts involved. This is especially pertinent to mathematics. Everyday language is useful for understanding many of the experiences and concepts that we use to live our lives. However, it is not very useful for describing and understanding many of the concepts involved in mathematics.

For instance, in the textbook we used in Year 8 the following definitions are offered for points and lines:

Undefined Terms

A point • has no dimension

  • marks a position in space

  • is usually denoted by a capital letter

A line • has one dimension

  • is an infinite set of points

  • extends indefinitely in both directions

  • only one straight line can pass through two given points

  • a *straight* line is usually denoted by the names of two points on the line

A model of the line PQ (or l):

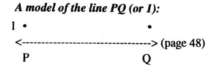

P   Q

After this set of definitions (the book goes on to define a set of lines, a plane, space), the students are asked to answer a set of multiple-choice questions based on understanding the concepts. Not surprisingly, most students cannot do this.

The student who reads these definitions cannot understand them unless he/she understands the meanings of the words "dimension," "space," "denoted," "infinite," and "extends." The definitions will not make sense unless explained in everyday language. Okay, I could do that—give them a lecture about what the definitions really mean. However, I consider the strategy to be fairly inefficient, because it does not actively involve the students. A more efficient way is to get the students to try to explain and understand these concepts in their own terms. This means talking to each other about them and trying to explain them in their own writing. This can be done on a classwide basis. However, doing this so that students can explain the concepts to other students adds interest and purpose to the discussions.

A group of students who worked on this section offered the following definitions to the class.

A dot

A dot is not like a point, it is a mark on the page. If you want to show a point you do a dot, for a point is invisible. A dot is a model of a point.

A line

A line is not a line, it is an invisible thing between two places, it cannot be seen. If it is drawn, then it becomes a model of a line. A model of a line is visible. A line goes on forever.

These definitions were well received and promoted a lot of discussion amongst the students, who were subsequently able to do the exercises with ease.

In the next example the students decided that the textbook definitions were too exact.

Definitions

Concurrent lines have a single point of intersection.

Collinear points lie on the same straight line.

Coplanar points (or lines) lie in the same plane.

Parallel lines are coplanar lines which do not intersect.

Skew lines are lines which are not coplanar and do not intersect.

A line is parallel to a plane if they have no point in common. (page 53)

The students rewrote some of these definitions and used examples and diagrams to illustrate what they meant.

Concurrent lines: are two or more lines which intersect (cross over each other) at one point and continue away from each other.

Collinear points: are two or more points which lie on the same line as each other, e.g.

A   B   C   D

Coplanar points or lines: lie in the same plane as each other.

Parallel lines: are two lines or more, which as long as they go they will never join because they are the same distance apart all the way. They are coplanar.

These students also rewrote the exercises provided to test the understanding of these concepts.

Sometimes the students completely rejected what the book had to offer and made up their own explanations and exercises. The following is an example of part of what one student offered his classmates for work on measurement.

Measurement

The whole idea of measurement is to be exact. For example:

———————————

This line is exactly 31½ mm long, not 30 or 31 but exactly 31½ mm.

The measurement of the blackboard in height is 115 cm or 1 metre and 15 cm. The width of the blackboard is 1 metre and 15½ cm.

Now I have set some work for you to measure, the same way as I have done.

1. The mobile trolley is ____ wide and ____ long and ____ in height.

2. The shelves on the wall are ____ in depth and ____ long and ____ wide.

3. A clock is ____ round as in [____] and ____ deep.

4. A teacher's collection box (orange)—the type the P.E. teachers use for log cards: it's ____ deep and ____ on the bottom and at the top from the top of the side to the other side is ____ .

This work should help you with your measurement.

Gavin

When the groups of students had finished revising their section, and had it checked by me, I then had their work printed, or they prepared it on overhead transparencies.

Each group then presented its work to the class, gave time to discuss the explanations and then set the appropriate exercises from the book, or from what they had prepared, for the students to finish during the lesson and for homework. These lessons were a great success. The students enjoyed being "teacher," and other students enjoyed being taught by students. Presenting information to other students in this way helps students to be more articulate about what they have learnt and gives them experience and confidence in explaining their ideas and learning to other people. Students openly admit this, and I'm sure that other teachers who have used this approach would support me in this claim.

Conclusion

After two terms of working on the course that the students and I had planned, I examined the amount of work done from the textbook in comparison to the amount of work done by other classes in the school. I found, to my delight, that we had covered the same amount of work as the other classes, although, of course, in a different sequence. We finished the year's work with most students covering the set Year 8 course, and some covering considerably more. I was very pleased with these results, and so were the students. I felt that, because the students and I had shared the responsibility for planning the course and topic work, we were more able to cope with the individual abilities that were present in the class. As I teach in a mixed ability situation, I found this result both remarkable and satisfying. In my opinion most students—fast, slow or average learners—benefited from being able to use their own judgment about their learning and to use this judgment to negotiate with me what and how they learnt in mathematics.

A Note on Barriers to Change

When a teacher offers a negotiable curriculum to students, he/she is sharing power with them. The teacher recognizes the basic democratic principle that people should have the right to help determine the activities in which they will participate. Over how much the students will have control is the negotiable factor and is determined by the teacher. By convention it is the teacher in whom control and authority within the classroom are vested. Because of this convention there are pressures within the conditioning of teachers, and within schools (and, indeed, within society), that act as barriers to a teacher's confidence in sharing that power.

Most teachers have been conditioned by their own schooling (primary, secondary and tertiary) and perhaps their teaching experience, to consider that in the classroom the decision-making input of the teacher is high while that of the student is low. Teachers traditionally make the decisions that concern learning, use of space, use of time, use of equipment, tone of behaviour and so on. The teacher who negotiates with students about these matters faces considerable amounts of rethinking in his/her attitude towards the relationship with, and responses to, the students.

Pressure from the school coincides with these conditions. Firstly, the decision-making model offered by the teacher may be in direct contradiction to the model recognized by the school. Industrial democracy is still fairly unusual within the administration of schools. The hierarchical nature of curriculum decisions still exists within schools, so the teacher may be faced with restrictions to, or disapproval of, negotiations he/she is undertaking with the students.

Secondly, the reactions of other classroom teachers to a teacher who is attempting to make changes within the classroom are varied. Some teachers, of course, react with interest and generally give support to the teacher. However, others react negatively because all that they hold important within the classroom is threatened. They are alarmed and critical of the change seen in the negotiating teacher's classroom. This group of teachers needs not to be large to cause, in various ways, considerable doubt in the teacher's mind about what he/she is doing.

- A lot of comments are made about the *noise level* of the classroom (this is what often attracts other teachers' attention first). The necessity for a fair amount of group and class discussion means that the classroom will be noisier than the norm at the time—especially when the norm is thirty still, silent students doing mathematics or whatever. Not all teachers recognize the value of talk in learning.

- There are sometimes undertones of criticism in these comments, because a noisy classroom is often considered indicative of the teacher's *"lack of control."* Other objections are raised because of the question of who is in control of the classroom. In fact, the teacher who is negotiating with his/ her students has an equally varied opinion about who should be in control of what happens in the classroom as those teachers who won't negotiate.

- When a teacher is seen *not to sequence* the content—that is, not to offer a certain prescription for learning, something by which all students *have* to learn—he/she will be criticised by those who don't recognise that people learn in different ways. It bothers them when they realise that the students are not performing uniform exercises, because they worry that the teacher cannot be maintaining "standards."

- Some teachers disapprove of the *less formal relationship* they see developing between the teacher and students in question.

I have described some of the objections that can be raised by other teachers because sometimes they are not made in the open. Traditionally, a person who has different ideas from most and tries to put them into practice comes across a lot of criticism. These criticisms need to be considered carefully and answered by using the theory on which the teaching is based. In fact, a teacher who is faced with these objections and is given a chance to explain him/herself, can use this opportunity to strengthen his/her articulation about teacher-student negotiation. The teacher can gain confidence in answering the issues raised by discussing them with teachers and others who support what he/she is doing. I found that discussing my ideas with the Curriculum and Learning Unit staff and with other teachers at my school was very important in helping me to develop confidence in practising the negotiating model, as well as in coping with barriers to change that arose in the classroom and the school.

Reference

Franklin, J., and K. Preece. 1973. *New Mainstream Mathematics,* Book 1. Melbourne: Longman-Cheshire.

14

Chicanos Have Math in Their Blood

Pre-Columbian Mathematics

Luis Ortiz-Franco

Editors' Notes: In this chapter, Luis Ortiz-Franco argues for the inclusion of ethnomathematics into our curricula to fulfill growing demands for multicultural education and to raise awareness of the rich cultural heritages of Chicanos. First Ortiz-Franco explains and vividly depicts the pre-Columbian vigesimal number system. Then he shows how it can be adapted to elementary, middle, and high school instruction. Ortiz-Franco believes this method can not only provide alternative strategies to math instruction, but can help raise the self-esteem of Chicanos. It reflects the pioneering work in critical ethnomathematics done by Ubi D'Ambrosio, Arthur Powell, and Marilyn Frankenstein.

Mathematics education dates its beginnings to the time when human beings began to quantify the objects and phenomena in their lives. Although the process of counting (one, two, three, . . .) was the same for different groups of people around the world, the symbols by which they represented specific quantities varied according to their own particular cultural conventions. Thus, the Babylonians, Romans, Hindus, Egyptians, Angolans, Chinese, Aztecs, Incas, Mayas, and other groups each wrote numbers differently.

Likewise, cultures that achieved a level of mathematical sophistication that allowed them to manipulate their number symbols to add, subtract, multiply, and divide and to perform other algorithms did so in different ways. Today, even within a single society, various groups of people (for example, accountants, physicists, engineers, mathematicians, chemists, and so on) view and manipulate mathematical quantities differently from one another. The study of the particular way that specific cultural or *ethno* groups—whether they are different national, ethnic, linguistic, age, or occupational groups or subgroups—go about the tasks of classifying, ordering, counting, measuring, and otherwise mathematizing their environment is called *ethnomathematics* (D'Ambrosio 1985a, 2; 1985b, 44).

The ethnomathematics of pre-Columbian cultures is a topic frequently overlooked in discussions about the cultural achievements of pre-Columbian civilizations and omitted from college-level textbooks on the history of mathematics. It is particularly important that we focus on pre-Columbian mathematics during the quincentennial of Columbus's arrival in the "New World." Such a focus broadens our perspectives on pre-Columbian cultures and may stimulate us to integrate new perspectives and topics into our classroom teaching. The ultimate beneficiaries of these educational practices will be North American society in general and North American children in particular.

The integration into school mathematics of pre-Columbian mathematics is important for both political and mathematical reasons. The teaching of the mathematical traditions of pre-Columbian cultures can contribute to achieve a crucial political goal, infusing multiculturalism into education. Students will thereby develop an appreciation for the diverse ways different cultures understand and perform mathematical tasks. This will expose students to the sophisticated mathematical traditions of other cultures and demonstrate that performing mathematics *is* a universal human activity.

For Chicano students, in particular, studying pre-Columbian mathematics will allow them to learn more about their ancestors in both cultural and mathematical contexts. This integrated approach can do much to instill pride in their culture and also increase their confidence in their ability to learn and do mathematics and, perhaps, later participate in mathematics-based careers. Thus, this topic can have a positive cognitive and affective impact on Chicano students.

Chicanos are *mestizo,* a blend of European and Mexican Indian ancestry. In this country, the cultural roots of Chicanos in pre-Columbian cultures is acknowledged at the social level but is usually ignored in the American educational system. In a scene in the movie *Stand and Deliver,* teacher Jaime Escalante attempts to motivate his Chicano mathematics students at Garfield High School in East Los Angeles by saying, "You *burros* have math in your blood."[1] Escalante's comment surely will seem sadly ironic to readers familiar with the statistics regarding the low educational achievement of many Chicano students and familiar with both the history of mathematics in Maya and Aztec societies and the relatively minuscule number of Chicanos who pursue mathematics-based careers in the United States.

Despite a long and distinguished heritage in the sciences, arts, and letters in their own culture, Chicanos are one of the least educated groups in this country. However, this impressive history of cultural achievement has been almost entirely ignored in U.S. schools for at least two reasons. First, the Western orientation of the educational process largely disregards the achievements of conquered indigenous civilizations and their descendants such as Mexican people. Second, as a result of this ethnocentric orientation, many teachers and other school officials in the U.S. are unaware of the mathematical accomplishments of pre-Columbian societies.

The purpose of this article is to discuss a pre-Columbian number system that played an important role in the cultural activities, such as commerce and dating historical events, and in the development of Mesoamerica. The term Mesoamerica refers to the geographical region that encompasses the area from northern-central Mexico to northern Costa Rica. In this essay, I discuss the Mesoamerican number system and the origins of the vigesimal number system, and make some instructional suggestions.

The Mesoamerican Number System

The Mesoamerican number system is a positional vigesimal (that is, base twenty) system. It employs only three symbols to write any whole number from zero to whatever quantity is desired. The three symbols are the figure:

representing zero; the dot:

•

representing the quantity of one; and the horizontal bar:

representing the quantity of five. To write the numbers zero to nineteen in this system, the two processes of grouping and addition are used (see Figure 14–1). Numbers 2 to 4 are written using an addition process. For the number 5, five dots are grouped into a horizontal bar. And, numbers 6 to 19 are written using the addition process.

For numbers larger than 19, a vertical, positional convention is used (see Figure 14–2). In this convention, the bottom level is for the units, the next level up is for the 20s, the third level up is for the 400s ($1 \times 20 \times 20$), the fourth level up is for the 8000s ($1 \times 20 \times 20 \times 20$), and so on in powers of 20. For instance, to write 20, we write the figure

in the first level and a dot

•

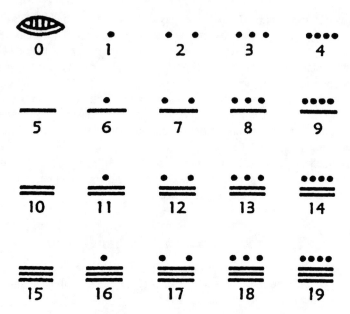

Figure 14–1. Mesoamerican numbers 0 to 19.

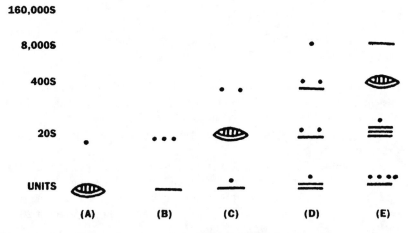

Figure 14–2. Examples of numbers beyond 19 in Mesoamerican notation. (a) 20; (b) 65; (c) 806; (d) 10,951; and (e) 40, 329.

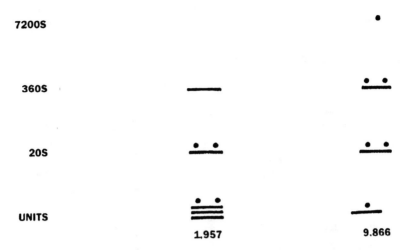

Figure 14–3. Two examples of chronological counts in the Mesoamerican system.

in the second level. To write 65, we write

• • •

in the second level, 3 × 20 = 60, and a

for five units, in the first level. These quantities, 20 and 65, and additional ones are illustrated in Figure 14–2.

This vigesimal number system was used by cultures of Mesoamerica for various everyday applications. Those cultures that used it in their calendars to record dates of events employed a modified version of the system. In this version, a unit in the third level had the value of 360 rather than 400 (see Figure 14–3). This was the result of multiplying the units in the second level by 18 to get to the third level, 1 × 20 × 18. Beyond the third level, the value of the units followed the vigesimal convention. For instance, units in the fourth level had the value of 7,200, which is equal to 1 × 20 × 18 × 20; units in the fifth level had the value of 144,000, or 1 × 20 × 18 × 20 × 20; and so on for subsequent levels. (For other further illustrations on the use of this calendar system, see Krause [1983], pp. 45–46. Although this number system is called Mayan, this system was used by cultures predating the Mayas, for example the Olmecs, Zapotecs, and others. See section below, "Origins of the Vigesimal System.")

This vigesimal system of numeration is practical to use and can easily be adapted to classroom instruction. For example, the operations of addition and subtraction are relatively straightforward processes. In the case of addition, one

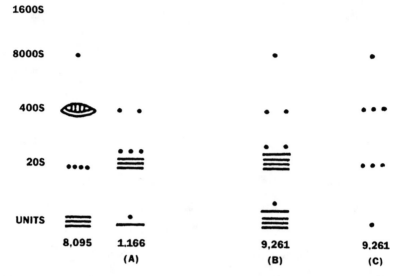

Figure 14–4. The sum of 8,095 plus 1,166: (b) shows the result 9,261 before grouping and (c) is the final result, after regrouping.

has to remember that since twenty units in a lower level are equivalent to one unit in the next level up, twenty units in a lower level are replaced with one dot in the level above it. Figure 14–4 shows the sum of 8,095 plus 1,166, before and after the grouping process.

In the case of subtraction, when borrowing is required, one unit from a higher level equals twenty units in the next lower level. The subtraction process of 40,329 − 10,951 is illustrated in Figure 14–5. Notice that in order to perform this subtraction example, borrowing is necessary. In the case of the vigesimal system, we call this process ungrouping. On the left of column (a), one unit is borrowed from the 8000s level, which then becomes 20 units in the 400s level on the left of column (b). Similarly, one unit is borrowed from the 20s level in column (a) and transferred to the units level as 20 in column (b). Therefore, column (b) shows the modified representation of 40,329, and column (c) illustrates the result of the subtraction 40,329 − 10,951.

These addition and subtraction examples point to rich mathematical experiences in which students can be engaged. Unfortunately, beyond these operations and associated algorithms, we do not know whether the Mesoamerican civilizations knew how to multiply, divide, or perform other mathematical algorithms with this vigesimal system. But we do know that the Mayas wrote books on paper just as we do. We know that for 1600 years before Columbus accidentally arrived in the "New World," the Mayas wrote and kept thousands of books in which they recorded their history and cultural achievements (Schele and Freidel 1990, 18 and 401). Tragically, however, the Spanish conquerors and missionaries burned and otherwise destroyed all of the Mayan libraries and

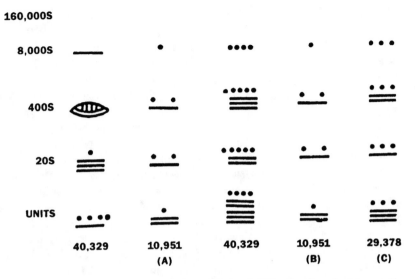

Figure 14–5. The subtraction 40,329 minus 10,951, showing the intermediate step (b) with borrowing process in 40,329 and the result 29,378 in (c).

archives. Possibly some of those destroyed books contained information on algorithms and other mathematical systems that pre-Columbian societies devised. We know that Mayan astronomers had calculated the cycles of the heavens so exactly that they could predict solar and lunar eclipses to the day, hundreds of years in advance. In fact, it was a Mayan astronomer who predicted, some 1200 years in advance, the solar eclipse that occurred on July 11, 1991 (*Newsweek* 1991, 58–62).

The Mayas knew the synodical revolution of Venus (Thompson 1966, 170; Morley, Brainerd, and Sharer 1983, 566). Some scholars argue that the Mayas also knew the synodical period of Mars and perhaps had parallel knowledge about Mercury, Jupiter, and Saturn (Morley, Brainerd, and Sharer 1983, 567). Given their ability to make these calculations as well as to predict celestial phenomena, it is reasonable to believe that they knew how to perform mathematical algorithms other than addition and subtraction. This belief is rooted in the origins and uses of their vigesimal number systems.

Origins of the Vigesimal Number System

Archaeologists and other scholars maintain that humans first inhabited North America around 30,000 years ago and, in particular, México about 9,000 years later (Lorenzo 1977, 102). Groups of hunters and gatherers roamed Mesoamerica for thousands of years before they became sedentary. Soustelle (1984, 4) pins down the advent of agriculture in Mesoamerica at approximately

4,000 B.C. However, the organized life that can be called civilization in the region began approximately 5,000 years ago (Schele and Freidel 1990, 37). The social evolution of Mesoamerica can be traced from the hunter-gatherers through the successive civilizations of the Olmecs, Zapotec, Mayas, Toltecs, Aztecs, and so forth.

The earliest evidence of numerical inscriptions that used positional systems of bars and dots has been traced to the Olmecs in approximately 1,200 B.C. (Soustelle 1984, 60). This date is significant, since some 800 years before Aristotle, Plato and Euclid (whose society did not have a positional number system) began making contributions to Western culture, the Olmecs were already using a positional system. It is worth noting that it was not until 499 A.D. that the Hindu-Arabic number notation using zero in a positional convention first occurred (Ganguli 1932, 251). The Zapotecs of Oaxaca used the Mesoamerican vigesimal system in their calendars between 900 and 400 B.C. (Soustelle 1984, 102–104). Between 400 B.C. and 300 B.C., the Izapan culture used the same convention (Stuart and Stuart 1983, 25–26). Later, the Mayas, to whom the vigesimal system is mistakenly attributed, used this system extensively, between A.D. 199 to 900. The Mayas developed their amazingly complex calendar system and astronomical sciences around this mathematical system hundreds of years before Galileo and Copernicus.

Recommendations to Teachers

It is vitally important that ethnomathematics is taught in the North American schools because such educational practices benefit both school children and society at large. The United States has experienced profound demographic changes in the last fifteen years that have significantly altered the cultural, racial, ethnic, and political landscape of the country. Current population projections indicate that the percentage of school-age children who are African American, Latino, Asian, and Native American will grow faster than the percentage of white school-age children. Accordingly, the demand for multiculturalism in education will increase to accomodate the realities of North American society. In the view of the National Association of State Boards of Education (NASBE), a multicultural learning environment is one in which multicultural perspectives in academic topics are integrated throughout the curriculum rather than being treated as "special" topics in schools. NASBE (circa 1992, p. 1) has observed, "Our ability to move schools and institutions into the next century rests on our ability to remove the obstacles that hinder multicultural learning environments." One of these obstacles is the absence of multicultural perspectives in mathematics education. By exposing children to ethnomathematics, we will increase their appreciation for the mathematical achievement of other cultures. Moreover, including ethnomathematics in mathematics curricula challenges the dominant perception of students and parents that only Western culture created mathematical knowledge. Thus, ethno-mathematics is a vehicle to provide our nation's students with a fuller and richer multicultural educational experience.

The pre-Columbian positional number system can be taught at various educational levels. As we have already seen, it could be included in the elementary school curriculum as a way to deepen how students understand the decimal system. In fact, the Mesoamerican system may be easier for children to grasp than the decimal system for at least two reasons. First, the vigesimal system is visual; and second, the representation of the quantities involve only three symbols—zero, one, and five—and manipulative materials can be adapted to give them physical representation.

For example, Dienes blocks can be adapted to the Mesoamerican base twenty system. Teachers can assign to the smallest blocks the value one, to the intermediate-sized blocks the value five, and to the larger blocks or to a group of four intermediate-sized blocks the value twenty. Alternatively, in classrooms that do not have Dienes blocks but have manipulative materials of different colors and sizes (rods or chips), different colors or sizes of rods or chips can be used for the three quantitative designations of one, five, and twenty.

When doing addition in this vigesimal system, teachers and students must remember the rule: one should not have more than twenty. Whenever there are more than twenty units in one cell, students must make a twenty-for-one replacement and place the one in the cell above. In the case of subtraction where borrowing is involved, one unit in a higher level is replaced by twenty units in the next level down. See Figures 14–4 and 14–5 for examples of how to do addition and subtraction in this vigesimal system.

At the middle school and high school levels, discussion of this number system can be included in social studies as well as in mathematics classes to broaded the students' appreciation of the cultural achievements of ancient peoples and the fate of conquered civilizations. Teachers can use this topic to illustrate that impressive mathematical achievements of Mesoamerican civilizations were ignored, devalued, or destroyed as part of the rationale for subjugation and domination. For presentations in social studies courses, a map of Mesoamerica is indispensable and can be obtained from the National Geographic Society or from some of the references listed at the end of this article (see, for example, Stuart and Stuart [1983, 21 and 51]). Teachers can consult other references for more details on the historical origins and uses of this numerical system and for more information on the pre-Columbian cultures who used it (see, for example, Morley, Brainerd, and Sharer [1983]; Ortiz-Franco and Magaña [1973]; and Thompson [1966]).

In mathematics classes at the middle school and high school levels, students can explore interesting mathematics through the Mesoamerican vigesimal system. Teachers can devise exercises comparing the polynomial representation of numbers in our decimal system and the vigesimal system. For example, students can explore interesting mathematics by relating powers of ten to the value of digits in numerals in the decimal number system and the value of units in the vigesimal system. The pattern to be observed is that while the value of a digit in the decimal system is multiplied by a power of ten that corresponds to the place of the digit of the numeral, the value of the same number of units in the same corresponding place in the vigesimal system is multiplied by a power of twenty. This can lead to discussions about powers of twenty as a product of powers of two and powers of ten to illustrate that the value of units in the vigesimal system increases exponentially faster than the value of these units in the corresponding place in the decimal system. This in turn can serve as a natural introduction to topics related to exponential growth and exponential functions.

Furthermore, in mathematics classes where students are already proficient with the usual algorithm for multiplication in the decimal system (grades 5–12), teachers can also include classroom activities or homework assignments requiring students to use their creativity when working with the vigesimal system. For instance, the teacher may break up the class into groups of three or four students each and ask the groups to generate ideas of how to carry out multiplication in this number system. This idea can be extended to include division, as well. These challenging assignments may turn into group projects that can last for an extended period of time. Including such extended projects or investigations is one way of implementing aspects of the *Curriculum and Evaluation Standards* of the National Council of Teachers of Mathematics. More importantly, these extended projects address what the *Curriculum and Evaluation Standards* ignores: the importance of doing mathematics in a multicultural context.

Given the sophisticated system of ancient Mesoamerican mathematics and the gross underrepresentation of Chicanos in mathematics-based careers in the United States, the comment of Jaime Escalante to his students is indeed sardonic. The legacy of racist discrimmination against the cultures and native peoples of Mesoamerica which resulted from the military conquests and colonization ushered in by Columbus's arrival in the "New World" has continued to this day in the imperialistic practices of U.S. society. It has resulted in an educational system in this country which effectively ignores the rich tradition of excellence in mathematics in the Chicano students' background and fails to instill in young Chicanos a sense of pride in their heritage and a positive self-image.

Despite all this, some modern Chicano mathematicians have made valuable contributions to applied and abstract mathematics—David Sánchez, Richard Griego, Manuel Berriozabal, Richard Tapia, and Bill Velez, to name a few. Their contributions should be used to encourage Chicano students to pursue the exceptional mathematical heritage of their pre-Columbian ancestors.

Note

1. For an understanding of the genesis of the statement, see Mathews [1988], p. 84. Mathews is an interesting source for information about Escalante and his other experiences at Garfield High School.

References

D'Ambrosio, Ubiritan. 1985a. "Ethnomathematics: What Might It Be?" *International Study Group on Ethnomathematics (ISGEm) Newsletter* 1(1): 2.

———. 1985b. "Ethnomathematics and Its Place in the History and Pedagogy of Mathematics." *For the Learning of Mathematics* 5(1): 44–48.

Ganguli, Saradakanta. 1932. "The Indian Origin of the Modern Place—Value Arithmetical Notation." *The American Mathematical Monthly* 39 (May): 251–256.

Krause, Marina C. 1983. *Multicultural Mathematics Materials.* Reston, VA: National Council of Teachers of Mathematics.

Lorenzo, José Luis. 1977. Los Origenes Mexicanos. *Historia General de México,* Tomo I. México, D.F.: El Colegio de México, 82–123.

Mathews, Jay. 1988. *Escalante: The Best Teacher in America.* New York: Henry Holt.

Morley, Sylvanus G., and George W. Brainerd, revised by Robert J. Sharer. 1983. *The Ancient Maya,* 4th ed. Palo Alto, CA: Stanford University Press.

National Association of State Boards of Education. 1992. *The American Tapestry: Educating a Nation.* Alexandria, VA: National Association of State Boards of Education.

National Council of Teachers of Mathematics. 1989. *Curriculum and Evaluation Standards for School Mathematics.* Reston, VA: National Council of Teachers of Mathematics.

Newsweek. 1991. "Mysteries of the Sun." 15 July, 58–62.

Ortiz-Franco, Luis, and Maria Magaña. 1973. "La Ciencia de los Antiguos Mexicanos: Una Bibliografia Selecta." *Aztlán: Chicano Journal of the Social Sciences and the Arts* 4(Spring): 195–203.

Schele, Linda, and David Friedel. 1990. *A Forest of Kings: The Untold Story of the Ancient Maya.* New York: William Morrow.

Soustelle, Jacques. 1984. *The Olmecs: The Oldest Civilization in México.* Trans. Helen R. Lane. Garden City, NY: Doubleday.

Stuart, George E., and Gene S. Stuart. 1983. *The Mysterious Maya.* Washington, DC: National Geographic Society.

Thompson, John Eric S. 1966. *The Rise and Fall of Maya Civilization,* 2nd ed. Norman, OK: University of Oklahoma Press.

15

Success and Mathematically Gifted Female Students

The Challenge Continues

Janice A. Leroux and Cheeying Ho

Editors' Notes: Janice A. Leroux and Cheeying Ho critique gender bias in high school math and examine the impact of social factors, attitudes, achievement motivation (female fear of success), formal educational experiences, support levels, and coed classrooms on female performance. In their study, students and teachers reported little gender difference in mathematical abilities, yet the researchers noted females had more mathematics anxiety and lower performances on tests. Leroux and Ho uncover social factors that contribute to gender differences and draw implications for the success of female students who study math.

Mathematics has increasingly become a greater focus of interest for parents due to the growing technological orientation of society (Chang, 1984). Mathematics is often regarded as the "critical filter" which determines entry into a host of careers requiring mathematical skills (Sells, 1978). Educators, therefore, need to develop approaches that will stimulate and encourage maximum participation in mathematics courses from both females and males. Programs for the mathematically gifted need to be structured so as to help both genders reach their potential in becoming creative mathematicians.

The term "mathematically gifted" has been used to describe three groups of students: (1) those who learn standard content very well, but have difficulty when taught at a faster pace or at deeper conceptual levels; (2) those who can learn more content and can reason at a higher level than average students; and (3) those who are extremely talented or precocious, and can learn with little formal instruction at a much higher content and abstract level (Chang, 1984). However, it is evident that to be truly gifted in mathematics, a student must be more than a "good exercise doer" or good at computations: she must demonstrate high-order reasoning skills. ". . . Mathematical knowledge (also) consists of the ability to perceive patterns and relationships, and to form concepts and generalizations about the perceived relationships" (Chang, 1984, p. 232).

As with other areas of giftedness, mathematical giftedness consists of three clusters: (1) above average ability, (2) creativity, and (3) task commitment. Creativity is seen as an important aspect of mathematical giftedness, therefore encouragement of and evaluation of creativity in problem solving should be an important component in gifted mathematics programs.

Gender Differences and Giftedness

Since ability is perceived essential for mathematical giftedness, the existence of gender differences in this area is an important consideration. Benbow and Stanley claim that "sex differences in achievement in and attitudes toward mathematics result from superior male mathematical ability, which may in turn be related to greater male ability in spatial tasks" (1980, p. 1264). They found that even in junior high school, females excel in computation while males excel on tasks requiring mathematical reasoning ability. These findings are observed in students who have identical backgrounds in mathematics, and who have had the same formal educational experiences.

These data apparently contradict the hypothesis put forth by Fennema and Sherman (1978) that differences in mathematics aptitude are due to differential course taking. They posited that if boys achieve more it is due to their having taken more courses in mathematics.

In another study, Benbow and Stanley found that there were no significant gender differences in grades earned in the classroom. However, some of their assumptions need to be questioned. Using the SAT-M scores as a valid and reliable judge of mathematical aptitude is questionable since performance in these types of timed tests is influenced by such a variety of external factors such as anxiety, risk-taking preferences and cognitive style (Eccles and Jacobs, 1986).

Concluding that both genders have had the same formal educational experiences in mathematics is also presumptuous (Gurney, 1992). Taking the same number of mathematics classes does not ensure equal formal educational experiences since it has been found that males receive much more attention from teachers than females do, and therefore receive more formal mathematics instruction (Eccles and Jacobs, 1986). As well, "boys are more likely than girls to have informal, mathematically related experiences such as playing with scientific toys, participating in mathematical games, and reading mathematical books" (Eccles and Jacobs, p. 369). Males were found to have learned considerable amounts of advanced mathematics either in a systematic way through mathematical games, puzzles, and books, thus developing their problem-solving skills and mathematical reasoning ability (Fox, 1974). Since few females study mathematics independently in a systematic way, or read mathematics books or play with mathematics puzzles and games, they really have less exposure to mathematical experiences than males do.

The talent searches conducted by the Study of Mathematically Precocious Youth (SMPY) at Johns Hopkins University every year have shown that males perform significantly better on the mathematical portion of the Scholastic Aptitude Test (SAT-M) than females. Not only do the males score higher than the females on average, but the greatest disparity is in the upper ranges of mathematical reasoning ability: the top scores were always made by males and more males scored in the higher limits (Benbow and Stanley, 1980). However, as Kolata states, "Too little is known about the development of mathematical reasoning ability and how to test for it to jump to the conclusion that these sex differences are genetically based rather than solely a result of social factors" (1980, p. 1235).

The researchers at Johns Hopkins believe, however, that social factors play a role in contributing to the differences in SAT-M scores. The talent searches conducted by SMPY probably attracted the most keen and able mathematics students. Because mathematics has been perceived in society as a more appropriate interest for boys than for girls (Cramer, 1989), it is more likely that able males participate in the talent searches more frequently than females.

Mathematics may also be seen as one of the more appropriate ways for males, especially gifted males, to demonstrate abstract thought, whereas for females, there are many more "socially responsible" options or avenues to express divergent thinking. Therefore, males who are gifted in these abstract ways of thinking may turn to mathematics whereas females may opt for other areas such as creative writing or shared leadership. Johnson and Lewman (1990) found that parents perceived their sons to be more interested and engaged in abstraction, curiosity, problem solving, and science/nature activities, and their daughters to be more interested in fine motor/art activities and verbal skills. Parents were perceiving their children's abilities along gender-stereotypical patterns even at an early stage. It is no surprise, then, that children grow up with perceptions of socially appropriate or inappropriate interests and behaviors.

Motivation and Achievement

Achievement motivation may be another factor that can explain sex differences in mathematics performance. Achievement motivation can be defined as one of the major determinants of an individual's striving for success, and is thought to be "a function of that individual's need for achievement, the expectation that the desired goal could be attained and the value of that goal" (Leder, 1984, p. 223). However, although the level of achievement motivation for males was consistent with their striving for success, findings were contradictory for females.

Horner (in Leder, 1984) suggested that the fear of success for females may have a strong influence on their actual attainment of success in certain areas because of societal stereotypes. Negative consequences such as unpopularity and anxiety or doubt about what is socially accepted female competence may detract girls from their goals and might lead to a lowering of performance standards (Leder, 1984; Silverman, 1986). Leder posited that "fear of success themes" apparent in the media included: 1) women need to work harder than men to do the same job; 2) women have problems with success and interpersonal relationships; and 3) success somehow just happens (Dweck and Licht, 1980). Such negative stereotypes may contribute to reasons "why fewer girls than boys opt for serious participation in special programs established to nurture and develop exceptional talents, and particularly in the traditional male areas of mathematics and science" (Leder, 1984, p. 228).

Visual spatial abilities have been found to be strongly correlated with mathematical reasoning ability (Benbow and Stanley, 1980; Higham and Navarre, 1984; Weiner and Robinson, 1986). However, Gallagher (in Dreyden and Gallagher, 1989) found that gender differences in spatial abilities virtually disappeared when time limits on spatial tests were removed. Dreyden and Gallagher then proposed that the cause of the gender gap differences in SAT-M results were due to the time limits given. They suggested that the mathematical ability of girls is comparable to that of boys but that girls may become affected by test anxiety due to factors such as: (1) familiarity of types of questions (the students in the study were gifted high school students, and often the gifted girls had taken fewer mathematics courses than the gifted boys); (2) phrasing of the questions; (3) risk-taking behaviors (boys are generally encouraged more than girls in mathematics and science classes to answer questions and to take risks). One goal of the SAT is to test performance under pressure—this pressure can produce different types of anxiety: facilitative and debilitative. Since boys usually have had more experience taking mathematics tests than girls, the SAT may produce facilitative anxiety in boys but debilitative anxiety in girls (Dreyden and Gallagher, 1989).

It was found that when times limits were lifted for the SAT, not only did both boys and girls score much higher than boys and girls who were timed, but the increase in score for the untimed girls was much greater than the increase in score for the untimed boys. Moreover, the difference in average scores between boys and girls reduced drastically when the time limits were eliminated. If differences found in SAT scores between males and females are due more to speed of performance rather than to actual mathematical ability, then educators must consciously teach and test in ways that respect differences in all students' ways of learning.

Strauss (1988) found that girls' mathematics averages dropped when boys entered the formerly all-girl classroom, although the females' scores on aptitude tests had not changed. This drop in achievement suggests that either the females' perceptions of their mathematics performance lowered in the presence of males, that teachers' perceptions of females' abilities somehow changed relative to males' abilities, or perhaps the teachers' teaching styles changed to favor the males. In any case, results suggest that a sex-segregated environment can help females to grow in understanding of self and of their potentials. All-female environments may help girls become aware of the issue of gender differences, allow them to feel less inhibited to express their interests and abilities, and to ensure a learning style more appropriate to their needs.

It is apparent from the literature that the controversies concerning gender differences in mathematics ability of gifted students exist. Therefore, in order to get a better idea of what gender differences persist within schools today, what may cause them, and what measure could be taken to eliminate them, 15 gifted female mathematics students were interviewed or completed questionnaires to describe their perception of the situation concerning gender differences in their gifted mathematics programs. A 20-item questionnaire formed the basis for both the written responses and the oral responses during the one hour interviews. (See Table 15–1.)

Seven females were interviewed personally and eight girls responded to the questionnaire. Along with responses from girls ages 14 to 16, four teachers of the gifted, a mathematics consultant, a principal, and a Ministry of Education official were interviewed.

Results

The gifted programs at the high schools in a large Ontario city consisted of 50 percent congregated classes and 50 percent in the regular (advanced) classroom. The subjects offered in the gifted program included mathematics, science, English, geography, and history at the junior high level, and mathematics, chemistry, biology, physics, geography, English (French at one school) at the senior high level. Students in the high school gifted program were strongly urged, especially at the junior high level, to take all the gifted courses, even if they were not gifted in one of those subjects. In junior grade school, students were tested at age eight and then entered into the gifted track if they placed at 98th percentile or higher.

At the high school level, the mathematics courses followed provincial guidelines, but the pace was faster and optional topics were covered in detail. As well, projects and independent learning activities were given, which were selected according to the interests of the learners. There was an emphasis on problem solving and on "learning little tricks, short cuts and fine points" (Mrs. G., mathematics teacher). Mathematics teachers tended to be mathematics specialists who were interested in teaching the gifted. They were "more accustomed to free thinking" (Linda, grade eleven student).

One noticeable outcome from the interviews was that almost all the students and teachers reported an equal ratio of girls to boys in the gifted mathematics program. This equal split in numbers had been a fairly recent occurrence

Table 15–1.

Interview Questions

1. What is it about mathematics that you enjoy? Why do you think you are good at mathematics?

2. Why did you decide to choose the gifted program in mathematics?

3. Why do you think mathematics is important?

4. How and when were you identified as a gifted mathematics student?

5. Is your gifted program full time or part time? (What courses are you taking in the gifted program?)

6. Does your gifted mathematics program include:
   —acceleration
   —enrichment
   —both? Explain.

7. Are your mathematics teachers specialized to teach and evaluate gifted mathematics students? Give an example.

8. Does your gifted program provide field trips, etc.? Do community experts take part in your program?

9. How does your program teach you to be creative?

10. What part do your parents play in being involved in the program? Are they encouraging to you as a girl to take part in the gifted mathematics program?

11. What is the ratio of girls to boys in the gifted program/mathematics class?

12. What do you feel your friends and peers think of you being in the gifted mathematics program?

13. Do you find that being in a gifted program takes time from your activities and social life?

14. How important is it to you that females have role models in mathematics and other areas? Are there enough?

15. What type of stereotyping have you felt with regards to girls taking mathematics? Do different teachers treat boys and girls differently?

16. Do boys and girls achieve differently? If so, why?

17. Do you consider yourself pretty self-confident?

18. Why do you think more girls should be encouraged to do better in mathematics?

19. How do you think more girls could be encouraged to do better in mathematics?

20. How do you feel about being labeled "gifted?"

in the program. In the past, there were generally more males enrolled in the gifted program at all levels. Reasons for this disparity included some parents' fear of allowing their daughters to take buses by themselves to attend another school for the program and the higher performance results of boys on the standardized tests which are used to identify the gifted children. Recently the gifted program has become more accessible in more community elementary schools, so girls and boys take part on a fairly equal basis.

Another consistent finding reported by both the females and the teachers was that the aptitude and level of achievement in mathematics of both girls and boys were equal. In general, the females and the teachers reported no difference between the girls' and the boys' mathematical ability and achievement. However, Mrs. G. pointed out that in her grade twelve class last year the top students were all boys: "Boys have insight and free thought . . . girls work harder to get to the top . . . ," but this year her top students were all girls. This teacher also believed that boys had better mathematical reasoning abilities, but she felt that this was due to earlier experiences boys had with toys and solid objects. Another teacher, Mr. D., reported that in his grade seven class there was a three to one ratio of boys to girls. He speculated the reason was due to the method of testing, which favored boys. Mr. D. found that although there were no differences in abilities or achievement between girls and boys, and that girls tended to be more methodical than boys and take more time to do their work. Boys, on the other hands, worked faster and left out questions or parts of their work. In his mathematics class, the most highly gifted students were boys, he concluded.

How Much Difference?

Although little difference was reported on mathematical achievement and ability between girls and boys, a difference between the sexes was apparent with regards to mathematics anxiety and performance on tests. Both the students and the teachers reported that females experienced more anxiety before tests than males. One teacher, Mr. B., reported a case of a drastic example of mathematics anxiety in a young girl who "became rigid" whenever numbers were mentioned. Through consultation with the girl's mother, Mr. B. decided to not mark anything wrong that the girl did in mathematics. Eventually the girl herself began to realize her own mistakes, and brought these to the attention of the teacher. His response then, was, "See, you know mathematics better than I do!"

This method worked to help this young student overcome her fear of mathematics by allowing her to see that she could do the work and understand it. Her parents were very language-oriented and though they did not discourage her from doing mathematics, he sensed they may not have been able to provide the support that was necessary for this girl to feel comfortable with mathematics. (This girl went on later to become the top student in her class.)

Likewise, Mrs. G. reported that girls showed their anxiety more, tended to "freeze up," and were more marks-conscious than boys were. She believed that the attitude of the teacher was very important. He or she must be "very careful not to intimidate."

In general, the female students interviewed either enjoyed high school mathematics a great deal and/or felt that they were good at it. Wendy said that she was good at mathematics because it "makes sense," and she has "no problems figuring it out." Both Wendy's parents are good at mathematics; Wendy's mother is a high school mathematics teacher.

Julie liked mathematics, believed she was good at it, and found it "fairly easy." Erin liked mathematics because she "likes facts," and it "comes easily" to her.

Linda, however, stated that she didn't like mathematics for the reason of it being too structured. She said that she has to "work at mathematics," and prefers English where she can give her own opinions. However, she does believe that mathematics is important because it "relates to other subjects."

Karen (grade eleven student taking grade twelve mathematics) likes mathematics because she can "memorize it." It's "right or wrong" and she can "learn formulas." She noted that mathematics is important for "practically everything." Other reasons given for liking mathematics included: "I like problem-solving" and "I feel confident in it" (Katie, grade eight); "I can think logically" and "there's always an answer" (Kerry, grade eight); and "I enjoy doing real hard problems and then solve them step by step" (Rachel, grade eight).

It appears that external influences may have a strong effect on these females' attitudes towards mathematics. The females who were in the gifted mathematics program all had women mathematics teachers. Several of them had had female mathematics teachers throughout high school. Although all of the females believed that mathematics was important for their university aspirations and that female role models in mathematics were important, one of the grade nine students, Julie, said that the gender of the mathematics teacher made no difference to her. That year, however, was the first time she had a male mathematics teacher. Linda felt that female role models were important for girls, but they were "more important to some." Wendy (grade eleven) said that female role models were "important" because they "make a career more attainable." She felt that female teachers were more approachable, and male teachers were more intimidating. However, she had only had female mathematics teachers in high school.

Some girls indicated that there weren't enough role models in mathematics. "Most females don't have role models" (Kerry, grade eight). "I still think there could be more. I think it is very important because all women are equal (to men) and deserve equal rights" (Kelly). Noted Lisa: "I think we're beginning to prove ourselves and I think we need as many people to look up to as possible."

Do Men and Women Teach Differently?

None of the females reported any noticeable stereotypes within the classroom, nor did they feel that male and female teachers treated male and female students differently (although most of the high school girls had mostly female mathematics teachers throughout high school). All the grade eight students claimed that they had never felt teachers treated girls and boys differently. The girls all asserted that boys were more outspoken than girls, often demanded more attention and were rowdier. The teachers were always equitable; they called on everyone in turn, including the quiet girls, and "tried to get everyone to answer questions by going up and down the rows" (Erin). Erin also claimed that her teacher seemed "more condescending" to boys and that girls were more reserved. Wendy said that she has heard of some teachers who were chauvinistic, talked down to students and "treated guys and girls differently." Rachel noted: "I've heard that girls who take mathematics are smart at studies and nothing else. I don't think they (the teachers) treat them (boys and girls) differently." It appeared that these respondents might have been somewhat inexperienced in recognizing the unfair practices that can inhibit full development of learning potential. This "personal denial" is not uncommon in youth (Frize, 1992).

Although no noticeable stereotypes were reported by teachers in the high school grades, Mr. B. mentioned that he noticed some stereotypes persisting among students. The boys still expected that the girls could not do some things such as build with the mechano sets or use computers, and the girls expected the boys to use them more. Cultural stereotypes were still tacitly supported by students and one wonders about the internal barriers which could inhibit females as a result.

Parental involvement seemed to play a large role for all the females. Most stated that parental encouragement was very important to them. Parents seemed happy that their daughters were in the gifted program. Linda claimed, however, that her parents were not particularly involved in the program and allowed her to make her own decisions, but they supported her. Wendy said that some of her girlfriends thought that they couldn't do mathematics and that this was because of past experiences and/or because they were not encouraged enough by their parents.

Most of the females declared that being in the gifted program did not take time away from doing extra-curricular activities and their social life. Most of them were involved in extra-curricular activities and several stated that being with their friends in the gifted program was an important aspect of their social lives. Erin suggested that some gifted females were not involved in extra-curricular activities because "maybe they're afraid of being laughed at . . . I don't know."

The girls all described themselves as fairly self-confident and all responded that is was "Okay" to be gifted. However, Mr. B. reported that he found the self-concept of gifted students generally low. "They can only see what they can't do." The girls reported that in general, they found their friends and peers were supportive of them or had respect for them for being in the gifted mathematics program. A few of them also stated that most of their friends did not think much about it or did not really care.

However, some went on to relate exceptions, such as, "Some other friends at another school thought I was a freak" (Linda). "Some friends were shocked at first" (Julie). Her non-gifted friends "feel she should do better," and some feel that she is an "elitist" (Wendy). In concluding, though, the girls felt that it made no difference to their friends what program they were in, and even the few negative reactions did not seem to deter or upset these gifted females to any great degree. The results affirm Leroux's study (1988) which found that females generally have feelings of positive interpersonal relations.

One of the females interviewed had just dropped the gifted program and another girl had just dropped her mathematics class. Laura dropped the gifted program upon entering high school because she didn't want to go to a different school (where the gifted program was offered) from her friends. She felt that she wouldn't be accepted by her friends or her new peers, she didn't really like the other students she knew in the program, and she was afraid of being "labeled." Although she felt she was quite good at mathematics, Laura "wasn't really interested" in it and it wasn't her favorite subject. She did feel that her parents' positive attitudes, acceptance, and encouragement were very important to her.

Marcia, along with several of her friends, had switched mathematics class from gifted to advanced while remaining in the gifted program in her other classes. She said that the gifted mathematics class followed the same curriculum as the advanced class, but was more difficult and the tests were harder. As a result, the marks she received were lower than the ones she would have received in an advanced class. "What's the point?" was her conclusion. Marcia reported that there were no differences in abilities and achievements between the sexes (the boys' marks were low also), nor were there any apparent stereotypes. She enjoyed the mathematics classes, but she was concerned about her mark. She now receives marks in the eighties and nineties, whereas in the gifted mathematics class, she was achieving in the seventies and eighties. It appeared that at one high school marking inequities could penalize a gifted student and possibly result in fewer university options in the future.

Discussion

It appeared that gender differences between females and males in one city's gifted mathematics program were changing in terms of numbers and achievement. The consistent findings of equal enrollment in the mathematics classes as well as equal achievement reported by both the students and the teachers showed that females in this small sample were proving their abilities in mathematics.

The results showed that certain factors are important to female achievement in mathematics. Female mathematics teachers, who also act as role models, are a significant influence. Teachers who treat both genders equally, provide a warm, uninhibiting environment, give equal attention to both females and males and are approachable, seem to provide the most "psychologically safe" environment that is conducive to girls' learning. Parental support and encouragement were also essential for the females' success. In general, the females who were in the gifted program like mathematics and believe that they are good at it. They tend to enjoy problem-solving, logical thinking, and getting correct answers. The females who reported that they did not like mathematics explained that they found it too structured, not personally relevant and they felt they were not good at it.

Despite the generally positive results, there were still some problems inherent in the gifted mathematics programs. Some females chose to drop the gifted mathematics classes because they were getting lower marks than they would have been getting in a regular advanced class. There must be a change in the grading and/or testing system so that students will not be penalized for taking gifted classes.

The females in the program thought that other girls chose not to take the gifted program because "they feel they need to be accepted," therefore implying that they wouldn't be accepted if they were in the gifted program. "They feel that they would be made fun of," they have "misconceptions about the program and probably don't realize the fulfillment" and they "were not encouraged by others." Although in some schools the gifted programs were well-accepted and seen in a positive and high-profile position, the gifted programs in other schools seemed to give the image of "elitist," "strange" or "not cool." All staff and students need to be educated concerning the nature of the gifted learner so that they become aware of, understanding and supportive of the need for congregated classes with specially trained teachers.

The gifted program should also allow and encourage students to take only the courses in the areas in which they are gifted. Students should not be forced to take all courses in the gifted program if they are only gifted in one area. Likewise, they should not be prevented from taking one course in the gifted program if they are talented only in that area and not in others.

To encourage more females into the gifted mathematics program, the females interviewed suggested "showing the neat aspects of mathematics," enticing more girls, and the need for "more discussion and feelings." Since females appear to have different learning styles than males (Gilligan, 1990), teachers need to transform instructional methods so they become more meaningful to females' ways of thinking.

Females often experience more anxiety and nervousness than males in taking tests. To help reduce this test anxiety, alternative testing measures may need to be taken, such as removing time limits, or allowing students to rewrite tests. More creative teaching methods and learning activities relating to real-life situations may interest more females in mathematics. Most of the females interviewed indicated that there was little, if any, way that their mathematics classes taught them to be creative, other than in problem-solving. All reported that there were no field trips taken or community experts brought into the mathematics class. Perhaps the addition of these activities would interest more students and increase the relevance of the course content. Teachers who can emphasize the connectedness of mathematics concepts across domains will also reach more students more successfully (Canadian Teachers' Federation, 1988).

Conclusion

Educators must continue to work at completely eliminating any barriers to equality of access as well as to equality of opportunity for both genders in mathematics programs. Continued encouragement from parents, significant mentors and teachers, as well as more female role models, will help attract females into mathematics. Allowing females the same formal and nonformal educational experiences in early mathematics activities, giving both females and males activities by which they can gain informal knowledge of spatial relations, providing a teaching environment and content relevance that foster female ways of learning, and using strategies that reduce mathematics anxiety, will ensure all students an equal opportunity at achieving success in mathematics. Incorporating social interactions, caring, and concern for others into the course content can also help females respect their own contributions across all subject disciplines. Females can be creatively gifted in mathematics if they are given the chance to develop their strengths and encouraged to risk new challenges in this important field.

References

Benbow, C. P., and Stanley, J. C. (1980) "Sex Differences in Mathematical Ability: Fact or Artifact?" *Science,* 210(12): 1262–1264.

Canadian Teachers' Federation. (1988) *The IDEA Book: A Resource for Improving the Participation and Success of Female Students in Math, Science and Technology.*

Chang, L. L. (1984) "Who are the Mathematically Gifted?" *Exceptional Child,* 31(3): 231–235.

Cramer, R. H. (1989) "Attitudes of Gifted Boys and Girls Towards Math: A Qualititive Study." *Roeper Review* 11(3): 128–130.

Dreyden, J. I., and Gallagher, S. A. (1989) "The Effects of Time and Direction Changes on the SAT Performance of Academically Talented Adolescents." *Journal for the Education of the Gifted,* 12(3): 187–204.

Dweck, C. S., and Licht, B. G. (1980) "Learned Helplessness and Intellectual Achievement." In J. Garber and M. E. P. Seligman (Eds.), *Human Helplessness.* New York: Academic.

Eccles, J. S., and Jacobs, J. E. (1986) "Social Forces Shape Math Attitudes and Performance." *Journal of Women in Culture and Society,* 11(21): 367–380.

Fennema, E. H., and Sherman, J. (1978) "Sex-related Differences and Related Factors: A Further Study." *Journal for Research in Mathematics Education,* 9(3): 189–203.

Fox, L. H. (1974) "Sex Differences in Mathematical Precocity: Bridging the Gap." In D. P. Keating (Ed.), *Intellectual Talent: Research and Development.* Baltimore: Johns Hopkins University Press, pp. 183–214.

Frize, M. (1992) *More Than Just Numbers.* Report of the Canadian Committee on Women in Engineering. Fredricton, NB: University of New Brunswick Press.

Gilligan, C., Lyons, N. P., and Hanmer, T. J. (Eds.). (1990) *Making Connections.* Cambridge, MA: Harvard University Press.

Gurney, P. J. (June 1992) "On the Association between Modes of Mental Representation and Mathematics Experience in Preservice Education Students." Unpublished dissertation, University of Ottawa.

Higham, S. J., and Navarre, J. (1984) "Gifted Adolescent Females Require Differential Treatment. *Journal for the Education of the Gifted,* 8(1): 43–58.

Johnson, L. J., and Lewman, B. S. (1990) "Parent Perceptions of the Talents of Young Gifted Boys and Girls." *Journal for the Education of The Gifted,* 13(2): 176–188.

Kolata, G. B. (1980) "Math and Sex: Are Girls Born with Less Ability?" *Science,* 210(12): 1234–1235.

Leder, G. C. (1984) "What Price Success?: The View from the Media." *Exceptional Child,* 31(3): 223–229.

Leroux, J. A. (1988) "Voices from the Classroom: Academic and Social Self-concepts of Gifted Adolescents." *Journal for the Education of The Gifted,* 11(3): 3–18.

Sells, L. W. (1978) "Mathematics—A Critical Filter." *Science Teacher,* 45(2): 28–29.

Silverman, L. K. (1986) "What Happens to the Gifted Girl?" In C. J. Maker (Ed.), *Defensible Programs for the Gifted.* Rockville, MD: Aspen Publishers, pp. 43–89.

Strauss, S. M. (1988) "Girls in the Mathematics Classroom: What's Happening with Our Best and Brightest?" *Mathematics Teacher,* 81(7): 533–537.

Weiner, N. C., and Robinson, S. E. (1986) "Cognitive Abilities, Personality and Gender Differences in Math Achievement of Gifted Adolescents." *Gifted Child Quarterly,* 30(2): 83–87.

16

Literacy, Democracy, and the Pledge of Allegiance

David Bloome with
Rachel Bloomekatz and Petra Sander

Editors' Notes: David Bloome invites us to consider how children can learn the tools, languages, and genres of writing necessary for active democratic participation. He realized this important connection between literacy and democracy when his eleven-year-old daughter, Rachel, struggled to write a petition to change her school's policy about the Pledge of Allegiance. Because Rachel had access to outside resources like a college library and a home computer, Bloome questions how educators can create the conditions in which all students can use writing for democracy. At the end of this chapter are dialogic responses to this essay. Appendix A is a letter to Ira Shor from Rachel Bloomekatz and Appendix B is "Three Teachers' Responses" to this article written in one of Ira Shor's classes.

In some elementary classrooms, teachers lead their students in the Pledge of Allegiance as part of their opening exercises. I (David Bloome) don't want to get into whether they should or shouldn't do so, as that isn't the point of this article, but there are some students and families who feel uncomfortable with the Pledge of Allegiance for various reasons. Our daughter Rachel felt uncomfortable about saying the Pledge of Allegiance in her classroom. So did some of her friends. Rachel frequently complained to us about it. We would listen and shrug our shoulders. There are lots of things in school that make kids feel uncomfortable; sometimes they just have to put up with them. We were proud enough of her being able to express herself and having a good explanation for her feelings. Some years earlier we had exchanged a series of letters and photocopies of state laws and court cases with the superintendent of schools about the Pledge of Allegiance when Rachel's older brother was forced to participate, but the question of student feelings got lost in the legal questions. We didn't tell that to Rachel.

At some point, Rachel's older brother told her she should start a petition. A few years earlier he had started a petition about spelling lessons, but he never got very far with it—he wrote it and brought it to school, but left it there. A couple of weeks later Rachel approached me: "Tell me how to write a petition." I gave her the barest of directions: "You state what you think is wrong and how you want it redressed." *Redressed?* Yes, that's the word I used; and no, she didn't understand what it meant. But I was busy doing something else, and she didn't ask me to explain. Her first few attempts at writing the petition missed the mark. The first attempt was only a sentence (similar to the first sentence of the final petition: "I am writing a petition for kids rights to say the pledge of allegiance or not"). There were no lines for others to sign the petition and no heading. I told her she had to explain why she was writing the petition; her older brother added suggestions as well. Subsequent attempts included more explanation. Rachel's older brother gave her more feedback and ideas than I did. Only when Rachel announced that she was ready to hand in the petition did I realize that she had not included space or lines for other students to sign. She had not understood what a petition was. I told her she needed lines on the petition and that she would have to ask the students in her class to sign.

Rachel's attempts at writing a petition raised many questions for me: Where do children learn the genres of writing needed for participation in a democracy? and What are those genres? Finally, she wrote a version that resembled a petition, to some degree.

Petition

I am writing a petition for kids rights to say the pledge of allegiance or not. I know kids do have a privilege if they want to say the pledge of allegiance or not. But they do have to stand look at the flag and listen to people say it. Also kids are saying the pledge of allegiance with out knowing what it means, and we did not review the definition of the of the pledge of allegiance in the beginning of the year.

Some kids don't like saying it, being there when people say it, or listening to people when they say it, because of religious beliefs, maybe have a different pledge or prayer at home, or don't like the meaning of it if they know the meaning of the pledge of allegiance.

Please sign your name if you agree.

It had a statement about her discomfort and a statement that students should have choices. It also had lines for her classmates to sign. She wrote it on a computer, and the only help she got from me in composing the text was that I showed her how to work the spell check and how to put lines in.

A few weeks later, Rachel took the petition to school. At first, it went back and forth between school and home without being taken out of her knapsack.

She told her friend Petra about it. Petra liked the idea and supported Rachel somewhat. Rachel began to get a few signatures, and as Petra saw Rachel get a few signatures, she decided to help. On the first day of getting signatures, a substitute teacher stopped Rachel and Petra and told them that students could only sign if they had their parents' permission. The next day I went with Rachel to the school to check the school policy. Rachel's teacher was not available, so we talked with the school principal. I'm not sure what he thought of the situation, but he treated Rachel and her petition with respect. He addressed Rachel—and I admired him for doing that. He asked her what she wanted, and she said that students should be allowed to leave the room or remain seated if they wanted. He told her that she could go ahead with her petition.

Over the next few weeks, Rachel and Petra sought their classmates' signatures on the petition. They got a lot of names at first. Then they tried to get the names of classmates who were absent or whom they hadn't seen in the hall or playground. On a daily basis, Rachel would tell us about getting another signature and who had not yet signed. It only became evident to us after a while that Rachel believed that the petition was only good if everyone signed. Rachel told us that was what the substitute teacher had told her. We talked with Rachel about whether or not there was a need to get everyone's signature, but I'm sure she understood that there wasn't. It was probably out of exhaustion that Rachel and Petra finally turned in the petition to their teacher with most, but not all, of the signatures of her classmates. The teacher talked with Rachel and Petra, and she listened to their petition. The teacher explained that students did not have to say the Pledge of Allegiance but that they should stand out of respect. The teacher also told them that she was not going to change the way she did class meetings (which included the Pledge of Allegiance as part of the opening exercises).

Rachel told us about her conversation and that she was disappointed with the outcome. We encouraged her to go to the principal and discuss the petition with him now that she and Petra had collected signatures. She thought that was a good idea, but it took several days before they approached the principal's office. Eventually, Rachel and Petra were able to get a meeting with him. Petra brought an article about the origins of the Pledge of Allegiance that her parents had given her. She and Rachel had read the article before meeting with the principal. He listened to them and then explained the state law to them and promised to look into the matter further. Petra and Rachel felt that there was nothing else they could do.

When they returned from the principal's office, about 7 of the 18 students who had signed the petition wanted to withdraw their signatures because they were afraid they would get in trouble. But by that time the principal had the petition.

The legal status of having to say the Pledge of Allegiance in school in Massachusetts is complex and confusing. In brief, there is a state law that requires the saying of the Pledge of Allegiance and assesses a minor fine if it is not said with sufficient frequency (*Massachusetts General Laws Annotated,*

v. 8B, ch. 71, s. 69, p. 419). However, that state law was found unconstitutional by a Massachusetts State Supreme Court ruling (*Decisions of the Supreme Judicial Court of Massachusetts*, v. 372, 1979, pp. 874–880) and later reaffirmed as unconstitutional by the state attorney general (see *Boston Globe* [1988, August 24], p. 15; *Boston Globe* [1988, August 26], p. 10). To the best of our understanding that is essentially how the situation remains, although there have been various efforts by the State Legislature to pass other laws related to the Pledge of Allegiance in schools.

After the meeting with the principal, Rachel, Petra, and I went to the University of Massachusetts library to look up what the law really was. This was not an easy task. It took us nearly 4 hours. We first went to the government section and talked to the reference librarian. He showed us the books where the state laws were and the supplements that described any subsequent actions or rulings. We found the state law mandating the saying of the Pledge or Allegiance and the possible fines for not doing so, but we found no indication of the State Supreme Court Ruling. We then went to the general reference section and talked with that reference librarian who directed us to the *Boston Globe* index. You may remember that the Pledge of Allegiance was a campaign issue in the 1988 presidential election. We looked in the *Boston Globe* index and then in the appropriate microfilm archives and photocopied articles describing the state law and the State Supreme Court ruling. Most important, the newspaper articles had the date of the ruling. Armed with these articles, we went back up to the government section. The reference librarian we had originally talked to earlier in the day was not there, so we had to explain the whole situation to another reference librarian. He helped us located the State Supreme Court decision. We photocopied it. We were exhausted.

At home, Rachel and Petra looked over the materials we had collected. They focused mostly on the newspaper articles—I don't think they read the State Supreme Court decision, other than scanning the title and abstract. But having it in hand seemed important to their reading and use of the newspaper articles. They decided to have another meeting with the principal and give him the articles and the State Supreme Court decision.

Again, several days passed without their actually approaching the principal's office. In fact, before they were able to make an appointment, the principal addressed their class. He had looked further into the issue and found out himself that there was a State Supreme Court ruling. He supported the teacher and felt that what she was doing was appropriate and respectful. However, since students are allowed to leave the classroom when they have strong feelings and beliefs about a particular activity (for example, some students hold strong religious beliefs and prefer not to be present during birthday parties), he felt that they should also be able to leave the room during the Pledge of Allegiance if they had their parents' permission. The teacher complimented Rachel and Petra for their research and hard work. During the rest of the school year, only three students chose to leave the room during the Pledge of Allegiance.

In many ways Rachel and Petra are very lucky. They had a teacher and principal who respected their feelings and their rights. In emotional terms, they could never have written the petition or persisted with it if their classroom and school were rigid, authoritarian places without a sense that the school also belongs to the students. They also had the time and support at home to write the petition, talk about what was happening, and research it in the library. They were lucky to have access to a library that had the resources they needed and that had reference librarians who treated them with the importance given to university students and professors. In addition, Petra's parents had a computer connection to a computer library and were able locate historical sources of information about the Pledge of Allegiance. Rachel and Petra were lucky to have the literacy skills needed and to have had an educational program that promoted literacy as an active skill.

When I reflect on Rachel's petition, it raises for me many disturbing questions. How successful can we claim our reading and writing programs to be if they don't give students access to the genres of writing (like petition writing or reading state laws and court decisions and rulings) needed in a democracy? Access to the genres of writing needs to be accompanied by access to the social and political strategies in which genres like petitions are embedded. Where do students learn those strategies? What if the university library had not been nearby? What if Rachel and Petra's parents had not had the specialized literacy skills needed to access and use a university library? What if there had been no reference librarians? What if their hours and numbers had been so cut back that they were not readily available to Rachel and Petra? What if the government microfilm section of the library had been closed? What if the library had not been open on the weekends? What if Rachel and Petra's teacher and principal had had no time to deal with their petition? What if, given other priorities or too many other students, they had no interest?

Rachel and Petra's petition and the actions that they took show us that in our society there is a close connection between democracy and literacy. But teaching students how to read and write does not necessarily help them learn how to use reading and writing for democracy. As educators, we must help students learn those genres of reading and writing associated with a democracy — genres like petition writing. And, we must include as part of learning to read and write in the genres of democracy those social and political strategies in which those genres are embedded (otherwise, petition writing can end up being little more than another oppressive worksheet or skills exercise). Most importantly, we must realize and insist that **all** students deserve and need the resources with which to learn how to use reading and writing for democracy.

Whatever educational implications can be derived from Rachel and Petra's Pledge of Allegiance petition experience, those implications probably do not lie in specific teaching strategies or in specific curriculum materials. Rather, implications are in the educational agendas we have for children's learning to use written language and how we conceptualize the sites of education. Rachel and Petra's petition experience shows that literacy learning—learning the forms, functions, and political strategies of using written language—requires sites beyond the classroom (in their case, home, library, university, playground) and educators beyond their teacher (in their case, parents, siblings, reference librarians, principal). Perhaps one implication for educators is that a vision of literacy education must include a broad complex of sites, texts, and educators—and not privilege only school sites, texts, and educators. Other educational implications will depend on who is doing the reading and what perspectives they bring to their reading. Teachers may see implications for responding to or encouraging uses of written language they had not previously considered; administrators may find a useful model of administrator response to students. A close examination of the events of Rachel and Petra's petition experience shows how fragile their use of written language for making change in their school was, and how easily they could have been turned back at so many points, given up, or become emotionally overburdened. So much support was needed from school, from home, from nearby libraries, from their community, and from their own strength of character for them to have been successful. Clearly, one educational implication for Rachel and Petra's petition experience is that as educators we must recognize the fragility of such literacy practices and find ways to provide the support and encouragement for them.

Part of what I learned from Rachel and Petra is that you cannot teach students everything about democracy and about using reading and writing for democracy—they must live it. One question we need to ask is whether, as teachers and educators, we are providing the resources and creating the conditions in which all students can live it.

References

Decisions of the Supreme Judicial Court of Massachusetts, v. 372, 1979, pp. 874–880. Boston, MA: Massachusetts Lawyers Weekly.

Dukakis assails Bush for criticism of Pledge of Allegiance law veto. (1988, August 24). *The Boston Globe,* p. 15.

Flag-waving on the pledge. (1988, August 26). *The Boston Globe,* p. 10.

Massachusetts General Laws Annotated, v. 8B, ch. 71, s. 69, p. 419. St. Paul, MN: West Publishing.

Appendix A:
Letter to Ira Shor from Rachel Bloomekatz

Dear Ira Shor,

Thank you for your letter regarding the petition. You asked how the principal and teacher acted toward me. Yes, my father was with me while I confronted the principal, asking him if I could circulate the petition. But I think he was more concerned that I was unpleased than that my father was sitting right next to me. Most of the time Petra and I were on our own, with our parents backing us up.

During this process we had classmates wanting to withdraw their signature because it was going to the principal. That was a scare for Petra and me but all in all it wasn't too frustrating circulating the petition. When the principal came into classroom, (after we gave him a copy of the supreme court ruling) and gave us notices saying that if our parents signed we were allowed to leave the room during the pledge, only three or four kids left the room but it was a great accomplishment to bend school policy. After this event the petition came up again. My class made a quilt, and in my quilt patch I included the petition; so did Petra. My older brother brought it up to his teacher. Their class didn't recite the pledge, but the principal didn't force it on every class. Our principal was nice. He played (my dad was wrong) trumpet in the band and eat lunch with kids. If he was not so nice I don't know what would have happened with the petition.

Doing this makes me feel that you can change the rules and that kids can over power teachers sometimes. I also feel that this was a great experience for me. In terms of using petitions to change problems also I showed myself and others that we count and we can make changes. Now I know how to run a petition so I would definitely use a petition to try and change other policies.

Thank you again for your wonderful letter.

Sincerely,

Rachel Bloomekatz

Appendix B:
Three Teachers' Responses

I.

This article really got under my skin. I felt that this premise that Bloome puts forth—that children need to be taught how to redress their government in a democracy in order for that form of government to be valid—utter hogwash. Furthermore, I do not think this is an innocent questioning of the Pledge of Allegiance by an eleven year old child as Bloome wants us to believe. This is a set-up that allows Bloome to posture on his own cause, not his daughter's. I will explain why I feel this way on these two points. First, children need to develop a certain level of critical thinking skills in order to feel that they are in a position individually of catalysts of change. They need to be able to express themselves in the written and oral forms that give them the experience that they can move and shake their environment. This does not necessarily entail learning how to write up a petition in Social Studies anymore than you need to have a lesson on how to write a recipe in order to give a friend your favorite chocolate chip cookie recipe. With a certain level of intelligence i.e. thinking skills, this activity can be self generated. . . . The second issue I have a problem with is Bloome's assertion that he is merely an impartial observer to his daughter's questioning. Come on, now. Bloome even admits that he was involved in a heated exchange with the superintendent of his son's school over that very same issue! Are we to believe that Rachel knew nothing of this issue that her father felt so emotionally about? I have a hard time believing that. In fact, I find the whole thrust of this article so weak that I can't imagine this being a real story. I think Bloome needed to get published and this was a convenient ax to grind. . . . Questions: (1) Why doesn't the author Bloome use his daughter's feelings for the Pledge of Allegiance as a springboard for her to find out what devotion (allegiance) to country has historically been about. Why don't you (Bloome) expose Rachel to the writings of Walt Whitman, Abraham Lincoln and Thomas Paine to see why people feel so strongly about our country and the beliefs it was founded on? (2) An 11-year-old and many adults need to be informed opinion makers. Why doesn't the author encourage positive activity such as having Rachel find out about how other nations use pledges and national anthems to promote love of country?

II.

Bloome's article was extremely illuminating in that I had never connected genres of writing in such a direct way with democracy. In fact, it seems to me that the educational agenda in this country is about learning a form of discipline that is actually the antithesis of democracy. . . . A perfect example can be

246

seen in the recitation of the Pledge. Students stand, place their hands on their hearts, face the flag and recite words they don't know the meaning of in a droning established rhythm like little robots. By Rachel's age (much earlier I expect) they sit, stand and perform meaningless tasks on command without thinking. . . . I am beginning more and more to believe that kids are not given access to the genres of writing needed for participation in a democracy for a reason. A petition is a potentially powerful tool of social and political change, and change is not in the educational or political agenda. If kids learned how to write petitions they *would* write petitions. All kinds of trouble would break out and kids might even wake up from that robot-like passivity that was so carefully cultivated.

III.

This article really upset me. It annoys me when people have a problem with saying the Pledge of Allegiance. We are lucky enough to be in this country. We should learn to appreciate all of our rights. For some people who do not want to say it, they should stand up and respect it.

There are a lot of kids in school who feel the same way as Rachel Bloomekatz. Most of them feel that way because they are just lazy and don't want to get up out of their seats.

Rachel seems to really be bothered about it and did a lot of research to express her feelings. Most kids don't do that.

We do need to teach children how to participate in government and how to express their feelings. This could be done in Social Studies classes where mock or realistic pieves are made up. Ex. Make a petition on the Death Penalty and send it to the governor.

I do agree with Bloome, that as educators we must help students learn genres of reading and writing associated with democracy.

17

Activism with Young Children

Louise Derman-Sparks

Editors' Notes: This excerpt from Louise Derman-Sparks' *Anti-Bias Curriculum* is a transcription of a meeting of the Anti-Bias Curriculum Task Force, which consists of day-care providers and preschool teachers. These experts discussed how they taught children to be assertive and empathetic, to recognize injustice, and to take constructive action against it. Throughout the dialogue, they provide concrete examples from their classrooms. They offer useful activities for young children and consider whether some children are too young to take action on issues, a question also raised during the controversy over Maria Sweeney's coverage of sweatshop abuses in her fourth-grade class (see Chapter 6, Appendices A and B).

Children learning to take action against unfair behaviors that occur in their own lives is at the heart of anti-bias education. Without this component, the curriculum loses its vitality and power. For children to feel good and confident about themselves, they need to be able to say, "That's not fair," or "I don't like that," if they are the target of prejudice or discrimination. For children to develop empathy and respect for diversity, they need to be able to say, "I don't like what you are doing" to a child who is abusing another child. If we teach children to recognize injustice, then we must also teach them that people can create positive change by working together.

Young children have an impressive capacity for learning how to be activists if adults provide activities that are relevant and developmentally appropriate. Through activism activities children build the confidence and skills for becoming adults who assert, in the face of injustice, "I have the responsibility to deal with it, I know how to deal with it, I will deal with it."

Many teachers and parents may be unaccustomed to doing activism with young children, so it is essential to carefully think through how to introduce this aspect of the curriculum. This chapter discusses the issues, goals, and kinds of activism activities meaningful to young children, through an edited transcript of an Anti-Bias Curriculum Task Force meeting.

Laying the Groundwork: Learning Assertion and Empathy with Each Other

Anti-bias activism begins in young children's daily interactions with each other. Learning to express their feelings to another child who has hurt them and to care when another child has been hurt creates the foundation upon which activism activities build. Anti-bias curriculum alerts us to helping children be assertive in situations that reflect bias or in situations of physical aggression.

MARIA (teacher of 2s): The first thing that we do is give children permission and support to speak their feelings about having an injustice done toward them. If they can't do it, we help them find words, even say the words for them. We want our children to get used to saying to each other, "I don't like it when you hit me," or "I don't like it when you call me a baby," or "Girls can *so* climb." They get daily practice in speaking up for their own rights.

REGENA (teacher of 2s): We have one 2½-year-old girl who is passive and fearful when another child takes something from her or picks a toy she wants. We're in the process of building up her courage. An adult stands right next to her and says to the other child, "You really need to listen to her words. There's something she wants to say," and then says to the first child, "You can say this in a strong voice. Tell them that you don't want. . . ."

MAE (preschool teacher): I have a similar situation with a 3½-year-old girl. She is able to stand up for herself with other girls but passively withdraws if a boy tells her she can't play. I am now intervening as soon as that happens. I bring her back and say, "I saw you wanted to play with the blocks, or sand, or whatever. Frank can't stop you. You tell him that you *are* going to play." The first few times she did it in a whisper, holding on to me. Recently she comes to get me and then says loudly, "I am going to play; you can't boss me." I hope soon she will be able to stand up on her own.

CORY (preschool teacher): Sometimes a child's been insulted, and I encourage the two children to talk about it, but the child who's been insulted doesn't want to talk. I might say, "Well, I really don't like what's happened myself, and I'd like to say something about it." And then I use whatever words are appropriate, like "When you said Rosa couldn't play with you because she looks funny, you were not fair to her. You hurt her and now she feels sad. What you did makes me feel sad too, and angry at you. In this classroom we are fair to each other," so that I model expressing feelings and don't let a situation like this go by without doing something about it.

MOLLY (kindergarten teacher): In kindergarten we do some very direct teaching about respecting each other's physical and emotional space, and about ways to assertively tell someone "no." We practice holding the offending child's wrists and saying what you feel as if you really mean it, whether you've been the recipient of abusive language or physical violence. I find that many of my kids begin by using a "wishy-washy" voice that wouldn't convince a cucumber. I want them to say it like they really mean it strong and firm.

FRANCOIS (child care teacher): By doing this we are saying to children, "You are respect-worthy human beings who have a right to your feelings, to express your feelings, to be listened to, to be taken seriously."

CORY: I think another important precursor of activism is children's developing the ability to care when another child is hurt or feels scared or sad. Usually children show empathy toward a child who is physically hurt, or feeling sad because of separating from a parent, or feeling sick. We need to help them also develop empathy for a child who is emotionally hurt by teasing, name calling, or rejection because of his or her gender, or race, or physical ability.

MAE: Learning to appreciate different needs or special needs of each other is another part of extending empathy. This is hard for preschoolers, but they are capable of learning if they see adults accepting a child's uniqueness, and not insisting that everyone act the same and do the same things. I also give children a lot of encouragement when I see them helping each other: "You're really showing your friend how much you care about her or him." I think we can build on this work, start with areas where preschoolers do show empathy, and then connect anti-bias issues to what they already do.

KAY (after-school care director/teacher): I teach my children to call on friends when they are faced with an unfair situation. For example, last week two boys were playing on the rope swing, and two girls were waiting for a long time. The girls kept asking for a turn, and the boys ignored them. I watched and waited to see what would happen. Finally, the girls came to me and complained. I asked them, "What should we do? *I* could go and stop them, but that won't help you in the future." One girl then said, "Maybe we could get some of our friends to help us." I responded, "Yes, that is a good idea." The two girls collected about four children, girls and boys, and with their friends around them told the boys to give them a turn. The boys got off the swings and complained to me that they had been chased off. I talked with the two boys about what they had done to create the need for the girls to get their friends to help them.

MOLLY: I absolutely agree about children learning to help each other. I have another example. Last year we had a White child who frequently used racial slurs against the Black children. I had been working with him for months, making it very clear that such language was not allowed. His behavior stopped finally. However, at a birthday party outside of school, he insulted Carol, one of the Black children, who came to school the next day very angry and hurt. I decided new action was necessary. I called the six Black children to a meeting, explaining to the other children that we had a special problem that was affecting the Black children and that if others wanted to they could also come. A few did. At the meeting I explained what had happened to Carol and asked what they thought we should do. All of the Black children told about times the White child had insulted them and how mad it made them. They had a lot of ideas about what to do—some more acceptable than others. One child told Carol that she should kick the White child in the balls if he called her names. I responded, "I cannot allow that action, even though I understand that you are angry enough to do it." Finally we agreed that the six Black children would meet with the White child, his mother, and myself as soon as he arrived and tell him that we never wanted to hear him say the N word again. By this time Carol was tooting on a cylinder-shaped block as if it was a trumpet, clearly feeling restored. I praised the children for their good work together. We did meet with the White child, and it did change his behavior for a while.

Friends learning to help each other deal with unfair situations prepare children for group activism activities.

Group Activism in the Classroom: Working Together to Create Change

While developing assertiveness and empathy are the activism goals for 2s and 3s, 4- and 5-year-olds are capable of working together to change biased situations beyond individual interactions with their peers. Group activism activities about concrete issues that are real to young children are empowering experiences. Through them children learn to interact with the world with initiative, responsibility, and strength. It is interesting to think about whether group activism activities also serve as a challenge to "superheroes." Instead of one superhuman figure (usually a White male) righting wrongs all by himself, activism activities teach children that real people, adults and children, can make life better by working together.

CORY: In the preschool we did an action around the multicultural dolls we bought from Lakeshore. One day, as I was using dolls to tell a story, one child commented, "They don't have any penises or vaginas." The other children checked out the dolls and agreed. We discussed whether it would be better if the dolls had either one or the other. The children felt that they would prefer to really know if the dolls were boys or girls. So, I suggested that we write to Lakeshore and tell them about our concern. The group dictated a letter, we sent it, and a few weeks later Lakeshore offered to replace our dolls with a new set that did have genitals. I felt that this was a very successful activity.

BILL (special education teacher): In my classroom (3- to 5-year-olds) we have an ongoing project dealing with the parking space for people with special needs at our school. It began a few years ago when a parent who was in a wheelchair had enormous difficulty getting to my classroom for a conference because there was no "handicapped" parking space at the school. I was furious; the irony of this happening in a school for physically disabled children added to my anger. I decided that the children in my class and I would remedy the situation.

I initiated the activity by taking the children to look at parking spaces for people with disabilities and asking them if they knew what the symbol stood for. We talked about why it is important to have a special parking spot for differently abled people, why it needed to be near the entrance of the school, and what would happen if a differently abled person who couldn't walk had to park far away. Then we looked at the parking lot at school, and the children couldn't find a special "handicapped" parking space. So, we agreed to make one from the spaces already on the lot. I got blue paint, made an H stencil to paint on the ground, and brought a "handicapped parking" sign for the other end. Everyone participated.

The next step was to deal with the people who inappropriately park in the spot. My classroom overlooks the parking lot so we could see when this happened. Many of the children suggested tickets—something they already knew about. Each child dictated a few tickets, and we either put the ticket on the car or gave it directly to the person. We haven't stopped all the able-bodied people from parking in the handicap space, but it has cut down on the number who do.

LISSA (child care center teacher): My favorite activism activity is the one I did on "flesh-colored" Curads™. One day, while getting an adhesive bandage for one of my 3-year-olds, the label "flesh-colored" suddenly hit me. So I said, "Look at this—it says on the box that these bandages are flesh-colored. That means they are the same color as our skin. Let's see if it is really true." We then put bandages on each child's arm and discovered that they were only like the color of some of the children, but not like the color of those with brown skin.

The next day I suggested that we do an experiment. We would invite other children from the Children's School to put on an adhesive bandage and see if it matched their skin. So, other children came to our yard and we took photos of each child's arm with a bandage on it. We made a chart and realized that the bandage didn't match a lot of children's skin.

On the third day I suggested that we write a letter to the company and tell them what we learned. The children dictated what they wanted to say, and I added an explanation of our experiment. We took a trip to the post office the next day to mail our letter. We also involved the parents, sending letters home about what we were doing, and talking about it when parents came to pick up their children.

We got a letter back from Colgate-Palmolive Co., which politely said, "We read your letter, but we don't think it's a problem. Enclosed find some transparent strips which are more flesh-colored." I felt it was important that we did the letter writing, even if the company didn't agree with us. We told them how we felt; they told us how they felt. I think the children felt it was a success because we could get transparent bandages. I let it go after that. Some children remember; I've heard them say, "This doesn't match me." Now I'm wondering if I should have taken another step such as saying to the children that if we still don't think it's fair, we can decide not to buy this brand anymore, or ask the parents to write letters too. We are just beginning. If we get the parents involved, then we are laying a longer lasting foundation.

MOLLY: One activity we did was to paint over a wall in a park that had racial slurs written on it. The day we saw it, I stopped the group and said, "Do you know what is written on this wall? It makes me very angry." I read the words, we talked about what they meant, how they are very hurtful to people. Then we talked about what we could do and decided to paint over the words, which we did the next day. We probably could have written to the Parks Department, telling them about the wall and what we did. It would have been interesting to see what kind of response we got.

LOUISE: A friend of mine, B. J. Richards, who teaches in New York City, told me about the following activity. One day, on a walk around their neighborhood, they came upon a sign, "Man Wanted," in a store window. They read the sign and talked about it, deciding it was unfair to women. They wrote a letter to the store owner and then visited him a few days later. He told them he thought they were right and would change the sign to "Person Wanted."

MOLLY: What else is common in children's lives? We could write to authors of children's books, either about what we like because we think it's fair, or about books that we think have stereotypes. We could write to toy manufacturers about the kinds of toys we want, or don't like, cereal manufacturers, TV shows. We could visit toy stores, bookstores, greeting card stores.

BILL: Sounds like good language arts activities as well as good activism activities.

MAE: How would you feel as a child if you wrote a letter or talked to a store manager and then it didn't do a bit of good? I deal with powerlessness a lot as an adult. I have a lot of trouble with some activism because I feel it's so hopeless.

SHARON: Is success a part of what needs to result in order to promote activism for young children?

A few voices at the same time: Right. Right.

MARIA: I'm hearing that you must have a positive outcome or else do nothing. Life isn't like that. There are ways of coping with not always winning, like with the adhesive bandage activity. The company didn't say they would make bandages that matched, or take the label "skin colored" off the box. Well, we can say, "Then I'm not buying your nasty bandages." That's success that's built into a situation that could be a failure.

REGENA: And that's what teaching children activism is all about. It doesn't necessarily have the outcome you want, but you have to keep on. Again, those are building blocks. You just have to keep putting one block on top of another until you get there.

Beyond the Classroom: Participating in Community Events

Is it appropriate for young children to participate in community-wide campaigns for social justice? The Anti-Bias Curriculum Task Force did not agree at the meeting. Some thought that if the issue was one the children could comprehend, and parents agreed, then joining a community-wide action would be a meaningful educational experience. Seeing many people coming together because they share a common conviction and are willing to stand up for what they believe can make quite a strong impression on a child. It provides role modeling and enhances children's sense of connection. On the other hand, some task force members questioned involving children in what are primarily adult issues. They pressed the group to think carefully through what might be appropriate or inappropriate community events in which to involve young children.

BILL: When Louise and I were teaching at a child care center, we took our 4- and 5-year-olds to some community demonstrations. For example, when a child care center in Echo Park was going to be closed by the city, the teachers went with the children and parents to a protest at the Los Angeles City Hall. We explained to our children that a friend of Louise's and mine, who was a teacher at a center just like ours, was upset because the city government was going to close her center. Her children and parents wanted to tell the city government people not to close their center, and they wanted us to help them. Our children wanted to go, and their parents agreed. It was very successful. The Echo Park Center was given another building and our children learned about standing up for their rights. We found this out when, a week later, our children—with a little help from school-aged siblings—made signs and picketed the teachers demanding to eat candy, which we did not allow. (We compromised with a candy time one afternoon a week!)

REGENA: In my experience too, children can understand a community action. When McDonald's was being boycotted by the NAACP, some of the families in my preschool class participated. Every morning I had one child say, "I still can't go to McDonald's," and we would talk about it.

MOLLY: Well, I think demonstrating about the closing of a child care center or boycotting McDonald's because of discrimination is a little different than, say, picketing the South African Embassy.

SHARON: Is that because you don't see apartheid in South Africa as a concern children can understand and care about?

KAY: I did a series of activities about the Nelson Mandela Tent City the college students set up at UCLA. We often take walks around the campus, and in the course of one of these walks we came upon the Tent City. The children (5- and 6-year-olds) were fascinated and wanted to know why it was there. I explained, simply and briefly, about apartheid in South Africa and why the students had set up Tent City. The children were able to relate what I said to our previous discussions about fairness and about civil rights struggles in this country.

As part of the environment, the college students had created a cemetery with gravestones of dead activists, including Steven Biko. I had previously taught them a song about Biko, so the children immediately recognized that name (some thought he was really buried there and I had to explain about that).

The group wanted to go back for several days and hang out with the college students. The Black children were particularly involved and excited. I then wrote a letter to the parents explaining about our first visit to Tent City and why we wanted to take the children a few more times. I asked for their responses, and it was unanimously supportive. It was an appropriate activity for my class because it was happening right on our campus and was a current issue children were hearing about from TV and their parents.

LOUISE: There are a few children's books about people working together for social change that support what our children do. One is called *Swimmy* (Lionni, 1973). It is about how a school of small fish stop a big fish from eating them. Another is about Mother Jones, a famous union organizer, who worked with children for better working conditions in the cotton mills during the time when child labor existed.

BILL: Another, *King of the Mountain* (Cassidy, 1980), is about children saving a big heap of dirt from a construction project they play on. The city wants to knock it down, but the children take action to save their "mountain."

LOUISE: Activism activities can include stories about historic heroes and heroines who have worked to stop injustice. But, I think it's important that we explain that it wasn't that hero or heroine alone who made change happen. No one is a leader without other people participating with them.

MAE: This discussion makes me feel a bit more comfortable about involving kindergarten-aged children in community action events.

MARIA: But you still aren't comfortable?

MAE: No. But I will try some activities and see.

Teacher as Activist

SHARON: If we ask children to be activists, don't we also have to be activists?

LOUISE: I think so. We need to look at our own attitudes and experiences in taking action against injustice by individuals and by institutions and what has kept us from acting. If a teacher thinks activism is wrong, it will be harder to implement this part of the anti-bias curriculum.

BILL: We don't want a "tourist" approach to activism—visit the problem, but don't get involved yourself.

MOLLY: I talk with children about "Here is something that bothers me very much—this is what I'm doing about it." It's sort of storytelling.

MARIA: I think activism means risk taking. I know that is so for myself. Through my parent education meeting, this year the parents know more about me than I think I've ever shared with any group of friends.

MAE: We can't teach more than what we are.

Inventing Activism Activities in Your Classroom

In every classroom and community, issues arise that can spark activism activities. Since these activities must be concrete and meaningful in the life of each group of children, there are no exact recipes. Each teacher has to create his or her own activities using the principles discussed in this chapter.

Young children's anti-bias interactions with each other are the first activism activities. Foster their developing empathy, their ability to express their needs, and their skills in standing up for themselves and other children.

Group activism activities should address issues that children understand and care about. Involve children in deciding what strategies to use.

Involve parents through informing them of, discussing, and encouraging participation in activism activities.

Teachers' own experiences as activists can strengthen their skills for doing activism activities with children.

You may find the examples in this chapter relevant to your class. Here are some further examples of possibilities:

Example 1

Your school is an all-White school in a middle-income community. You have done a number of activities about physical differences and similarities. The children became particularly interested in the dolls with disabilities. You tell them that you noticed that the local bookstore (or toy store) doesn't have books about people with special physical situations (the toy store doesn't have dolls with disabilities). You ask the children what they think about that, helping them see that other children will miss out on the chance to learn what they have been learning. You and the children may decide to ask the store manager in a letter to visit your school and see your books and dolls; or you may decide to write and ask the manager if you can visit and show her or him your materials. What you will do next depends on how the store manager responds and your follow-up discussions with the children. If she or he is not interested, you may decide to involve parents and other preschool teachers in sending letters. If the manager cooperates, you may want to send letters telling preschool teachers and parents that new materials about differently abled people will be available at that store.

Example 2

You are in a Head Start program with a diverse group of children: Black, Mexican-American, White. You realize that you have mainly White dolls, and want to diversify them, but do not have a budget for purchasing new dolls. You raise the problem with the children, comparing the diversity among them with the token diversity among the dolls—do they think we need more dolls to be fair? You then suggest that they, the staff, and their parents can help make cloth dolls at a workshop and at home. Children can dictate a letter to parents explaining the problem and inviting them to a workshop of parents and staff. Children can go on a trip with teachers to buy materials. Get dark, medium, and light brown, sand color, and beige cotton; a variety of colors and materials for hair, including wool; check pattern books for dolls or find someone who already makes dolls to help. Figure out tasks the children can do. After the workshop, some parents may be able to continue to help at home. Make little gifts with the children to send to all the parents who have participated in the project.

Example 3

You are in a child care center where a number of the children are Vietnamese and Korean immigrants. You do not have books or tapes or materials in the children's languages. You need the help of people who are bilingual to make tapes reading children's books, to make signs for materials, to make alphabet and number posters, and to teach you key words. Discuss the problem with the

children—involve them in writing letters to leaders in the Vietnamese and
Korean communities who would know of people who can help. Then write
letters to these people asking if they can help with specific jobs.

Example 4

The neighborhood in which your children live does not have a decent playground. You have heard that some community people are organizing to get
funds to develop a new playground. Discuss the problem with the children, go
on a field trip to playgrounds in other neighborhoods, and then talk about the
lack in their own neighborhood. Contact the community organizing group and
figure out how the children can help. This may include letter writing, speaking to city officials, helping to plan equipment, suggesting ideas for accessi-
bility. This same series of activities could also tackle the need for a traffic
light, or for curb ramps.

Adaptation

To invent activism activities:

- Be alert for unfair practices in your school or neighborhood that directly
  affect your children's lives. You may be the first to identify the problem, or
  the children may bring a problem to your attention.

- Consider the interests and dynamics of your group of children. Do they
  care about the problem? What kind of actions would work with them?

- Consider your comfort. Is the issue one you feel comfortable addressing?
  What strategies do you prefer?

- Consider the parents' comfort. Do you want their agreement beforehand?
  Do you just plan to inform them of your plans? Do you want to include
  them in the activity?

- Try out the activity. If it works, great! If it doesn't, try again with a different activity!

References

Cassidy, G. (1980). *King of the mountain*. New York: Leisure Books.

Lionni, L. (1973). *Swimmy*. New York: Knopf.

About the Editors

Ira Shor has a dual appointment as Professor of English at the City University of New York Graduate School and at the College of Staten Island. His *Critical Teaching and Everyday Life* was the first booklength treatment of Freirean literacy in the United States. He worked with Paulo Freire for a number of years and coauthored with Freire his first "talking book," *A Pedagogy for Liberation.* Shor, whose most recent book is *When Students Have Power*, speaks widely around the country. He grew up in the working class of New York City.

Caroline Pari is Assistant Professor of English and Basic Writing Coordinator at Borough of Manhattan Community College, CUNY. She received her Ph.D. from CUNY, specializing in Composition and Rhetoric, Women's Studies, and nineteenth-century women's writing. Pari has contributed to *Teaching Working Class*, edited by Sherry Linkon, and *Attending to the Margins*, edited by Michelle Hall Kells and Valerie Balester. She is a native of Queens, New York, and lives there with her husband.

Acknowledgements for borrowed material continued from p. ii.

"Discovering Columbus: Rereading the Past" by William Bigelow originally appeared in *Rethinking Schools* 4:1 (Fall 1989): 12–13. Reprinted with permission.

"Columbus, A Hero?: Rethinking Columbus in an Elementary Classroom" by Maria Sweeney originally appeared in *Radical Teacher* No. 43: 25–29. Reprinted by permission of *Radical Teacher*, P.O. Box 383316, Cambridge, MA 02238.

"Pupils' Script on Workers Is Ruled Out" by Evelyn Nieves originally appeared in *The New York Times* 6/26/97. Copyright © 1997 by The New York Times Company. Reprinted by permission.

"Banned in Jersey, Welcomed on Broadway" by Stan Karp originally appeared in *Rethinking Schools* 12.2 (Winter 1997–98): 14–15. Reprinted with permission.

"Beyond Thanksgiving: Teaching About Native Americans of New England" by Rosemary Agoglia originally appeared in *Radical Teacher* No. 43: 6–9. Reprinted by permission of *Radical Teacher*, P.O. Box 383316, Cambridge, MA 02238.

"On the Road to Cultural Bias: A Critique of *The Oregon Trail* CD-ROM" by William Bigelow originally appeared in *Rethinking Schools* 10.1 (Fall 1995): 14–18. Reprinted with permission.

"What Happened to the Golden Door?" by Linda Christensen originally appeared in *Rethinking Schools* 11.1 (Fall 1996): 1, 4–5, 20, 21. Reprinted with permission.

"The Human Lives Behind the Labels: The Global Sweatshop, Nike, and the Race to the Bottom" by William Bigelow originally appeared in *Rethinking Schools* 11.4 (Summer 1997): 1, 12–16. Reprinted with permission.

"Tales from an Untracked Class" by Linda Christensen originally appeared in *Rethinking Schools* 7.2 (Winter 1992–93): 1, 19–22. Reprinted with permission.

"Teaching Math Across the Curriculum" by Bob Peterson originally appeared as "Number Numbness: Teaching Math Across the Curriculum" in *Rethinking Schools* 10.1 (Fall 1995): 1, 4–5. Reprinted with permission.

"Negotiating Mathematics" by Susan Hyde originally appeared in *Negotiating the Curriculum* by Garth Boomer, Nancy Lester, Cynthia Onore, and John Cook. Copyright © 1992. Reprinted by permission of Falmer Press, A member of the Taylor & Francis Group.

"Chicanos Have Math in Their Blood: Pre-Columbian Mathematics" by Luis Ortiz-Franco originally appeared in *Radical Teacher* No. 43: 10–14. Reprinted by permission of *Radical Teacher*, P.O. Box 383316, Cambridge, MA 02238.

"Success and Mathematically Gifted Female Students: The Challenge Continues" by Janice A. Leroux and Cheeying Ho originally appeared in *Feminist Teacher* 7.2: 42–48. Reprinted with permission.

"Literacy, Democracy, and the Pledge of Allegiance" by David Bloome with Rachel Bloomekatz and Petra Sander originally appeared in *Language Arts* Vol. 70, December 1993: 655–658. Copyright © 1993 by the National Council of Teachers of English. Reprinted with permission.

"Activism with Young Children" by Louise Derman-Sparks originally appeared in *Anti-Bias Curriculum.* Reprinted by permission of Louise Derman-Sparks, Director of Anti Bias Multicultural Leadership Project, Pacific Oaks College.